William Jeynes, PhD

Divorce, Family Structure, and the Academic Success of Children

More pre-publication
REVIEWS, COMMENTARIES, EVALUATIONS . . .

"**H**ooray for Jeynes! This research-er has taken on a not so popu-lar, yet all too important, topic—the impact of nontraditional family struc-tures on students' academic achieve-ment—and he has done so with re-spect, integrity, and grace. My col-leagues and I are committed to doing whatever it takes to ensure learning and success for all of our students. However, without knowing key find-ings like those Jeynes shares, our hands are somewhat tied. Jeynes pro-vides us with a scholarly work that has significant implications for to-day's teachers and school leaders. Hats off to William Jeynes for his work.

The implication of Jeynes' work for educators seems clear: teachers, ad-ministrators, and other school person-nel need to be aware of inherent challenges that seem to exist for stu-dents from less traditional family backgrounds. If we are better aware of the ways that family structures tend to affect academic performance, we can be better equipped to provide the type of support and intervention program-ming needed to ensure learning and success for all within our schools."

Bruce Allen Brotzman, EdD
Principal,
Rock Bridge High School,
Columbia, MO

The Haworth Press®
New York • London • Oxford

Divorce, Family Structure, and the Academic Success of Children

THE HAWORTH PRESS
Divorce and Remarriage
Craig A. Everett, PhD
Editor

New, Recent, and Forthcoming Titles:

The Effects of Family Structure on the Academic Achievement of Adolescents by William Jeynes

Divorce, Annulments, and the Catholic Church: Healing or Hurtful? by Richard J. Jenks

Titles of Related Interest:

The Therapist's Notebook for Children and Adolescents: Homework, Handouts, and Activities for Use in Psychotherapy edited by Catherine Ford Sori and Lorna L. Hecker

Women's Stories of Divorce at Childbirth: When the Baby Rocks the Cradle by Hilary Hoge

Clinical Epiphanies in Marital and Family Therapy: A Practitioner's Casebook of Therapeutic Insights, Perceptions, and Breakthroughs by David A. Baptiste Jr.

Couples Therapy, Second Edition by Linda Berg-Cross

Divorce and the Next Generation: Effects on Young Adults' Patterns of Intimacy and Expectations for Marriage edited by Craig A. Everett

Family Therapy and Mental Health: Innovations in Theory and Practice by Malcolm M. McFarlane

Marital and Sexual Lifestyles in the United States: Attitudes, Behaviors, and Relationships in Social Context by Linda P. Rouse

Together Through Thick and Thin: A Multinational Picture of Long-Term Marriages by Shlomo A. Sharlin, Florence Kaslow, and Helga Hammerschmidt

Basic Concepts in Family Therapy: An Introductory Text, Second Edition by Linda Berg-Cross

Divorce, Family Structure, and the Academic Success of Children

William Jeynes, PhD

The Haworth Press®
New York • London • Oxford

The Haworth Press, Inc., 10 Alice Street, Binghamton, NY 13904-1580.

Cover design by Anastasia Litwak.

Cover design concept by Craig A. Everett.

Library of Congress Cataloging-in-Publication Data

Jeynes, William.
    Divorce, family structure, and the academic success of children / William Jeynes.
      p. cm.
    Includes bibliographical references and index.
    ISBN 0-7890-1486-6 (alk. paper)—ISBN 0-7890-1487-4 (pbk. : alk. paper)
    1. Children of divorced parents—Education—United States. 2. Children of single parents—Education—United States. 3. Home and school—United States. 4. Academic achievement—United States. 5. Educational surveys—United States. I. Title.

LCS159.3.U6 J49 2002
306.43'2—dc21
                                                      2001046325

CONTENTS

ABOUT THE AUTHOR

William Jeynes, PhD, is Associate Professor of Education, California State University at Long Beach. He earned his doctoral degree in education from the University of Chicago, his EdM from Harvard University, and his BA in psychology and economics from the University of Wisconsin at Madison. He has published a number of articles on the effect of parental divorce and family structure on children's academic achievement.

Foreword

The release of the Coleman Report in 1966 alarmed many Americans about the importance of the family in terms of determining a child's level of academic achievement. The Coleman Report concluded that the family circumstances a child came from had a far greater impact on that child's academic achievement than the quality of the child's school. Coleman's research indicated that even the most academically demanding and/or the wealthiest school could not affect a student's ability to learn the way the family could. *Divorce, Family Structure, and the Academic Success of Children,* is, in many respects, probably the most complete work of its kind, examining the effects of parental divorce, remarriage, and other family structures on the academic achievement of adolescents.

Four aspects of this book make it a particularly important addition to family research and educational psychology. First, Jeynes addresses important methodological issues that few social scientists dare to examine. Second, the research in this book examines certain family structures that are both very important and unique, e.g., children of divorce living with neither parent. Third, the author uses a highly respected nationwide data set, the National Educational Longitudinal Study (NELS), to determine the results. Fourth, Jeynes is one of the first researchers to dedicate an entire book to the relationship between parental family structure and the academic achievement of children.

The first important contribution of this work, regarding addressing essential methodological issues, is especially apparent. One issue that is especially important is how a researcher controls for socioeconomic status. Jeynes points out that whether one controls for socioeconomic status and how that is undertaken can dramatically change the results one obtains for the effects of divorce and remarriage. Jeynes presents convincing evidence that the means by which most researchers control for socioeconomic status results in significantly understating the effects of parental divorce on adolescents. He further argues that many social scientists have a very simplistic notion of the significance of socioeconomic status, and that a much more sophisticated and realistic view of socioeconomic status is needed. The good news, according to this book, is that numerous researchers in the natural sciences are already addressing this issue and some researchers with overlapping interests in the medical and psychological fields (e.g., psychiatrists) are also beginning to address this problem. From a methodological standpoint, social scientists have usually learned about research methodology from the example set by natural scientists. It would appear that properly controlling for socioeconomic status is another area of endeavor in which this learning can take place.

From the analyses in this book, it is clear that one must be careful not to attribute too much merit to particular studies, in terms of coming to specific conclusions about the effects of divorce and remarriage on children. The results that emerge from a particular study may have more to do with how a study was structured, for whatever reason, than the actual impact of divorce and/or remarriage. Other analyses undertaken indicate that insufficiently distinguishing between certain family structures can produce misleading results. In addition, determining the effects of divorce by combining children from remarried families with those from intact families, can produce results that understate the effects of parental divorce. All of the methodological issues presented here can have considerable impact on how one interprets the impact of parental divorce on academic achievement.

The fact that Jeynes examines family structures and situations that are unique is a second important contribution. Jeynes is one of the few researchers to examine the effects of a child of divorce living with neither parent. In doing this, the author recognizes the fact that many children from broken homes live in orphanages, with foster parents, or with other relatives. Jeynes argues convincingly that one cannot truly understand the effects of divorce unless he or she includes these children in the analyses. Jeynes also examines the effects of other family structures including living in a home with an unwed parent, a widowed parent, a cohabiting couple, and so forth. The examination of the effects of these other family structures helps place the effects of parental divorce on academic achievement in its proper context. Analyses of family situations involving mobility are also examined. The question that is being addressed is whether family physical mobility explains the downward impact that parental remarriage exerts on student academic achievement. Although this is the assertion of McLanahan and Sandefur (1994) in *Growing Up with a Single Parent: What Hurts, What Helps,* Jeynes presents a means of testing this hypothesis. He addresses this hypothesis objectively, logically, and in a balanced fashion. One gets the impression that the author is not determined to prove or disprove any particular theory, but simply seeks to uncover the truth.

The use of the NELS data set is also an important contribution of this work. This is one of the most highly respected data sets that uses a nationwide stratified random sample. The vast majority of studies examining the effects of parental divorce, remarriage, and other family structures do not use a nationally representative random sample. Using the NELS data set is important because it enhances the likelihood that the findings used in these analyses can be generalized to the United States as a whole and it reduces the incidence of sampling bias.

This book provides a gold mine of information regarding the relationship between family structure and academic achievement. Over the years, countless educators, parents, and social scientists have acknowledged the need to understand the relationship between parental family structure and student academic achievement. Although researchers such as Judith Wallerstein, E. Mavis Hetherington, Paul Amato, and others have emphasized the importance of this relationship, this book goes into as great a depth in studying this relationship as any that is available.

As Jeynes points out, the research community is improving its ability to effectively determine the effects of parental divorce, remarriage, and other family structures on the academic achievement of children. This is an important contribution in this quest. It calls for social scientists to develop a more sophisticated approach to understanding the effects of family life and takes a major step in this direction.

Herb Walberg
Research Professor of Education
University of Illinois at Chicago,
Distinguished Visiting Scholar
Stanford University Hoover Institute

Preface

The goal of this book is to examine the relationship between parental family structure, especially parental divorce and/or remarriage, and the academic achievement of children. Very few books are dedicated to examining this very important topic and almost none examine issues of research methodology relevant to this area of study. It is my hope that this book will be a useful tool for educators, researchers, professionals, and parents who desire to examine this relevant and practical area of study. Our society has become too complex to rigidly divide into parental and school-based influences. A broad range of research now supports the notion that children usually perform the best in school when parents and schools work together. Nearly every educator knows that he or she can only lead a child so far if the child comes from an intolerable family background. Ultimately, what takes place in the home affects a child in the school and what the child experiences in school can also affect the child's life outside the school.

Much has been written about the need to raise the academic achievement of students from minority backgrounds. Although these publications can be useful, they tend to define "minority" in terms of skin color and other external characteristics. However, other minority groups deserve America's attention as well. Their status as minorities may not be so easily discerned because they cannot be defined as such on the basis of skin color. One of these minority groups is children from nonintact families. Although this group of children is not readily identified by certain external characteristics, they nevertheless face their own set of unique circumstances of which American educators, researchers, and parents should become more aware. To become more effective in educating this nation's children, there is a need to become more sensitive to the distinct backgrounds that children come from. Although these backgrounds are defined partially by ethnicity and culture, they are but a portion of the factors at work affecting the personalities and the educational abilities of children.

This book examines the relationship between parental family structure, especially divorce and remarriage, and academic achievement in as complete a way as any book on the market. In addition, this book examines some of the most debated theories within the family sciences, including the role of residential mobility, socioeconomic status, and so forth. Ultimately, the findings of the research undertaken will likely answer many questions about the effects of divorce and remarriage. Nevertheless, the research findings will doubtlessly cause one to have many questions as well. It is my belief that both the answers and the questions are healthy outcomes. Certainly, the inquiring mind desires answers. However, there is also a certain advantage to having additional questions and to questioning whether some of the answers we assume to be true are really answers at all. For example, one might conclude after reading the chapters about residential mobility and socioeconomic status, that the research community probably does not know much about the reasons for the impact of parental divorce and remarriage on adolescent academic achievement. To the extent that this is true, it may be a good thing. To the extent that people realize that the truth they believe is insufficient, they begin a journey toward finding a greater degree of truth. It is finding the truth and experiencing the freedom and wisdom that accompany the truth, that defines what is hopefully a person's ultimate quest. It is the author's hope that this book will be an important rung on the ladder in the search for understanding the effects of parental divorce, remarriage, and other family structures on the academic achievement of children.

Acknowledgments

I am very thankful to many individuals who played a large role in making this work possible. I want to thank Craig Everett for his investment of time, support, and his editorial comments. Craig's work and dedication is an inspiration to all who are familiar with him. I also want to thank numerous people in the academic community for their help and assistance in statistical analyses, especially those at the University of Chicago and Harvard University. I want to especially thank the late Bob Jewell for his encouragement in this project. Bob Jewell has been an unceasing source of encouragement during my time here and has always served to lift up my spirits. Two other academicians who never ceased to inspire and encourage me are Chris Ullman and Wendy Naylor. I also want to thank several dear friends of mine whose encouragement with respect to this project touched me deeply. Among these dear friends are: Jean Donohue, Jon Yoshihara, and Don Doleshal. Thank you so much for your support!

I am incredibly blessed to have been married for fifteen years to my wife, Hyelee, whose support has been exemplary. Without her prayers and support, this work never could have been completed. I am also blessed and honored to have three wonderful boys, whom I thank for their love and inspiration. The support of my wife and children gave me the encouragement I needed to rely on God's strength and providence to complete this project. I am forever grateful.

Chapter 1

Historical Background of the Study

The research studies presented in this book attempt to examine the effects of family structure, and especially parental divorce, on the academic achievement of adolescents from a number of different perspectives. This book traces the development of the study of the effects of parental family structure from its incipiency. It will examine the major debates and controversies that surround this field of study. The research presented in this book will investigate the effects of divorce and remarriage using a variety of approaches. It will also examine how other, less common, parental family structures impact the academic outcomes of children. Through it all, one needs to remember that by examining this research, the purpose of this book is not merely to engage in some intellectual exercise. These studies involve the lives of real students and real families. As social scientists examine such issues, it is hoped that the products of all the work in the last century, this century, and beyond, will strengthen students, parents, families, teachers, our nation, and the world.

CHRONOLOGICAL HIGHLIGHTS

The study of the relationship between family structure and academic achievement started many years ago. H.E.G. Sutherland (1930) undertook the first such study, in which he found a difference in the IQ between one- and two-parent children. Sutherland did not distinguish between the kinds of one-parent families. Hence, it is difficult to distinguish how much his results measured the effects of any specific family structure on academic achievement. Nevertheless, Sutherland's work launched the study of the relationship between family configuration and academic achievement. Fortes (1933) conducted some of the first research on stepfamilies at about the same time. He examined the relationship between "stepparenthood and juvenile delinquency" (p. 153). Fortes uncovered differences in the likelihood of stepchildren versus children from intact families committing delinquent acts. Nevertheless, the differences Fortes discovered were smaller than in previous studies. Although these major research inquiries took place during the first half of the 1930s, educators and social scientists initiated few studies on single parenthood and remarriage until just after World War II. The dearth of studies prior to World War II probably finds its roots in the fact that single parenthood occurred only on rare occasions prior to World War II.

After World War II sociologists and educators expressed new interest in the effects of single parenthood and remarriage. Because the departure of many young men into military service temporarily created many single-parent homes, World War II played a large role in the birth of this area of study. In addition, because of the pressures of extended wartime marital separation, there arose a temporary surge in the divorce rate. As a result, "father absence" studies emerged in increasing frequency during the first twenty years following this period.

William Smith (1945) wrote on the unique psychological adjustments facing the stepchild. Ivan Nye (1952) undertook an often-quoted study that took into consideration the interplay of other variables relevant to single-parenthood. He examined such factors as gender, sibling number, and whether the mother worked as intervening variables. Although Nye's study focused on "adjustment" rather than "achievement," his study produced two especially noteworthy results. First, Nye's results demonstrated "a significant association . . . with broken homes, on the average, showing poorer adolescent-parent adjustment" (p. 330). Nye noted, however, that the differences did not appear as great as some believed. Second, contrary to what many Americans believe, Nye found that children from "mother only" families "showed better adjustment than those with a 'stepfather'" (p. 330). Although Nye's work represented the most ambitious of the immediate post-World War II period, Nye, like so many of his contemporaries, lumped all the broken homes into one category. Therefore, we have no way of knowing how much of the effect stems from one-parent families in which one parent has passed away, and families in which divorce or other factors were at work. This distinction carried particular importance, because the ratio of each of these two causes of single-parent status were considerably different in 1952 than they are today.

Carlsmith (1964,1973) conducted a study which sought to measure the effect of parental absence on academic achievement in college students. In these cases all the instances of parental absence resulted from World War II military duty. Carlsmith found that students who experienced father absence suffered in academic achievement only if the military service necessitated an extended absence. Although many studies on divorce cite the Carlsmith study, some questions exist as to the extent that findings from temporary father-absence studies are applicable to the divorce and remarriage scenario. Salzman (1987), for example, conducted a meta-analysis in which she found that divorce had a major effect on educational achievement, but that father absence due to military service had none.

With the rising divorce rates of the 1960s and 1970s, researchers redoubled their efforts to further understand the effects of divorce on academic achievement. E. Mavis Hetherington and Judith Wallerstein contributed a great deal to the groundwork for research in divorce. Hetherington initiated several studies during the 1970s-1990s indicating that children from one-parent families trail children from intact homes in achievement and psychological adjustment (Hetherington 1972, 1973, 1989; Shok and Jurich, 1992). Hetherington also contributed a great deal to the knowledge of the effect of divorce on girls, discovering that adolescent girls from one-parent homes tend to exhibit more forms of "provocative" behavior with males than girls from intact homes (Hetherington 1972, 1973). Hetherington (1989) also found that a child's adjustment to divorce depends, in part, on the child's temperament.

Judith Wallerstein and colleagues conducted a longitudinal study on sixty volunteer families and 131 children ranging in age from three to eighteen. Wallerstein studied these families "intensively during a six-week period near the time of marital separation" and then again during follow-up studies after eighteen months, five years, ten years, and twenty-five years following the separation (Wallerstein and Lewis, 1998, p. 370). Numerous researchers applauded Wallerstein's longitudinal study as one of the most significant contributions to the body of research on divorce (Collins, 1981; Corsica, 1980;

Heyman, 1992). Wallerstein found divorce's impact on educational achievement remained substantial even five to ten years after the initial separation (Wallerstein and Blakeslee, 1989; Wallerstein and Kelly, 1980). Wallerstein estimated that 40 percent of the children in her study were "underachievers" (Wallerstein, 1987; Wallerstein and Lewis, 1998).

Despite its many strengths, the Wallerstein longitudinal study contains two weaknesses: (1) since the researchers used volunteers, one cannot easily ascertain whether the results are generalizable; and (2) since Wallerstein and her colleagues offered counseling advice to those that participated in the study, they acknowledged that this weakness could have somewhat weakened the effects of divorce in their study (Wallerstein and Kelly, 1980; Wallerstein and Lewis, 1998). In other words, the existence of counseling may have reduced the effects for divorce to a smaller level than might have otherwise been the case. But beyond this, the question of the extent that their volunteers constituted a representative sample leads one to conclude that there exists a need to make certain that future studies of this kind are representative.

The extent to which a sample is determined randomly poses even more of a problem on research into stepfamilies than it does one-parent families. Ganong and Coleman (1984) found that only 15 to 16 percent of the studies on stepfamilies used a random sample. Bernard's (1942) study, comparing personality differences among children from intact and reconstituted families, also used purely volunteers. Ironically, Bernard's work is one of the most cited works on remarriage in all of the research literature. Yet by the 1980s, several researchers started to point out that all of Bernard's subjects were either friends of his or acquaintances of those friends (Collins, 1981; Corsica, 1980).

Throughout the period that researchers have investigated divorce and remarriage, three types of subject pools generally used were: (1) volunteers; (2) random samples; and (3) a clinical population. Not surprisingly, a meta-analysis by Amato and Keith (1991) indicated that clinical populations generally yielded the largest effects, volunteers the smallest effects, and random samples moderate effects. The reasoning behind Amato's results is quite intuitive. If one examines a clinical population, he or she is more likely to find the most extreme cases of the detrimental effects of divorce. These clinical studies may only accurately tell us that the worst case scenarios in one-parent families are more severe than the worst case scenarios in intact families. Studies using volunteers present almost the reverse problem. The volunteers used are often college students and acquaintances of the researcher who tend to be well-adjusted and almost by definition have overcome some of the obstacles normally associated with divorce and remarriage. With these facts in mind, the need for representative samples appears obvious.

In the 1980s and 1990s, researchers redoubled their attempts to make sure their samples were more representative of the general population. Researchers availed themselves of the results of national surveys in order to obtain a more representative and larger sample of students.

Sally Banks Zakariya (1982) summarized the results of one of the first of these studies. This study, cosponsored by the National Association of Elementary School Principals (NAESP), and the Institute of Development of Educational Activities, found that children from one-parent homes showed "lower school achievement in school than their two-parent classmates" (Zakariya, 1982, p. 36). Zakariya also noted that children in stepfamilies achieved at a level between these two groups, but not significantly different from either one. Guidubaldi et al., (1983) conducted a nationwide NAESP study using a vast array of achievement measures and reported statistically significant differences in achievement between students from one- and two-parent families, even when controlling for family income level. McLanahan and Sandefur (1994) also found significant differences for academic achievement between one- and two-parent families. They investigated a few additional areas that Guidubaldi and colleagues did not examine. First, McLanahan and Sandefur did distinctly investigate the achievement of children from reconstituted families. They noted that children from these families achieved at the same level as children from single-parent families. But McLanahan and Sandefur generally failed to distinguish among the different types of stepfamilies. Second, McLanahan and Sandefur controlled for socioeconomic status (SES) in a more sophisticated way than Guidubaldi and colleagues. Although Guidubaldi and colleagues merely *controlled* for SES, McLanahan and Sandefur sought to determine divorce's impact on the SES level. In addition, McLanahan and Sandefur's study looked at SES as more than merely a certain level of income.

Overall, the examination of divorce and remarriage still represents a young science. It constitutes a discipline that still suffers from a high incidence of methodological problems and questions. Researchers are just now coming to grips with how to best measure those things that are easiest to quantify. Yet the progress in using more precise methodology, especially within the past few years, is undeniable. Given this trend, more progress seems likely in the coming years.

HISTORICAL AND CONTEMPORARY FACTS REGARDING FAMILY STRUCTURE

Facts Regarding Divorce

Being familiar with both the historical and contemporary facts about divorce carries importance for a number of reasons: (1) it helps us converse about divorce and remarriage in an intelligent and objective manner; (2) it helps us understand how widespread divorce is in its influence; and (3) it helps us understand some of unique challenges that confront our society that did not face us in past generations.

Historical Background

Until the early 1960s, Americans maintained a very different attitude toward divorce than is found today. Until this time, the vast majority of Americans believed that in order to keep the children from being hurt, divorce should be avoided in all but the most extreme circumstances. Psychologists and ministers alike taught that marital differences could be worked out if a married couple made a sufficient effort. Frequently, those who initiated divorce were considered selfish, placing their own needs ahead of their family (Furstenberg and Cherlin, 1991).

In 1900 only 3 percent of all couples divorced (Cherlin, 1978). In fact, until the 1930s most remarriages were due to the death of a spouse (Cherlin, 1978). Even including those children who had lost a parent due to death, the percentage of children in single-parent homes remained in the single digits until the early 1960s (Ahlburg and DeVita, 1992; Fitzpatrick, 1993). But beginning in 1962-1963, the percentage began to soar, rising to about 50 percent by 1970 and almost tripling from a rate of about 2.1 per 1,000 population to about 5.5 per thousand by 1991 (Ahlburg and DeVita, 1992). Currently, about 25 percent of children live in single-parent homes and roughly 50 to 60 percent will live in single-parent homes at some time in their childhood (Ahlburg and DeVita, 1992; Heyman, 1992). The statistics are even more sobering for African Americans. In 1960, 67 percent of African-American children lived in intact families. By 1980, this percentage declined to 42 percent, and by 1991, only 36 percent of these children lived in intact families (Ahlburg and DeVita, 1992; Bumpass, Sweet, and Martin, 1990).

Several prominent theories attempt to explain the dramatic rise in the number of couples filing for divorce. Most of these theories focus on one or two major themes. First, adults, prior to the 1960s, placed a higher priority on the welfare of their family (and especially their children) than they do today. Second, the industrial revolution created a societal structure conducive to higher rates of divorce.

A considerable amount of evidence supports both of these statements, although some facts remain unexplained. Historical studies, for example, surveying the history of fatherhood in America have been especially useful in understanding the changing attitudes that Americans have toward the family. These historical studies indicate, for example, that fathers in the late eighteenth and early nineteenth century committed a level of time and energy in the raising of their children that would be unfathomable in most American families today (Furstenberg, 1988). The rising percentage of mothers with young children in the workforce indicates that a declining number of mothers believe that child rearing represents a full-time job and that it may be more difficult than in the past for some families to live on one income. Even as late as 1940, only one in seven married women worked outside the home, and the ratio stood considerably lower for women married with young children (Furstenberg and Cherlin, 1991). The priorities of American fathers and mothers have changed and are still changing.

Evidence also suggests that industrialization has played a role in rising divorce rates, although the evidence is less persuasive. Generally speaking, when a nation becomes industrialized, its divorce rate tends to rise (Goode, 1992). Many European nations, for example, have experienced significant increases in their rates of divorce since World War II (McLanahan and Sandefur, 1994). Surely, increased interaction with the opposite sex and greater financial independence among women tend to accompany industrialization. Each of these trends would appear to increase the likelihood of divorce.

Nevertheless, there exist some shortcomings to theories that rely strongly on the link between divorce and industrialization. First, between the years 1890 and the late 1970s, two nations enjoyed greater levels of economic growth and industrialization than any other: Japan and the United States. Yet the divorce rates of both of these nations went in entirely different directions. While the divorce rate of the United States rose substantially, the divorce rate in Japan actually *fell* during this time (Goode, 1992). In addition, while other European nations did experience a rise in their divorce rates, the U.S. rate rose dramatically since 1962 (Hobbs and Lippman, 1990). Between 1960 and 1990, the U.S. divorce rate rose 12 percentage points. The divorce rate increases of the major European nations ranged from between 1 and 10 percentage points, with the average resting roughly halfway in between (McLanahan and Sandefur, 1994). Today, the United States holds the highest divorce rate in the world, with a rate 64 percent higher than second place Great Britain (Hobbs and Lippman, 1990). Therefore, while industrialization played some role in the increase of divorce rates, other factors help explain why the United States stands as the divorce capital of the world.

Interesting Facts

The near 50 percent divorce rate that exists in America today is of concern to many psychologists and researchers because of the many people affected by it. In a Harris poll adults were asked, "What is most important in life?" Ninety-six percent of those surveyed responded "to have a good family life" (Stinnett and DeFrain, 1985, pp. 3-4). In a similar Gallup poll, "eight of every ten people" called family "one of the most important or the most important facet of their lives" (Stinnett and DeFrain, 1985, pp. 3-4). Surely, divorce causes grand disappointment and hurt in an area so important to many people.

Fifty percent of the marriages that took place in 1970 will likely end in divorce (Block, Block, and Gjerde, 1986). This figure is a direct consequence of rising divorce rates. From 1970 to 1990, while marriage rates declined 30 percent, divorce rates surged ahead 40 percent (Ahlburg and DeVita, 1992). From 1980 onward, the number of divorces per year generally fluctuated between 1.1 to 1.5 million (Fitzpatrick, 1993; Zill, 1994). During that time, the divorce rate finally appeared to stabilize, after years of dramatic growth (Cherlin, 1988). Yet simply examining the rise in divorce rates starting in the 1960s does not communicate the extent to which children have suffered during this time. In 1950, only 46 percent of the divorces that took place involved children (Cherlin, 1978). By 1974, this figure rose to 60 percent (Cherlin, 1978). Estimates are that in the future, 70 percent of the divorces taking place may involve children under the age of eighteen (Block, Block, and Gjerde, 1986). Hence, not only have divorce rates risen in the past few decades, but so has the propensity for a divorce to involve children. Many of these children are young children. The average duration of a marriage that ends in divorce stands at only about 6.5 to 7 years (Chadwick and Heaton, 1992).

The result of these trends is that there has been a significant demographic change in the percentage of American children living with *both* natural parents. The percentage of children who eventually live with single parents was limited to less than 10 percent (and much of this figure was due to the death of a parent) for most of U.S. history (Fitzpatrick, 1993; McLanahan, 1999). The percentage rose to 33 percent by 1981, and 43 percent by 1993 (Zill, 1994). Estimates indicate that between 50 to 60 percent of young children will eventually live in a one-parent family (Bumpass, 1984; Glick, 1980; Heyman, 1992). Some researchers emphasize *only* the percentage of children in single-parent homes *at this moment.* This figure stands at about 23 to 25 percent (Cherlin, 1988; Fitzpatrick, 1993). But citing only this figure overlooks the millions of children who experienced *both* a divorce and a remarriage in their household. A growing number of researchers argue that the experience of remarriage in the household is also very traumatic for children (Bray, 1999; Deater-Deckhard and Dunn, 1999; Hetherington, 1999; Jeynes, 1998a, 1999b; Wallerstein, Corbin, and Lewis, 1988). Beyond this, we should not forget the number of children who experience divorce in their household more than once over the course of their childhood. Bumpass (1984) notes that "about half of the children who go through a divorce and remarriage, will experience the breakup of the new family as well" (p. 71). Second marriages with children are especially prone to end up in divorce (Avenevoli, Sessa, and Steinberg, 1999; Booth and Dunn, 1994; Wallerstein and Blakeslee, 1989). McLanahan (1999) and Heyman (1992) found that the more changes in a family structure a child experienced, the more likely he or she would perform poorly in school. Anderson, Hetherington, and Clingempeel (1999) found that the number of transitions also affects other social functions among children.

Divorce rates do differ among different groups of people and in different circumstances. Divorce tends to fluctuate somewhat with the business cycle, decreasing during times of recession (Goode, 1982; Haskey, 1984). Divorce also takes place more frequently among people of the lower economic strata (Hoem, 1997). This latter fact emerges as the main reason why researchers have tended to overcontrol for SES. Some researchers thought the SES variable reflected only the tendency for those with a low SES to divorce more often. What they neglected to consider, however, is the fact that divorce *causes* a drop in the SES level.

Facts Regarding Never-Married Parents

The percentage of women with out-of-wedlock births has also soared in the last thirty years. Much of this rise finds its roots in the changes of sexual behavior of the last thirty to thirty-five years. Surveys conducted in the 1950s indicated that roughly 20 percent of women reported having sex before marriage (Garfinkel and McLanahan, 1986). That percentage jumped to 32 percent by 1967 and to 60 percent by 1973 (Garfinkel and McLanahan, 1986). In 1950, only 4 percent of all births were to unwed mothers, but by 1984, 21 percent of all births were to unwed mothers (Cherlin, 1988). By 1990, the percentage stood at 30 percent (Zill and Nord, 1994). For whites, the percentages stood at 2 percent in 1950, 13 percent in 1984, and 22 percent in 1990 (Cherlin, 1988; Zill and Nord, 1994).

In terms of the issue at hand, we should regard these trends as important for a number of reasons. First, in addition to the increased propensity to divorce, out-of-wedlock births constitute a major contributing factor to the rise in single-parent homes in America. Second, because out-of-wedlock births contribute to this growing number of single-parent households, the need for researchers to distinguish between the *different kinds* of single-parent households becomes imperative. Third, evidence indicates that children of divorce are much more likely to have out-of-wedlock births (Kiernan and Hobcraft, 1997; Stevenson and Black, 1995). Therefore, the growing percentage of children who experience parental divorce will increase the likelihood that the "epidemic" of single-parent households will last well into the next century.

Chapter 2

Research Regarding the Effects of Family Structure on Children

THE EFFECTS OF DIVORCE ON ACADEMIC ACHIEVEMENT: RESEARCH RESULTS

The bulk of evidence supporting an effect of divorce upon academic achievement is quite vast. Studies on the effect of divorce on academic achievement almost always fall into one of three categories, in terms of their results: (1) those studies that show a statistically significant effect favoring intact families over children from one-parent homes; (2) studies that show a statistically *insignificant* advantage favoring children from intact families; and (3) studies that show no statistically significant effect between children according to family structure. Studies with results different from these three categories are extremely rare. Gilner's (1988) meta-analysis, for example, found only one study favoring one-parent families over two-parent families. Studies finding even insignificant results favoring children from one-parent families are also very rare (Gilner, 1988).

Studies Showing Statistically Significant Differences Favoring Children from Two-Parent Families

Research on the impact of divorce on educational achievement indicates that the academic advantage for children from intact families holds for various ages and using various means of measurement.

Guidubaldi and Perry (1984), for example, found large differences in achievement as early as kindergarten. Couch and Lillard (1997) and Mednick and colleagues (1990) found that considerable advantages exist for children from intact families even into the college years. Most research studies investigated the impact that divorce had

13

on academic achievement for more than a year, although most studies focused on either elementary or secondary school. The result is that a voluminous amount of data exists for all grade levels confirming the extent of divorce's impact on achievement. A study sponsored by the NAESP (1980) may represent the most extensive research, in terms of examining both elementary and secondary school students. This study found a large gap between the Grade Point Average (GPA) of children from one-and two-parent homes. Jenkins and Guidubaldi (1997) and Shreeve and associates (1986) also examined several grade levels and found that the effects of divorce proved quite consistent across grade levels. Jenkins and Guidubaldi (1997) examined grades one, three, and five, Shreeve looked at grades seven to twelve, and Elliot and Richards (1991) examined students aged seven to sixteen. Elliot and Richards, like the NAESP study, considered both elementary and secondary students and found consistent significant effects favoring intact families. Other elementary school studies have typically focused on between one and five grade levels and generally found statistically significant results favoring children from intact families (Allen and Tadlock, 1986; Roizblatt, Rivera, and Fuchs, 1997).

Researchers analyzing the effects of divorce on students in junior high school and high school generally look at a more restricted sample of age levels. For example, Wood, Chapin, and Hannah (1988) studied high school seniors, Fitzpatrick (1993) examined high school juniors, and Peckham (1989) focused on sophomores. Some studies drew their data from two grade levels (e.g., Mednick et al., 1990; Milne et al., 1986), but only a handful of studies considered a broader age range of high school students (Elliot and Richards, 1991; Jeynes, 1998b). Part of the reason for this specificity in the research on high school students may rest in the fact that most people associate the teenage years with considerable change. Indeed, evidence suggests that a good deal of the behavioral changes associated with divorce emerge during the teenage years. Therefore, some researchers probably want to isolate when these changes take place. Once again, no matter what the grade level, divorce shows a consistent effect on academic achievement among students in both junior high school and high school (Kurdek and Sinclair, 1988; McLanahan and Sandefur, 1994; Metcalf and Gaier, 1987).

The studies that found statistically significant effects used a vast array of measurements. Among them were GPA measurements, IQ tests, the California Achievement Test (CAT), Miller Analogies Test (MAT), various other measures of reading and mathematics achievement, as well as teacher ratings.

Shinn (1978) noted that three-quarters of the studies she examined in her meta-analysis showed statistically significant effects. One should note, however, that some of the researchers complained that the variance in achievement test scores (or GPA, etc.) accounted for by the impact of divorce was rather low. Kurdek and Sinclair (1988), for example, found that their divorce model accounted for only 7 percent of the variance in academic performance among the eighth-graders that they studied.

Studies Showing Statistically Insignificant Differences Favoring Children from Two-Parent Families

The vast majority of studies that show no statistically significant differences in achievement show results that nevertheless point in the expected direction of favoring children from intact families. These studies usually fall into one of two categories: (a) those studies demonstrating *only* statistically insignificant differences favoring children from intact families; and (b) those studies showing *mixed* results in which statistically significant differences existed for some groups of children, but not others. Other recent studies also suffer from this limitation (e.g., Wadsby and Svedin, 1996).

A number of the studies indicating insignificant differences in the expected direction share a common weakness in that they used small sample sizes. For example, Hoffman and Zippco (1986) used just seventeen subjects in their study of ten- and twelve-year-olds; and Massey (1987) used thirty-three subjects in analyzing the effects of divorce on fifth graders.

Other studies, however, used larger sample sizes, but still produced results above the .05 probability level. Solomon and colleagues' (1972) results using fifth-grade African-American children raised the possibility that divorce may not impact the lives of black children as much as it does white children. These results, however, approached but did not exceed statistical significance. Biggs (1986) examined 250 fourth-grade children and also uncovered statistically insignificant results.

Studies that yielded mixed results (i.e., some differences that were statistically significant and others that were not) did not evince any predictable pattern. Kaye (1988/1989), for example, found that boys suffered more academically than girls as a result of divorce. Other researchers have found differences by gender, although not as clear-cut as those found by Kaye (Nigel, 1998).

Some studies indicated that the effects of divorce may prove significant for children of some ages, but not for others (Santrock, 1972), or for some ages *more* than others (Canziani, 1996; Hetherington, 1993; Kalter and Rembar, 1981; Swartzman-Schatman and Schinke, 1993).

Although many researchers agree that divorce produces differential impacts on children depending on their gender and age, the relationship is often complex and depends on a multitude of other variables.

Studies That Show No Statistically Significant Effect Between Children According to Family Structure

Although they are few in number, some studies show neither a statistically significant nor an insignificant difference in academic achievement favoring children from intact families. (Cortes and Fleming, 1968; Beer, 1989). Most of the studies that yield such results actually do not reveal the direction of their insignificant findings. Hence, it would be presumptuous to assume a direction for the majority of these insignificant differences. Once again, the small sample size used in some of these studies may help explain why significant differences did not result (Beer, 1989).

Researchers debate about whether different effects exist for different academic subjects. Some studies suggest that divorce influences all academic achievement in all subjects equally or almost equally (Guidubaldi et al., 1983; Kaye, 1988/1989). Other studies indicate that father absence may particularly hurt math scores (Carlsmith, 1973).

Researchers also debate about whether divorce influences student grades or standardized test scores more than the other. In their research synthesis of 1981, Hetherington and colleagues concluded that divorce impacts school grades more than it does standardized tests (Hetherington, Camara, and Featherman, 1981). If their conclusion is correct, this effect could result from any number of different dynamics. These possible dynamics include: (a) undesirable working and/or behavioral patterns that produce a larger drag on grades than they do on standardized test scores; (b) a possible "Pygmalion effect," in which the expectations of teachers may exert downward pressure on the grades of single-parent students (Rosenthal and Jacobson, 1968); and (c) the notion that grades might measure something different than standardized tests. Jeynes (1998b) used the NELS data set to see if Hetherington's results could be confirmed. He found that while parental divorce impacted school grades more than it did standardized tests for eighth graders, the reverse is true for the twelfth-grade level.

THE EFFECTS OF REMARRIAGE FOLLOWING DIVORCE ON ACADEMIC ACHIEVEMENT

Research on stepfamilies stands at a much less advanced stage than research on single-parent families (Furstenberg, 1988; Wertlieb, 1997). The primary reason for this is because few studies on stepfamilies have been done (Booth and Dunn, 1994; Emery, 1988; Ganong and Coleman, 1994; Jeynes, 1998a; Wertlieb, 1997). Studies that have been done on stepfamilies often suffer from many weaknesses. The vast majority did not use a random sample. This limitation poses even more of a problem on research into stepfamilies than it does with one-parent families. Ganong and Coleman (1984) evaluated thirty-eight studies specifically dealing with the effects of remarriage on children. Of these thirty-eight studies, only six used a random sample. Only one of the studies in their review used *both* a random sample and had academic achievement as a dependent variable. Bernard's (1942) study, which compared personality differences among children from intact and reconstituted families, also used purely friends and acquaintances. Other studies suffer from similar shortcomings. Duberman (1975) examined only Caucasian stepfamilies. In addition, as Heyman (1992) notes, many studies that included children from stepfamilies can yield no information specific to stepfamilies, because they are lumped into the same category with children from intact families. A main reason for this failure to distinguish stepfamilies from other family structures rests in the assumption that remarriage is a positive experience for children. Therefore, the only distinction of family structures that was necessary was between children from one-parent and two-parent families.

As a consequence of all these limitations in the research, little is known about the effect of remarriage on the academic achievement and emotional well-being of children (Booth and Dunn, 1994; Furstenberg, 1988; Jeynes, 1998a; Wertlieb, 1997).

Although there exists considerable consensus among family theorists regarding the negative effects of divorce upon children both psychologically and in terms of academic achievement (Dawson, 1991; Dornbusch et al., 1987; Downey and Powell, 1993), the same consensus does not exist regarding the effects of remarriage. A large degree of this lack of agreement stems from these problems in the literature on stepfamilies.

As the research literature on reconstituted families has proliferated, a growing number of social scientists have concluded that the positive effects of remarriage have been exaggerated. Nevertheless, Ganong and Coleman (1984) noted that some sociologists are very insistent that remarriage does not perniciously impact children. Indeed, some researchers remain unconvinced that children from reconstituted homes are any worse off, in any respect, than children from intact families (Beer, 1992; MacDonald and DeMaris, 1995).

In recent years, however, social scientists have accumulated a sizable amount of evidence indicating that remarriage may have ill-effects on many children. Many children demonstrate reluctance in accepting a new parental figure (Deater-Deckhard and Dunn, 1999; Fine, Coleman, and Ganong, 1999; Ganong et al., 1999; Hetherington, 1999; Pagani et al., 1998; Thomson, McLanahan, and Curtin, 1992). Children in reconstituted families often struggle with rivalries with their stepbrothers and stepsisters, as well as jealous feelings toward their new stepparent (Anderson and Rice, 1992). William Smith (1945) also noted, "When a stepparent enters a new home, there is a danger of favoritism. A parent usually is partial to his or her own children. A stepfather compares his child with the wife's own child to the disadvantage of the latter" (p. 239). Stepchildren often feel that the stepparent monopolizes the time and energy of the natural parent (Amato, 1987; Kelly, 1992; Walsh, 1992). McLanahan and Sandefur (1994) used three nationwide data sets in their analysis and concluded that children from stepfamilies were much more mobile (i.e., likely to move away from their homes) than children from other families. McLanahan and Sandefur (1994) believe this mobility constitutes a major handicap for children from reconstituted families. In addition, children often suffer because remarriage often produces an increased tension between the biological parents (Walsh, 1992).

All in all, the research indicates that children in reconstituted families suffer because they often live in an unstable environment of increased mobility, adapting to difficult new roles and relationships, (Hetherington and Jodl, 1994; McLanahan and Sandefur, 1994) and frequently unstable remarriages (Booth and Edwards, 1992; Popenoe, 1994). As a result, many children from reconstituted homes become frustrated and show a greater tendency to be aggressive, anxious, and unhappy than children from intact families (Elliot and Richards, 1991; Nunn, Parish, and Worthing, 1993; Wallerstein and Lewis, 1998). Given these tendencies, it is not surprising that Duberman's (1975) often-cited study on the reconstituted family found that remarried parents rate "child rearing" as the number one problem of living in a reconstituted family.

Some moderating influences may exist in the challenges that stepchildren face such as the age of the child, the length of time that the child has lived in a reconstituted home, and the extent of the communication between the stepchild and the stepparent (Anderson, Lindner, and Bennion, 1992; Walsh, 1992; White, 1994). Nevertheless, there is considerable value in acknowledging and sensitizing oneself to the challenges that most stepchildren face. A longitudinal study by Hetherington (1992) indicated that adolescents and stepsons may find a new parental authority more difficult than younger children and girls, respectively. Indeed, the overall body of research on stepfamilies confirms the notion that younger children generally adjust better to their stepfamilies than older children do (Hetherington, Stanley-Hagan, and Anderson, 1989). Gender differences, in the effect of remarriage on children, do not show a consistent pattern from one study to another, favoring boys or girls. Many theorists who believe remarriage can have a positive effect, claim that remarriage should especially benefit boys because most remarriages will involve the reintroduction of a father figure into the boy's home (Cherlin, et al., 1991; Zaslow, 1988, 1989). However, the results of studies examining the effects of remarriage only sporadically support this perspective. Whether academic measures or psychological measures are used, some studies indicate that girls struggle more than boys in adjusting to the presence of a stepparent (Baltes, Featherman, and

Lerner, 1990; Beer 1992; Hetherington, 1989; Zaslow, 1988, 1989). Kalter (1977) reviewed the records of 400 children referred for outpatient psychiatric evaluation and found a much higher proportion of girls than boys coming from reconstituted families. Kalter concludes: "The high rate of occurrence of girls from stepparent, typically stepfather, homes subsequent to divorce indicates that girls whose divorced mothers remarry could constitute a group of children particularly at risk" (p. 47). The fact that Kalter refers to girls living with stepfathers is especially noteworthy. As Brenda Maddox observed in her classic book, *The Half-Parent,* "Sexual attraction between stepparents and stepchildren can be a major complication in stepfamilies . . . . The real reason why sex becomes an issue is that the incest taboo, the organizing principle of family life is missing. Nobody in a stepfamily knows what the ground rules are" (p. 91).

Despite the concerns raised by these findings, other studies suggest that daughters may actually benefit from the act of parental remarriage (MacDonald and DeMaris, 1995; Nunn, Parish, and Worthing, 1993). The research to date regarding gender differences in the effects of remarriage appears inconclusive.

THE EMOTIONAL AND PSYCHOLOGICAL EFFECTS OF DIVORCE ON CHILDREN

Researchers agree that one should not treat separately the relationship between divorce and academic achievement on the one hand, and the overall effects of divorce on child development, on the other. In fact, some of the keys to understanding the link between divorce and academic achievement rest in some of these other effects. Researchers agree that divorce, almost by definition, results in: (1) more stress upon the children involved; and (2) less parental support (Bruce, 1998; DeGarmo and Forgatch, 1999; Hetherington, 1999; McLanahan and Sandefur, 1994; Uhlenberg and Eggebeen, 1986). Recently, McLanahan and Sandefur (1994) noted that lack of community support may also play a role in hindering ideal child development. They noted that following a divorce, the child often moves to a new community. As a result, the absence of supportive friends and the parent's lack of knowledge of community resources will often make adjustment more difficult for the child.

More Stress upon the Children

Several researchers, without qualification, refer to the divorce experience as the most stressful time of a child's life (NAESP, 1980; Thomas and Forehand, 1993; Wallerstein and Kelly, 1980; Wertlieb, 1997). Moles (1982) went so far to say that the effect of this stress on the life of the child waxes even greater in the case of divorce than it does with a parent's death. After all, divorce results in a sudden and *voluntary* (on the part of the parents) imbalance in the family system (Gilner, 1988). The voluntary nature of divorce (in contrast to most deaths) creates a sense of parental betrayal in the hearts of many children (Corsica, 1980), as well as anger (Dreman, Spielberger, and Fried, 1999). Many children feel lonely (Wallerstein and Lewis, 1998) and many of them feel their needs are not met (Wallerstein and Kelly, 1980). Nevertheless, one can also argue that in the case of divorce there often is at least some access to the absent parent. In contrast, when a parent dies, no such access is possible. Hence, of these two unfortunate events, one would be hard pressed to say which hurts the child more.

Divorce produces a great deal of stress in the life of the single parent, often causing the parent to become depressed (Dreman, Spielberger, and Fried, 1999; Forgatch, Patterson, and Ray, 1996; Wallerstein and Kelly, 1980; Cortes and Fleming, 1968). Bronfenbrenner (1979) and Wallerstein and Kelly (1980) asserted that what affects the mother invariably affects the child. Some researchers believe that children from divorced homes do not differ from children from intact homes in their psychological adjustment overall (Wilson et al., 1975), or at least in the long run (Dunlop and Burns, 1995). But such conclusions are rare. Although few would dispute the notion that different children respond in different ways to divorce (Hetherington, 1999), there remains a widely held belief that children from single-parent families have a harder time adjusting in life overall (Amato, 1999; DeGarmo and Forgatch, 1999; Hetherington, 1999; McLanahan, 1999).

Several studies confirm the belief that children from divorced homes encounter greater difficulty in adjusting psychologically and otherwise. Research indicates that among eighteen- to twenty-two-year-olds from homes experiencing divorce, 41 percent had received psychological help (Fitzpatrick, 1993). Similarly, Kalter's (1977) research indicated that "children of divorce, appeared at nearly twice the rate of their occurrence in the general population" at his psychiatric clinic (p. 40). Various psychological studies performed in recent years tend to confirm these results (Emery, Kitzmann, and Waldron, 1999; Wertlieb, 1997). If it is true that the impact of divorce on the parents affects the children, these findings should not surprise us. Divorced men are eighteen times as likely to seek psychological help than married men (Luepnitz, 1978). Of course, these results may exaggerate the impact of divorce. One can argue that men with significant psychological problems are more likely to get a divorce than those who do not suffer from these problems. Nevertheless, it seems likely that a significant portion of the men seeking psychological help did so because of problems resulting from the divorce. Hetherington (1989) believed that most children recover from divorce within two to three years, but most longitudinal studies contradict this claim (Love-Clark, 1984; Wallerstein and Lewis, 1998). These results have caused even those researchers who asserted that divorce had an effect over a short length of time to readjust their views (Hetherington, Cox, and Cox, 1985).

The typical effects of divorce on a child have some similarities with the effects of the 1973 oil crisis on the U.S. economy (Norman, 1995). Today, the oil crisis is over. But most economists agree that the U.S. economy has never been the same since that time. Economists refer to the post-World War II time of prosperity as covering the period 1945-1973. Since 1973, the growth in the U.S. Gross Domestic Product (GDP) has slowed substantially. In a similar way, the "divorce crisis" a child faced may have happened years ago. Although the crisis is over, many children of divorce are never quite the same. Wallerstein and Kelly found that divorce created substantial problems for children even ten years following the marital breakup (Wallerstein and Kelly, 1980; Wallerstein and Lewis, 1998). A growing number of studies suggest that the effects of divorce on children extend well into adulthood (Amato, 1999; Haurin, 1992; Wertlieb, 1997; Werner and Smith, 1992).

Naturally, the extent of the effects of divorce vary from child to child (Hetherington, 1999; Linker, Stolberg, and Green, 1999). Such factors as the number of changes in the marital structure (Anderson, Hetherington, and Clingempeel, 1999) and the number of times a family moves (McLanahan and Sandefur, 1994) can exacerbate or attenuate the effects of divorce.

Given this wide range of data on the stressful effects of divorce on children, psychologists believe a "crisis model" best conceptualizes its influence (Baltes, Featherman, and Lerner, 1990). Garmezy and Rutter (1983) further added that if other stresses, in addition to divorce, arise in the child's life, the combined effects of the two stresses are geometric in their increased effect rather than additive. They claim, "The combined effects of the two together was greater than the sum of the two considered separately" (Garmezy and Rutter, 1983, p. 22).

Less Parental Support

Less parental support takes a number of different forms. First, less parental support means less parental involvement in the child's life, schoolwork, etc. (McLanahan and Sandefur, 1994; Zill and Nord, 1994). Second, there emerges less parental supervision (McLanahan and Sandefur, 1994). Third, with less parental support also comes less parental control (McLanahan and Sandefur, 1994). Fourth, single parents tend to spend less time with their children (Gilner, 1988). As a result of this, children from single-parent homes generally have less access to the adults in their home in terms of asking for help with schoolwork (Gross, 1982), etc. Wallerstein and Kelly's (1980) research indicates that in a home in which parents are divorced the children receive "little help from their parents." Wallerstein and Kelly aver that the primary reason for this tendency rests in the fact that divorce has caused "radical alterations" in the lives of the parents. Therefore, the parents tend "to focus their attention on their own troubles" (p. 36). Of course marital problems *begin* before the onset of divorce. As a consequence, McLanahan and Sandefur (1994) noted that at least some of the tendency for single parents to spend less time helping their children in schoolwork could predate divorce.

The increased stress that parents experience likely contributes to a reduction in all four of the aspects of parental support (less involvement, supervision, control, and time). In addition, Garfinkel and McLanahan (1986) and others noted that the proportion of mothers working outside the home tends to rise prodigiously after a divorce (Garfinkel and McLanahan, 1986; Zill and Nord, 1994). This fact could also lead to decreased parental support. Even if an increase in work hours does not produce a direct influence, it can lead to a "task overload" in which the single parent faces too many concurrent responsibilities (Gilner, 1988).

Most family theorists believe that the decline in parental support, although often involuntary, leads to certain behaviors in children that are conducive to bad grades. Numerous researchers note that children whose parents are divorced tend to show more problems in the areas of: (a) absenteeism and tardiness (Fitzpatrick, 1993; NAESP staff, 1980); (b) a lower self-concept (Robinson, 1997; Rosenthal and Hansen, 1980); (c) suspensions and disciplinary problems (Hett, 1983; NAESP staff, 1980); and (d) general school behavior (Dornbusch et al., 1985; Zill, Morrison, and Coiro, 1993). The divorce literature also indicates that children of divorce tend to (e) suffer the greatest academic decline in their areas of greatest strength previous to the divorce (Heyman, 1992); and (f) appear to be less obedient to their parents (Dornbusch et al., 1985).

Behavioral Problems

In addition to the academic effects of divorce on children are various undesirable social behaviors which are highly correlated with divorce. Frequently, educators and sociologists avoid even the mention of these behaviors because they do not wish to be insensitive. However, as McLanahan and Sandefur (1994) noted, it is the very avoidance of dialogue on these issues that is insensitive. To the extent that divorce causes children to hurt, professionals in any field of endeavor ought to do what they can to minimize that hurt. Educators and sociologists ought to join those in the clergy and marriage/family counseling in doing what they can to address the hurt that divorce causes in children.

Various research studies indicate that girls of divorced parents are more likely to give birth out of wedlock (Garfinkel and McLanahan, 1986; McLanahan and Sandefur, 1994; Stevenson and Black, 1995; Wallerstein and Lewis, 1998; Zill and Rogers, 1988). Evidence also suggests that girls of divorced parents manifest more provocative sexually oriented behavior than their counterparts from intact marriages (Gabardi and Rosen, 1992; Hetherington, 1973). Short (1998) found that boys from single-parent homes also engaged in more aggressive behavior than boys from two-parent homes.

An abundance of literature is available regarding what undesirable social behaviors prove more prevalent among children of divorce.

Several studies indicate a higher incidence of juvenile delinquency (Emery et al., 1999; Fitzpatrick, 1993; Moore, 1988); disciplinary problems (Dornbusch et al., 1985); emotional problems (Fitzpatrick, 1993; Hetherington, 1999); and overall behavioral problems (Amato, 1999). Some researchers claim that once SES and other factors are controlled for, the differences vanish (Santrock, 1972). Many educators and psychologists, however, disagree with this perspective.

Two of the most disturbing factors that researchers have found in children of divorce are the relationships between: (1) divorce and suicide (Dineen, 1990; Lester, 1986; Stack, 1989; Trovato, 1986, 1987; Wasserman, 1984) and (2) divorce and homicide (Kowalski and Stack, 1992). These findings indicate that the increased incidence of divorce may go a long way in explaining the soaring rates of juvenile suicide and homicide which have become part of the American scene since the early 1960s (Barton, 1994; U.S. Department of Justice, 1993; Zill and Rogers, 1988). Some of the research in this area has focused on the relationship between divorce rates and suicide and homicide rates as a whole (Gould et al., 1998; Trovato, 1986; Wasserman, 1984). Other studies have found that children of divorce, specifically, are more likely to engage in acts of this kind than their counterparts in intact families (Dineen, 1990; Moore, 1988, 1995).

CIRCUMSTANCES THAT CAN INFLUENCE
THE EFFECTS OF DIVORCE

Although social scientists often approach divorce as a singular phenomenon, many variables exist that influence the severity of the divorce for the child. None of these variables make divorce less of a negative event for the child. In addition, different variables will have differing impacts on each child. Nevertheless, certain variables can increase or decrease the severity of divorce, as experienced by children. Researchers have found that the following factors prove especially weighty when understanding the influence of divorce upon children.

How Parental Stress Affects Children

The extent to which the divorce impacts the parents often determines the extent to which the divorce impacts the child. Bronfenbrenner (1979) and Robinson (1997) assert that what significantly influences one member of the family will ultimately affect other members of the family. Brigitte Mednick and colleagues found that a mother's level of discontentment negatively correlated with achievement test scores (Mednick et al., 1990). Along similar lines, Brady and Forehand (1988) found that high levels of maternal depression correlated with psychological maladjustment in children. Forgatch, Patterson, and Ray (1996) found that maternal depression can have a negative psychological impact on children. How a parent feels and behaves in the aftermath of a divorce depends, of course, on the circumstances surrounding the divorce. First, marriages ending in divorce due to adultery, for example, are especially stressful (Lawson, 1988). In the case of adultery, the innocent parent feels a sense of betrayal because the marriage partner has not kept the marital vows (Lawson, 1988). For example, a husband often encounters a particularly hard time when he feels victimized by his wife leaving him to engage in an affair with another man (Jeynes, 1998b). Even though the wife is guilty of adultery, the law usually requires the husband to pay alimony and child support, and the wife usually gets custody of the children (Garfinkel and McLanahan, 1986; Maccoby, 1992; Maccoby, Buchanon, Mnookin, and Dornbusch, 1993).

Second, divorces that involve physical abuse also involve high levels of stress. The victim (usually the woman) must come to grips with the fact that the man she married is quite different from the man she knows now (Lawson, 1988).

Third, divorce proves especially painful for those marriage partners who really do not want the divorce, but would prefer to work together to make the marital relationship better. In many cases, the marriage partner who is not filing for divorce experiences a sense of helplessness and in some cases unpleasant surprise, which makes divorce more difficult (Davis and Murch, 1988; Robinson, 1997).

Most of all, divorce presents an especially stressful and saddening experience for the children involved (Ayoub, Deutsch, and Maraganore, 1999; Mednick et al., 1990; Robinson, 1997; Wallerstein and Lewis, 1998). As a result, children frequently look to the custodial parent to help relieve that stress. But to the extent that the custodial parent also wrestles with depression and stress, it becomes difficult for that parent to ameliorate the feelings of depression and stress experienced by the children.

How Parents Treat Children

How the parents treat the children plays a role in determining the extent to which divorce affects children involved (Ayoub, Deutsch, and Maraganore, 1999; Linker, Stolberg, and Green, 1999). The quality of parenting that a child receives is often more cumbersome to assess than it might appear at first glance. The quality of parenting, in some important respects, depends on the quality of the relationship between the parents (Amato, 1993; Mechanic and Hansell, 1989; Twaite, Silitsky, and Luchow, 1998). Children frequently feel that the parents treat them as pawns in the midst of an emotional chess match, intensifying their sense of feeling caught between parents (Buchanon, Maccoby, and Dornbusch, 1991; Schlesinger, 1975; Twaite, Silitsky, and Luchow, 1998).

Most parents seek to provide a loving atmosphere for their children. The child's discipline or lack of discipline is an important issue, especially because Gallup poll results indicate that Americans believe this issue constitutes "the main fault of parents in raising children" (Chadwick and Heaton, 1992, p. 76). This has implications not only for potential behavioral problems, but in school achievement as well. In the 1993 National Households Education Survey, only 38 percent of sixth to twelfth grade students said that their friends thought it was important to work hard in school (as cited in Zill and Nord, 1994). In general, parental involvement does positively correlate with family income (Zill and Nord, 1994). Nevertheless, because one parent must now fulfill many of the responsibilities normally done by two parents, this is difficult.

Custodial Arrangement and Level of Cooperation Between Parents

Approximately 90 percent of children of divorce live with their mother following the divorce (Hetherington, 1993). Although undecided issues remain on the differential impact of maternal and paternal custody according to the gender of the child, a growing number of social scientists instead choose to argue that boys and girls need *both* their mother and father (Acock and Kiecolt, 1989; McLanahan and Sandefur, 1994). Although psychologists and sociologists emphasize the effects of father absence on sons, theorists are now increasingly appreciating the effect of father absence on daughters (Peckam, 1989). The reality is that children long for their parents to reunite and if they do not, they yearn to have ongoing close relationships with each parent (Wallerstein and Kelly, 1980). In recognizing the need that children have for both parents, social scientists have begun to examine the notion of joint custody more seriously. Research indicates that children generally prefer joint custody over one-parent custodial rights (Shiller, 1986; Wallerstein and Blakeslee, 1989). The verdict is not yet in on whether joint custody produces better adjusted children, i.e., the results thus far are inconclusive (Emery, 1988; Gilner, 1988; Wallerstein and Blakeslee, 1989;). Presently, only about 22 percent of divorced couples obtain joint custody (U.S. Department of Health, 1998). In his study on joint custody, Lichtenstein (1990) notes: "Mutual access of children and parents to each other was seen as joint custody's main benefit, while frequent interaction with the ex-spouse was the major drawback." Lichtenstein goes on to note that 88 percent of the parents examined in his study were satisfied with joint custody (Lichtenstein, 1990, p. xii).

Camara and Resnick (1988) emphasize that "the degree of interparental cooperation in the postdivorce period" helps determine "the children's psychosocial adjustment" (pp. 191-192). Some debate exists over whether joint custody makes parental cooperation easier (Maccoby, 1992). To the extent that joint custody facilitates this cooperation, it may represent a healthy alternative to single-parent custody.

Support from Relatives and Peers for the Child and the Custodial Parent

Children who have suffered through a parental divorce, over which they have had no control, are in great need of emotional support. The support of relatives and peers can help a child more effectively endure the divorce experience. One should note, however, that the presence of relatives and peers does not necessarily connote support. Research indicates that using a grandmother as a parental substitute may do more harm than good (McLanahan and Sandefur, 1994). A child's peers can also obtain too much influence in a child's life and do damage (Lasch, 1977). Peers can have views different from a child's parents and can engage in activities that pull the child of divorce away from the family (Coleman, 1989; Zill and Nord, 1994). But to the extent that a child's siblings and friends do maintain values consistent with those of the parents, they can help him or her endure the changes that have taken place in his or her family (Hetherington, 1989).

Custodial Parents Who Move Frequently

Thirty-eight percent of custodial mothers move within the first year following a divorce (Garfinkel and McLanahan, 1986). Research indicates that fathers who do not live with their children are even more mobile than mothers with children (McLanahan and Sandefur, 1994). McLanahan and Sandefur (1994) found that mobility correlates negatively with academic achievement. When a family moves, it moves away from many of the support systems that served to alleviate some of the more severe effects of divorce (McLanahan and Sandefur, 1994). In addition, when a father moves frequently, the relocation often results in living farther from the children than was previously the case. As a result, the children often have less access to the benefits that come with having a father. Hence, when we examine the effects of mobility, we should note not only whether the custodial parent has moved, but also whether the noncustodial parent has moved.

Using data from two national data sets, the High School and Beyond data set and the Panel Study of Income Dynamics (PSID), McLanahan and Sandefur (1994) found that single-parent families moved considerably more often than two-parent families, and that stepfamilies moved most of all. The tendency for divorced families (single-parent and reconstituted) to move more frequently than intact families proves especially salient during the time of a child's secondary school education (NAESP staff, 1980). One can argue that moving during this time might do more harm than moving at an earlier age, because the roots of the child in the community are probably deeper at this older age.

Given these results, McLanahan and Sandefur (1994) conclude "middle-class parents should . . . minimize the number of times the child changes schools or neighborhoods. They should do this . . . to lower the risk that her grade-point average and interest in a college education will decline" (p. 5).

THE INFLUENCE OF TIME
ON THE EFFECTS OF DIVORCE

Studies indicate that the element of time along a number of dimensions can play an interesting role in determining how much impact divorce has on the educational achievement of children. The three most studied dimensions include: (1) the age of a child at the time of the divorce; (2) the number of years since the divorce has taken place, (or a related category—the number of years in a one-parent family); and (3) the long-term effects of divorce.

Age of the Child at the Time of the Divorce

A great deal of debate persists about whether divorce differentially affects children, depending on their age at the time of the divorce. For the most part, social scientists have considered three central hypotheses when examining this issue:

1. *The cumulative effect hypothesis*—this perspective asserts that "the earlier the parental divorce occurs in the child's life, the more profound its impact will be" (Twaite, Silitsky, and Luchow, 1998, p. 109).
2. *The critical state hypothesis*—those espousing this viewpoint believe that the first two to three years of a child's life are the most critical to ensuring the normal development of a child. Therefore, a divorce taking place at this age would have considerably greater impact than for any other age. Freudian psychologists tend to support this view (Twaite, Silitsky, and Luchow, 1998, p. 109).
3. *The recency hypothesis*—declares that divorce constitutes a trauma from which the child can recover within a year or two (Kalter and Rembar, 1981).

Now that more significant research has been done concerning the long-term impact of divorce, virtually no social scientist takes the third hypothesis very seriously. Wallerstein's often-cited longitudinal study of children of divorced parents found that divorce had significant effects on children even ten and twenty-five years following the divorce (Wallerstein, 1987; Wallerstein and Lewis, 1998). Love-Clark's (1984) meta-analysis also found that the average effect size for divorce on both academic achievement and psychological adjustment measures remained considerable even seven to eight years after the divorce. More will be discussed on this topic later in this chapter.

The other two theories would appear to agree that divorce would hurt one- to three-year-olds more than all other age groups. Those advocating *the cumulative effect hypothesis* would go a step further, however, and predict that elementary school children would be hurt more than secondary school children, and so on. Those adhering to the *critical state hypothesis* would not make this latter prediction, because in both cases the marital breakup occurred after the critical first two to three years of development.

The weight of evidence suggests that there may be a somewhat larger effect for divorce when it occurs early in a child's life. Santrock (1972) found that divorce produced the most negative impact on cognitive functioning when it occurred during the first two years of a child's life. Love-Clark's (1984) meta-analysis indicated that the mean effect for divorce was greater for children whose parents had divorced between the ages of two and six than for children whose parents divorced between the ages of seven and twelve or thirteen and eighteen (Love-Clark, 1984).

As a result of this research and other findings, many theorists believe, as a matter of fact, that divorce hits young children the hardest (Cherlin, 1988; Gilner, 1988). However, Ellis and Russell (1992) and Grant and colleagues (1993) found that, in the long-term, children whose parents had divorced when they were young fared better than those who divorced when they were older. But a sizable body of research also challenges this view. Sutton-Smith, Rosenberg, and Landy (1968) found that father absence hurt children more when it took place between the ages of five and nine than when it occurred between the ages of zero and four, and other studies indicate that divorce hurts children of all ages equally (Mednick et al., 1990; Shinn, 1978).

These somewhat conflicting results have led some researchers to examine other factors that could play an intervening role in the relationship between the effect of divorce and the age of the child at its onset. McLanahan and Sandefur (1994) found some indication that the timing of the divorce might be more important for girls than for boys. Luepnitz (1978) found that effects of divorce interact with birth order.

In all this debate it should be noted that no credible researcher argues that the effect for divorce proves greater when the time of the breakup occurs later (versus earlier) in a child's life. On the basis of this evidence William Goode (1982) concludes: "While the evidence is suggestive that earlier absence may be more detrimental than later, there is no clear and significant association" (p. 92).

Although the current level of evidence is less than definitive, the methodology used in two recent studies may help clarify just how much of an effect the timing of a divorce has on the life of a child. First, Kalter and Rembar (1981) undertook an insightful study in which they measured the effect of divorce using a vast array of dependent variables. What they found is that the *kind* of effect that divorce has on a child tends to vary with the age of the child at the time of divorce. Kalter and Rembar (1981) conclude: "Divorce timing was unrelated to overall level of adjustment, but was associated significantly with different constellations of emotional-behavioral difficulties" (pp. 87-88). For example, children were most likely to steal if the parents divorced during their adolescent years. Children were most likely to engage in acts of aggression if the divorce occurred during the early years of their lives. The study did not find any differences in academic achievement among children whose parents divorced at various points in their lives. It also indicated that social scientists might arrive at very different conclusions in their analyses, depending on the dependent variables they use. This could (1) indicate that the relationship between the impact of divorce and the child's age at divorce could be more complicated than theorists previously believed, and (2) explain at least one reason why different studies report different results.

In a second study, McLanahan and Sandefur (1994) examined a nationally representative sample and examined the issue of children's ages at the time of "first disruption." The idea indicates that it is quite possible for older children to have experienced two or more parental divorces over their childhood. Research has shown that children who experience more than one marital disruption generally fare less well academically than those who have experienced one disruption (Heyman, 1992). To the extent that older children are more likely to have experienced more than one parental divorce, unless a study specifies "the amount of time since the *first* disruption," deceiving results could emerge (Heyman, 1992, p. 39). If researchers simply inquire how old children were at the time of *the* divorce, the answers they receive might well pertain to the second or third divorce, rather than the first.

Number of Years Since a Divorce Occurred

Various studies indicate that children suffer most severely during the first two years following a marital disruption (Hetherington, 1999; Kinard and Reinherz, 1986). Recent research indicates, however, that the effects of divorce do *not* gradually dissipate each year following the marital dissolution (Love-Clark, 1984; Wallerstein, 1984; Wallerstein and Lewis, 1998). In fact, a meta-analysis by Love-Clark (1984) indicated that after five years the effects of divorce once again start to increase and continue to increase for some time. Other studies confirm this trend found in this meta-analysis (Wallerstein, 1987).

Long-Term Effects of Divorce

As divorce research has broadened and covered a more extended time, theorists have begun to understand that "divorce" is really not a single event, but rather an ongoing one (Amato, 1999; Wallerstein and Lewis, 1998). As a result, the effects of divorce last considerably longer than was first hypothesized. In fact, some researchers point out that divorce has some parallels to death itself (Wallerstein and Blakeslee, 1989). Indeed, as with death, one cannot return to "square one" once a divorce has taken place (Wallerstein and Blakeslee, 1989).

Even though the most traumatic period of a divorce occurs at the time of the marital separation, other stresses occur following this period which make divorce an ongoing experience. First, the children continue to suffer from the ongoing absence of a parent (Wallerstein and Lewis, 1998). Second, a strain in relationships usually remains even when the children grow up (Umberson, 1992; Wallerstein and Lewis, 1998). Third, husbands and wives can still feel bitter toward each other years after the divorce (Wallerstein and Blakeslee, 1989). These ongoing stressful experiences produce any number of long-term behavioral changes in children, even into their adult years. For example, as teenagers and adults, children of divorce are more likely to have a nervous breakdown, seek professional counseling, and go through a divorce themselves (Collier, 1991; Karney and Bradbury, 1995; Stevenson and Black, 1995; Wertlieb, 1997). Children of divorce are more likely to possess lower occupational status as adults and are more likely to be unemployed (Garfinkel and McLanahan, 1986; McLanahan and Sandefur, 1994; Wallerstein and Lewis, 1998). Children of divorce are also more likely to eventually commit suicide (Preston, 1984). Phillips and Asbury (1993) note that, "Divorce-related childhood conflicts that have been suppressed are often reactivated by the important real life choices faced by college students . . ." (p. 204).

Indeed, research indicates that the long-term effects of divorce may last for decades and appear considerably more vast than originally believed (Amato and Keith, 1991, 1999; Fitzpatrick, 1993). Ultimately, the individual characteristics of each child of divorce help determine precisely what the long-term effects of divorce are (Hetherington, Stanley-Hagan, and Anderson, 1989). Nevertheless, the effects of divorce do display certain patterns which are dependent on the timing of the divorce, the length of time since the separation transpired, and the age of the child at the time of the divorce. To the extent that we understand the interaction of divorce with these variables, we possess a better understanding of the influence of divorce on children. However, there is still much about these interactions that we do not understand. Certainly one of the challenges of the coming years will be to uncover more specifically how divorce, time, and the age of the child all interact.

THE EFFECTS OF DIVORCE BY RACE

One of the most interesting questions regarding divorce involves whether the effects of divorce and remarriage differ by race, particularly between African Americans and whites. Social scientists have a particular concern about the effects of divorce, remarriage, and single parenthood on the African-American community as a whole. The concern arises because of some sobering statistics. Eighty-six percent of African-American youth will spend time in a single-parent home, compared to 45 percent for whites (Garfinkel and McLanahan, 1986). Over half of African Americans *presently* live in a single-parent home compared to 14 to 15 percent for whites (Ahlburg and DeVita, 1996; Chadwick and Heaton, 1992; Garfinkel and McLanahan, 1986; Laosa (1988). Approximately 25 percent of Hispanic children and 30 percent of Native American children live in single-parent families, while only 12 percent of Asian children live in that situation (Ahlburg and DeVita, 1996; Laosa, 1988). Actually, it has only been relatively recently that most black children lived in single-parent homes. In the 1960s, about 67 percent of black children lived in two-parent homes; by 1980 this number fell to 42 percent and by 1991 it stood at 36 percent (Ahlburg and DeVita, 1992). A considerable number of the black children abiding in single-parent homes are there as a result of the rise in births to unwed black mothers (Ahlburg and DeVita, 1996; Zill and Rogers, 1988).

Three decades ago, Democratic Senator Daniel Patrick Moynihan expressed alarm over the apparent disintegration of the black family structure (Lasch, 1977; McLanahan and Sandefur, 1994; U.S. Department of Labor, 1967). Some sociologists and family theorists defended the black family by asserting that the situation did not even approach the severity that Moynihan claimed (Stevens, 1982; Worthington, 1988). Instead, these theorists believe, the extended family structure evident in and around many African-American households acts as a support to a child, in the absence of a parent (Stevens, 1982; Worthington, 1988). Unfortunately, recent research indicates that a considerable degree of child care given by any relative other than a mother or father does not positively impact academic achievement and psychological adjustment (versus being cared for solely by a single parent) and may even impede such development (McLanahan and Sandefur, 1994).

Given the exceptional percentage of African-American children living in single-parent homes, the extent of divorce's impact on these children becomes especially important. However, certain facts show that divorce might produce a less deleterious effects in African Americans than in whites. First, while a higher percentage of black women than white women work outside the home in the case of two-parent homes, the *opposite* is true among single-parent homes (Laosa, 1988). According to parental absence theory, the fact that black single-parent women are more likely than their white counterparts to stay at home with their children could mitigate the effect of divorce on the academic performance of black children. Second, men's earning advantage over women is less for African Americans than for whites (Laosa, 1988). Hence, in the 90 percent of the cases in which divorce produces a change in a child's household composition from a two-parent family to a mother-only family, the African-American child would experience less of a drop in household income than his or her white counterpart. Third, some researchers point out that children from lower-income families may suffer less from the dissolution of a family through divorce than children from middle-and upper-income families (McLanahan and Sandefur, 1994). Given that a higher percentage of blacks than whites have a lower SES, some argue that the trend may also apply to blacks. The change in family income, on average, would be less drastic for lower-income families than for middle- and upper-income families.

Research into these issues has produced mixed results. Some studies produced results showing that divorce did not seem to affect the academic achievement of African Americans at all (Cortes and Fleming, 1968). Kinard and Reinherz (1986) found a statistically negative effect for divorce on black males, but not on black females. Most studies, however, have found statistically significant effects for divorce on academic achievement, often extending for many years (Phillips and Asbury, 1993; Salzman, 1987).

Given that the majority of studies have shown that divorce works adversely on the achievement levels of black children, the question becomes whether the intensity of the effect is greater, the same, or less for blacks than for whites. Some social scientists in the 1970s and early 1980s believed, on the basis of their research, that divorce might produce greater harm to white than black academic achievement (Shinn, 1978; Svanum, Bringle, and McLaughlin, 1982). However, Jenkins and Guidubaldi (1997) found that the effects of divorce were greater for black children than for white children. As mentioned earlier, Stephanie Salzman's (1987) meta-analysis went a long way in resolving the matter. Salzman found no statistically significant difference by race.

Studies conducted since the time of Salzman's meta-analysis have not contributed much more to the debate concerning racial differences in achievement in the aftermath of marital dissolution. Garfinkel and McLanahan, for example, have shown that even in their own analyses the direction of the effect for race is not always consistent. For example, in one of their studies, based on the Michigan PSID they "found that living in a mother-only family decreased the likelihood of completing high school by about 3 percentage points for white children and 13 percentage points for African Americans. These differences represent substantial proportion decreases in the likelihood of graduation: about 42 percent for whites and 70 percent for African Americans" (Garfinkel and McLanahan, 1986, p. 28). Yet in *Growing Up With a Single Parent: What Hurts, What Helps* (1994), McLanahan and Sandefur reported:

> The proportionate increase in risk associated with family disruption is much smaller for African Americans and Hispanics than for whites. Family disruption increases the chances of school failure by 2.5 [times] for the average white child, 2.0 [times] for the average Hispanic child, and 1.8 for the average black child. (p. 59)

Given the fact that: (1) researchers nearly always study the influence of divorce on the education attainment of minority children only at the low-income level, and (2) a rapidly expanding number of minority families now enjoy the fruits of middle- and upper-class life, more research needs to be done to determine the consequences of divorce on the academic achievement of minority children.

If researchers do not yet understand the relative consequences of divorce for minority children, the same truth holds to an even greater degree regarding the impact of remarriage on the academic achievement of minority children. Social scientists know that white children whose parents divorce are more likely to enter into a stepfamily (58 percent) than black children (37 percent) whose parents divorce (Furstenberg, 1988). The primary reason for this according to Furstenberg (1988) is that "the marriage pool for black women is much less attractive providing a lower incentive to divorce and remarry" (p. 247). Research indicates that wealthier people (especially males) have a higher propensity to remarry than do lower-income people (Duberman, 1975; Hannan, Tuma, and Groeneveld, 1977). This result makes perfect sense. A single parent with children would be unlikely to marry someone whom he or she did not think could adequately support the children.

Chapter 3

Methodological Issues in Research on Divorce and Family Structure

THEORY AND RESEARCH LITERATURE

Although a general agreement exists among researchers that divorce does negatively impact academic achievement for children, there is a considerable degree of variation among sociologists, psychologists, and educators regarding just how much of an effect divorce creates. Unfortunately, a large portion of this disagreement may find its roots in the methodology used in the studies themselves rather than a large degree of variance in the effects of divorce and remarriage. For example, in the 1960s most studies on the effects of divorce did not sufficiently control for SES (Hetherington, Camara, and Featherman, 1981). As a result, effects attributed to divorce were high (Amato and Keith, 1991; Salzman, 1987). Herzog and Sudia (1971) criticized many early studies for not sufficiently controlling for SES. In response to these criticisms, studies in the 1970s frequently incorporated substantive controls for SES. In their meta-analyses, Amato and Keith (1991) and Salzman (1987) noted that the effects of divorce on academic achievement and other measures dropped substantially during the 1970s. Amato and Keith (1991) asserted that this trend indicated that because of the increased acceptance of divorce, its negative influences may be receding. Although this constitutes a possible explanation for the drop in effects, the sudden and sharp nature of the drop may point to other explanations.

Milne (1989) noted that many studies underestimated the effects of divorce by failing to acknowledge that one of its major impacts was that it substantially reduced the SES level of the household in which a child lives. Increasingly, other researchers have agreed with

Milne's observations (Downey, 1995; Heyman, 1992; Jeynes, 1998b; McLanahan and Sandefur, 1994). One recent series of research analyses, incorporating Milne's suggestions, yielded large effects for divorce (Jeynes, 1998c).

Another methodological concern involves the tendency for various studies to use an insufficient differentiation of the subjects under study (Kleist, 1999). The most common insufficient differentiation involves studying one-parent versus two-parent families. In numerous studies, stepfamilies are included under the category of two-parent families. Most studies that measured the academic achievement of children from stepfamilies indicated that they scored either somewhat higher, about the same, or in some cases somewhat lower than children from one-parent families (Amato and Ochiltree, 1987; Elliot and Richards, 1991; Zakariya, 1982). Hence, studies that lump children from stepfamilies together with children from intact families will tend to understate the effect of divorce. Even when researchers do distinguish children from stepfamilies from intact families, they frequently fail to differentiate between those children who have lost a biological parent due to death and those who have lost a parent due to divorce (Bray and Berger, 1993; Darden and Zimmerman, 1992). Finally, studies that examine stepfamilies frequently do not use representative samples (Corsica, 1980; Ganong and Coleman, 1999).

There appears to be good reason to address these methodological issues regarding family income (and SES) and stepfamilies.

RELEVANT RESEARCH SYNTHESES AND META-ANALYSES

Certain advantages exist in meta-analysis that make the results from this approach especially relevant for a literature review. These advantages emerge as a positive consequence of synthesizing existing studies and weeding out studies of poor quality, both of which are done in meta-analytic research. The values of meta-analyses are: (1) they generally result in increased precision and reliability in the results; (2) the possibility arises of testing hypotheses that have not been tested in primary studies; and (3) researchers can address questions regarding trends that take place over time that otherwise could not be addressed (Cooper and Hedges, 1994).

Herzog and Sudia (1971) presented the first real overview of the divorce literature. However, their analysis included virtually no quantitative analysis and did not examine the studies in much detail. Herzog and Sudia concluded that children from single-parent families trailed children from intact families in academic achievement, but they asserted that this gap resulted almost entirely from differences in SES levels.

The next two meta-analyses used vote-counting procedures and analyzed the studies in greater detail than the Herzog and Sudia study. Shinn (1978), and Hetherington, Camara, and Featherman (1981), unlike Herzog and Sudia, came to the conclusion that divorce did have an effect on academic achievement. However, as Moles (1982) pointed out, twenty-three of the fifty-four studies examined by Shinn were published after the Herzog and Sudia review. The Shinn (1978) and Hetherington, Camara, and Featherman (1981) analyses examined nearly the same set of studies. Like Herzog and Sudia, both Shinn and Hetherington, Camara, and Featherman complained of the methodological inadequacies of a majority of the studies. Therefore, only a minority of the studies met the methodological criteria set by both Shinn and Hetherington, Camara, and Featherman. Shinn observed:

> Various methodological problems plague research on father absence. Primary among them is the definition of terms. Frequently, father absence is examined without regard to the reason for absence, its length, the child's age at its onset. . . . Temporary absence is not always distinguished from permanent loss. (p. 295)

Both meta-analyses maintained similar requirements for controlling for SES and other key variables in order to qualify for their meta-analysis. Because both of these studies took place only three years apart and held to similar methodological requirements, they looked at roughly the same sets of studies. Ironically, some differences emerged in their conclusions. Both Shinn and Hetherington, Camara, and Featherman concluded that children from one-parent families scored lower in terms of GPA and academic achievement than their counterparts. However, Hetherington and colleagues believed that the average difference in achievement test scores was not large enough to warrant much consideration.

Our review of studies using aptitude and achievement tests as measures of cognitive functioning of children suggests that children in one-parent homes score lower on standardized tests than do children from two-parent homes. However, these differences are usually small (less than 1 year difference). (Hetherington, Camara, and Featherman, 1981, p. 27)

Hetherington, Camara, and Featherman reported larger differences in grades.

If Hetherington's conclusion is correct, it would suggest a possible "Pygmalion effect," in which the expectations of teachers may put a downward pressure on the grades of single-parent students (Rosenthal and Jacobson, 1968). The Pygmalion effect was first elaborated on in a study undertaken by Rosenthal and Jacobson (1968), based on their research in San Francisco schools. In this study, Rosenthal and Jacobson communicated to the teachers that they had determined, on the basis of standardized tests, that 20 percent of their students were "special." Actually, the students designated as "special" were randomly selected and were, on average, no different from the rest of the students. Rosenthal and Jacobson reported that the 20 percent of the students designated as "special" improved in their academic achievement over the school year more than the remaining 80 percent. Their conclusion, therefore, was that teacher expectations had played a prominent role in explaining that improvement.

Shinn (1978), in contrast, reported that family structure played an important role in determining both grades and achievement. Although she found about the same difference in achievement test scores as Hetherington, Camara, and Featherman (1981), Shinn believed this to be quite significant. Gilner (1988) performed a research synthesis including some additional studies performed in the 1980s, which tended to support Shinn's conclusions. Nevertheless, the finding of a possible "Pygmalion effect" set the stage for addressing this and other questions in quantitative meta-analyses in the 1980s.

Shinn's (1978) finding that the effect of divorce on whites might be greater than for African Americans also aroused the curiosity of those seeking involvement in quantitative meta-analysis.

Four major quantitative meta-analyses were undertaken during the 1980s and 1990s which examined the effects of divorce on academic achievement: Amato and Keith, 1991; Love-Clark, 1984; McKee, 1992; Salzman 1987. All of these quantitative meta-analyses yielded statistically significant effects favoring children from intact families. However, beyond this, the actual effects varied widely. Salzman (1987) found an effect size of .31 for the relationship between divorce/separation *and academic achievement*. Amato and Keith (1991) and McKee (1992) both found overall effect sizes of less than .2. However, it should be noted that the Amato and Keith meta-analysis differs from the others in that it drew its conclusions only from studies that examined long-term effects of divorce (i.e., on adults whose parents divorced when they were children). In the McKee study, the effect size for *academic achievement,* specifically, was the lowest of all, a mere .11. Love-Clark (1984) found an average effect size of .53 for *cognitive* measures, but only .26 for social psychological measures.

Overall, the effect sizes for the relationship between divorce and academic achievement ranged from .11 to .53. In addition, there appeared to be no discernible trend as to whether the effects of divorce proved greater using achievement or psychological adjustment measures. In a field in which so much variation resides in methodology, such results should be surprising.

Regarding a possible "Pygmalion effect" in grades, as opposed to achievement tests, Salzman (1987) differentiated between the two in her meta-analysis and found no significant difference. In fact, the effect size for achievement tests stood at a slightly higher level (.30) than for grades (.29).*

Concerning race, Salzman (1987) found several provocative results which may raise more questions than answers. Salzman found that for those studies that differentiated by race, the effect size for African Americans was marginally greater than for whites, .24 versus .22 respectively.* Nevertheless, Salzman found that lower-class whites suffered slightly more than lower-class African Americans from the effects of divorce, with effect sizes of .31 and .29 respectively.* It should be noted that these differences do not exceed a statistically significant level of probability. Unfortunately, Salzman could not undertake any racial comparisons at the middle- and upper-class level, because at that

*Effect sizes include all kinds of one-parent families. The vast majority were from homes where divorce occurred. Comparison data were not available for divorced homes.

time no study had ever examined the effects of divorce specifically for African Americans at anything other than the lower-class level. Salzman's results certainly sensitized researchers to the need to move away from stereotyping certain races as falling into the low-income category, and to study racial differences at all income levels. Beyond this, Salzman's results likely indicated one of two possibilities: (1) racial differences may not exist; or (2) there may be some kind of interaction between race and income level that because of the dearth of studies along these lines, has not yet been uncovered.

Despite enjoying the fruits of post-World War II advances in methodology used in research on family structure, many inadequacies remain in this body of research. Unlike the 1960s, 1970s, and early 1980s, few educators argue that parental family structure has no impact on academic achievement. However, the question remains as to just how much of an impact parental family structure has, and researchers cannot accurately answer this question until they *reasonably control* for SES. Virtually all of the research before 1994 operated at one of two extremes in this regard. Past studies either controlled for SES in a perfunctory manner, or overcontrolled for SES in a way that overlooked divorce's direct impact on SES. Neither extreme will do. Researchers need to control for SES in a way that reflects reality.

Perhaps even more unfortunate is the fact that educators and sociologists know so little about the effect of many of the less common family structures on the educational achievement of children. For example, social scientists know relatively little about the effects of parental remarriage on the academic achievement of children, even though remarriage rates have been soaring for decades. To date, the National Assessment of Educational Progress (NAEP) does not differentiate between reconstituted families and intact families when it reports data on divorce's impact on achievement. In addition, while a vast majority of Americans acknowledge the negative impact of single-parent homes, Americans show much less consensus regarding the impact of the reconstituted family (Chadwick and Heaton, 1992).

These methodological problems affect the theories and data that arise from these studies. Specifically, the failure to properly distinguish between family structures and to consider each family structure's impact on SES (and family income) has produced a tendency for socioeconomic theorists to overstate the causal role of SES and understate the role of family structure, especially divorce, in academic achievement. In addition, addressing these methodological concerns will make it easier to test whether family income plays as much of a causal role, as socioeconomic theorists suppose, in determining the educational achievement of children of divorce. This issue will be elaborated on in the following sections.

METHODS

Population

In discussing methodological concerns, we will look at a study that includes students who participated in the National Education Longitudinal Study (NELS) for the years 1988, 1990, and 1992. The NELS research project was sponsored by the U.S. Department of Education's National Center for Education Statistics. The NELS research project may well represent the most comprehensive longitudinal study ever undertaken in the United States. The National Opinion Research Center (NORC) and NORC subcontractors designed the study. The Educational Testing Service (ETS) designed the achievement tests used in the study.

In 1988, using a "two stage stratified probability design" the researchers selected a nationally representative sample of schools and eighth grade students (U.S. Department of Education, 1992, p. 14). The first stage produced 1,734 school selections and 1,052 of those schools ended up participating in the study. The latter number included 815 public and 237 private schools. "The second stage produced a random selection of 26,432 eighth grade students," among the participating sampled schools (U.S. Dept. of Education, 1992, p. 14). Of these students, 24,599 participated in the study. On average, twenty-three students from each school participated in the study. Questionnaires, regarding a vast array of topics, were given to students, parents, and teachers. This study utilized the results from the student and parent questionnaires. Achievement tests in mathematics, reading, science, and social studies (history, civics, and geography) were also given to the students. These tests were "curriculum based cognitive tests that used item overlapping methods to measure" academic achievement (U.S. Dept. of Education, 1992, p. 14). This study will focus on the student questionnaire, the test results, and the school data that accompany the results of the questionnaire.

The goal of the NELS researchers was to follow up on these eighth graders in two-year intervals in 1990 and 1992. The first follow-up in 1990 surveyed not only those students still enrolled in school, but those who had dropped out since the time of the "base year" (1988) study. The selection of the students participating in the 1990 follow-up study proceeded in two stages. The first stage involved "the selection of 21,474 (students) who were in the eighth grade NELS: sample in 1988. These students were termed 'core' students" (U.S. Dept. of Education, 1992, p. 14). To compensate for the decline in sample size from 1988 due to students who had transferred out of the schools and other reasons, this "core" group was then added to through a process called "freshening." This process added 1,229 tenth graders (1,043 of these were found to be eligible) to the total sample size. Students then filled out a questionnaire that was similar in nature to the one they had completed in 1988. Achievement tests were again administered and data on the schools involved were again collected.

A similar two-stage sampling technique was used in choosing the student sample for the 1992 follow-up study. The "core" group consisted of those students who were in the tenth-grade sample in the first follow-up. Then, 364 twelfth graders (243 of whom were found to be eligible) were added to the "core group" to produce a total sample size of 18,726. Students then filled out a questionnaire similar to the ones completed in 1988 and 1990. Achievement tests were again administered and data on the schools involved were again collected.

Family Structure Variables

Family structure variables were based on using the NELS variables for marital status, family composition, and determining whether a parent was dead or alive.

In determining the family structure variables, any responses that were contradictory (e.g., responses that indicated the natural parents were married *and* that the natural father was dead) were deleted and included in a variable called "delete" to measure the effect for the observations that were deleted in various analyses. I will elaborate on this "delete" variable later in this section. Similarly, a variable called "miss" was designed to account for the effect of missing data for the family structure variable. The primary variables used in this analysis were as follows.

Divorce

Any child whose natural parents had been divorced, whether the custodial parent(s) had since remarried or not had the value 1 for this variable. All other children had the value 0 for this variable. Including this variable in the analysis allowed us to consider the difference in scores between children of divorce and children from intact families.

The primary regression analyses examined households of divorced parents in which the child lived with at least one natural parent, but regression analyses were also performed to include situations in which the child lived with neither natural parent.

Remarried

In the regression analyses, which examined only the effects of divorce and any subsequent remarriage, the remarriage variable *only* included the effect for remarriage following divorce. In the regression analyses, which examined the effects of several family structures, the remarriage variable included the effect of remarriage following the death of a spouse, as well as following divorce. In each case the remarriage dummy variable was coded as 1 when remarriage had taken place. Other children were coded as 0 for this variable. Including this variable in the analysis allowed us to consider the difference in scores between children who have experienced parental remarriage and children from intact families.

Widowed

Any child who had lost one or both of his or her natural parents due to death had the value 1 for this variable. All other children had the value 0 for this variable. Including this variable in the analysis allowed us to consider differences in scores between children who have experienced the death of a parent and children from intact families.

It should be noted that some children had a parent who was *both* divorced and dead. This group was coded as "yes" for the widowed variable but not for the divorce variable for two reasons: (1) among stepfamilies it was not always possible to determine whether a couple had divorced before one of them had died; and (2) if parents who had died and divorced had been included, it would confound the effect for divorce. In such cases, the effect of divorce *and* death would almost surely exceed the effect for divorce alone.

This procedure probably resulted in a slight understatement of the effect for divorce. Research has demonstrated repeatedly that divorced people are more prone to commit suicide and have a shorter life span than never-divorced couples (Stack, 1980; Trovato, 1986; Wasserman, 1984). This procedure may also slightly overstate the effect for widowhood. Nevertheless, because the main focus of this study is on divorce/remarriage, I would prefer to arrive at a conservative effect for divorce rather than to overstate that effect.

Never-Married Single

This family structure applied to any mother-only or father-only family in which the parent had never married. Children from this type of family structure had the value 1 for this variable, while all other children had 0. This variable in the equation allowed us to consider differences in scores between children who live with an unwed single parent and children from intact families.

Cohabitation

This variable applied to any situation in which the child resided in a household in which the couple caring for the child was not legally married. Children from this type of family structure had the value 1 for this variable, while all other children had the value 0. This variable in the equation allowed us to consider differences in scores between children whose parent(s) lived together with another adult and children from intact families.

Separation

This variable applied to any marriage in which the marital couple was separated. Children from this type of family structure had the value 1 for this variable, while other children had the value 0. This variable in the equation allowed us to consider differences in scores between children whose parents are separated and children from intact families.

Academic Achievement Variables

Grade Point Average

Grade point average was calculated as the average of the students' self-reported grades covering four subjects (English, math, social studies, and science). For the 1988 data set, the following numerical values were assigned each letter grade: A = 4; B = 3; C = 2; D = 1; and mostly below D = .5. The mean was taken of all the "nonmissing values of these four variables" and was "equally weighted" (U.S. Department of Education, 1992, Appendix H, p. 16).

In the 1992 data set, GPA was calculated rather differently. For this data set, grades were tabulated on a 0 to 100 basis. Credit was also given for advanced placement courses. As a result, the actual range of scores was 0 to 108.98. The GPA data for 1992, unlike the 1988 figures, were not on a 4.0 scale.

This variable allows us to consider a student's academic achievement in school.

Standardized Tests

Standardized test scores were obtained using tests developed by ETS. IRT scores (Item Response Theory scores) were obtained for the reading comprehension test, the mathematics comprehension test, the social studies (history/citizenship/geography) comprehension test, the science comprehension test, and the test composite (reading and math test results combined).

Held Back

This variable was coded with the value 1 if a student had been held back a grade at any time in his or her life. Other students were coded with the value 0.

Basic Core

This variable was coded with the value 1 if a twelfth-grade student had taken the basic core courses identified by the NAEP (National Assessment of Educational Progress). This basic core program consisted of: four years of English courses; three years of social studies courses; three years of science courses; three years of math courses; two years of foreign language courses; and one half-year of computer science courses. Other students were coded with the value 0.

Dropout

This variable was coded with the value 1 if a student dropped out of school during the 1988-1990 and 1988-1992 periods. Other students were coded with the value 0. This variable allowed us to consider whether there were any differences in the likelihood of a child dropping out of school among children from different family structures.

Other Independent Variables

Variables Involving Socioeconomic Status

The socioeconomic status of a child's family was determined "using parent questionnaire data, when available" (U.S. Department of Education, 1992, Appendix I, p. 5). Five components comprised the socioeconomic status variables: (1) father's level of education; (2) mother's level of education; (3) father's occupation; (4) mother's occupation; and (5) family income. The occupational data were recoded using the Duncan SEI (Socioeconomic Index) scale, which was also used in the High School and Beyond survey. If any of the components were missing from the parent questionnaire, equivalent or related questions were used from the student questionnaire to determine SES. Three coded SES variables were used.

Variables Involving Race

For each variable measuring race (Asian, Hispanic, black, and Native American), a student was coded with a 1 if he or she was a member of this race and coded with a 0, if he or she was not.

Gender

This variable was coded with the value 1 for a female. Males were coded with the value 0. This variable allowed us to consider differences in scores between females and males.

Other Variables Under Consideration

Other analyses not presented in this book considered variables such as whether a student attended a public or private school, whether the student came from a large family, and various interactions between variables. These results were not presented because they did not have much impact on the primary variables being examined.

Deleted

This included any student's family structure that was not included in a particular analysis either because: (1) it was not being studied in a particular analysis, or (2) because the student's answer was contradictory in some way, e.g., the student answered that his or her parents were presently married, but one of them was dead. Under either of these circumstances this variable was coded with the value 1. Otherwise, this variable was coded with the value 0.

Missing Data Variables

A "missing" data variable was included for family structure to ascertain the effect of students whose missing answers made the determination of the family structure impossible. Generally, more than one NELS question was needed to ascertain a student's family structure. If a student's answer for any one of these questions was not answered, the family structure could not be determined and the family structure was coded as "missing."

Missing data variables were also used for other student attributes such as race if less than all or virtually all of the students answered the relevant uestion(s). Missing variables were coded with the value 1 when this information was missing; otherwise they were coded with the value 0.

MODELS

Two regression models were used in analyzing the effect of divorce, remarriage, and other family variables on academic achievement. Although there were variations of these two models used at various points in the analyses, these two models set the framework for all the analyses undertaken in this study. Both models and their variations included variables for family structure as well as for both missing and deleted data. I will refer to the variables just listed as the *central variables*. The models and their variations differ in terms of whether they included variables for SES, race, and gender. (1) Both variations of the full model include variables for race and gender, whereas neither variation of the basic model includes these variables. (2) Both the basic and full model have two variations. One variation of each model includes variables for SES, while the other does not.

Model 1: The Basic Model

The two variations of the basic model include the central variables, but do not include variables for race or gender. The basic model takes two forms:

1. *Basic Model.* This variation of the basic model includes *only* the central variables, i.e., it does not include variables for SES, race, or gender.
2. *Basic Model with SES variables included.* This variation of the basic model includes the central variables *plus* the SES variables.

The use of the basic model is important for the following reasons:

1. To obtain overall effects for divorce and remarriage.
2. To use models that are the most commonly used by family researchers so that the results of this study can be understood in reference to the work that other family researchers have done. If controls are used in a family research study, race, sex, and SES are the most common ones used.

Model 2: The Full Model

The two variations of the full model include the central variables and, *unlike* the basic model, include variables for race and gender.

1. *Full Model*—This variation of the full model includes the central variables and variables for race and gender, but does not include variables for SES.
2. *Full Model with SES*—This variation of the full model includes the central variables and variables for race, gender, and SES.

Important Note: In many of the studies undertaken, only the full model is used. In this case, the models are referred to as the SES model and the No-SES model.

Limitations

A number of limitations arise common to examining large data sets, such as NELS, and virtually any study examining the effects of divorce. Although none of these limitations are particularly serious, they should be noted. They apply to each of the studies undertaken in this work.

As in almost any study, there are certain relevant characteristics of the sample that one would like to know about, but are not accessible. In this study, the most important of these characteristics of the sample involved those students who dropped out of the study. A fair number of students dropped out of the NELS sample at some point during the 1988-1992 period for various reasons which included moving to another school or moving to a different location, etc. Past studies that have examined how such dropouts from a study differ from the remainder of a sample indicate that (1) this group of students generally performs less well academically than the remainder of a given sample, and (2) this group has a disproportionately high percentage of students coming from divorced or reconstituted homes. These facts combined will probably cause the effects for divorce to be lower in this analysis than they otherwise would be if we had access to the group of students that dropped out of this study. This is probably the most important limitation of this study.

It would also be desirable to have reliable measures of parental conflict, the age of the child at the time of divorce, and the length of time since the divorce. The NELS study did not make this information available. Reliable measures of parental conflict are difficult to obtain, because of the subjective nature of such conflict. However, information on the length of time since the divorce would be particularly interesting, because research indicates that the effects of divorce on academic achievement may or may not slowly decrease with time after the third or fourth year following the divorce (Wallerstein and Blakeslee, 1989). It would also be advantageous for every study on divorce to have more information about the predivorce families. Research indicates that some of the effects of divorce occur prior to the actual act of divorce (Neighbors, Forehand, and Armistead, 1992). Hence, some of the children in "intact" families may reside in families in which separation or divorce is about to take place. This fact probably mildly biases the results of this study in the direction of understating the effects of divorce.

Also, for the purposes of this study, the family income aspect of SES was defined in actual terms rather than in terms of per-capita income or living standards. Living standards were impossible to determine from the NELS questionnaire. Using a per capita income measure is not only difficult to determine, it fails to consider economies of scale. An ideal measure of family income as a component of SES *might* include a measure that considered the distribution of income among the household (Lazear and Michael, 1988). However, even this model would have a hard time wrestling with the fact that many big ticket items are purchased with every family member in mind. The benefits from such items are not distributed equally. Given the limitations of the other measures, it would appear that actual family income is the preferable, albeit imperfect, measure for the family income component of SES.

Chapter 4

The Problems with Using
Socioeconomic Status in Research

One of the most crucial debates that has been ongoing among those examining the effects of divorce on family structure has been how to best control for socioeconomic status (SES). This debate first rose to prominence in the early 1970s (Herzog and Sudia, 1971). However, as statistical analysis has become more sophisticated in recent years, it has emerged once again (Acock and Kiecolt, 1989; Boes, 1995; Jeynes, 1998c; Kinard and Reinherz, 1986; McLanahan and Sandefur, 1994). The initial debate about SES arose because Herzog and Sudia (1971) objected to some of the conclusions of many of the studies done up until that point, asserting that the studies did not sufficiently control for SES. A significant number of the early studies on the effects of the divorce either nominally controlled for SES or included no control for SES at all. Usually, a measure of SES has three major components: (a) family income; (b) parental education; and (c) parental occupation. Herzog and Sudia (1971) argued that too many studies on the effects of parental divorce excluded one or more of these components.

As a result of the objections made by Herzog and Sudia, virtually all of the researchers examining the effects of absence of a parent on academic achievement have controlled for SES in a much more elaborate way than their early predecessors (Hetherington, 1999; McCombs and Forehand, 1989; McLanahan and Sandefur, 1994). Now that most researchers control for SES, the regression coefficients that most of them find for divorce are smaller in absolute value than those obtained prior to 1971 (Amato and Keith, 1991). A growing number of researchers point out that how SES is controlled can affect the ultimate results of a given study (Robinson, 1992; Warren, Sheridan, and Hauser,

1998; Wieczorek and Hanson, 1997). Therefore, it is possible that the decline in statistical effects for divorce, beginning in the early 1970s, may have had to do more with changes in the methodology used by researchers in controlling for SES than in an actual decline in the effects for divorce.

THE IMPORTANCE OF USING SES VARIABLES

Most social scientists view the issue of controlling for SES as very important. In assessing the quality of research, social scientists often examine whether a given study controlled for SES. There is little doubt that SES is highly correlated with any number of different academic and other results (Scott-Jones and Clark, 1986). Nevertheless, a significant number of researchers have pointed out that social scientists have often been too quick to assume that if SES correlates with another variable, SES is acting as a causal variable (Meddings et al., 1998; Morag et al., 1998; Sobel, 1998). For example, if a researcher found a strong correlation between the number of telephones in a household and the academic outcomes of children, one would hardly recommend that the solution to America's educational inadequacies would be for families to purchase more telephones at the department store. Rather, the presence of a certain number of telephones in a household often reflects the SES of the household. Households with a high SES would tend to possess more telephones than would households of low SES.

Given the importance that virtually all social scientists place on controlling for SES, the inclusion of SES as a controlling variable(s) is almost taken for granted. Studies that control for SES are considered superior to those that do not (Jeynes, 1998c; Tate and Gibson, 1980; Williams, Takeuchi, and Adair, 1992). There is little question that the inclusion of variables to account for SES is often warranted and can be of great service in understanding the results of many studies (Lichtenstein et al., 1993; Link, Lennon, and Dohrenwend, 1993). Nevertheless, many researchers point out that the typical use of SES variables is either: (1) too simplified (Adler, 1995; Gottfredson, McNeil, and Gottfredson, 1991; Valkonen, 1993; Wright et al., 1999; Ximenes and Araujo, 1995), or (2) used in too vague a way that overlooks the underlying dynamics of numerous variables (Prandy, 1998; Scott-Jones and Clark, 1986; Warren, Sheridan, and Hauser, 1998).

The Problems with Using SES Variables

First, the issue about whether the typical conception and use of SES is oversimplified is essential to acknowledge in any study and in studies on family structure in particular. Sobal (1991) and Milne (1989) note that including variables for SES can cause complications in any study because SES is a "catchall" variable which reflects far more than simply income, education, and occupational status. SES reflects all the human qualities that contribute to a certain level of income, education, and occupational status. It reflects an individual's degree of intelligence, diligence, perseverance, determination, passion for life, slothfulness, luck, work ethic, interpersonal skills, communicative skills, materialism, investment acumen, quality of family upbringing, present family structure, love for reading, love for his or her family, like or dislike for learning, and so forth. Huang (1999) argues that one's SES level states as much about one's psychological status, self-esteem, and locus of control as it does about anything. Friedman and Ali (1997) assert that the failure to acknowledge that SES is a "catchall" variable frequently leads to overestimating the influence of SES. Sobel (1998) believes that it is unfortunate that the vast majority of researchers, in practice, do not regard SES as a "catchall" variable, but as a variable that reflects only economic, educational, and occupational realities. As a result, when SES is demonstrated to have a major impact on various facets of life, social scientists tend to view the solution to the problem in purely economic and educational terms.

Sobel (1998), Sobal (1994), Stunkard and Sorenson (1993) also believe that although SES is generally regarded as a causal attribute, in reality, it is usually more a product of the other causal factors such as those listed earlier. When SES is regarded as a causal factor rather than as a product of other causal agents, social scientists view SES in too simplistic a fashion. They often fail to acknowledge obvious causal agents that are often acting to either raise or lower SES. Adler (1995) asserts that a plethora of psychosocial factors which influence one's SES level and yet are frequently ignored in statistical analysis.

When individuals possess a certain level of SES, it reflects the activity of a countless number of causal agents which enable them to attain or hinder them from attaining a certain level of education, occupational status, and income. Yet this reality is often ignored. When these factors are not ignored, researchers have often found that SES plays less of a causal role than was originally imagined. Friedman and Ali (1997), for example, found that when the causal agents acting upon SES are considered, SES is not related to illegal drug use. Other research has confirmed these findings (Hoffman and Johnson, 1998; Jeynes, 1999c). Tittle and Meier (1991) considered similar causal agents and found that SES was not consistently related to delinquency. Gottfredson, McNeil, and Gottfredson (1991) also found that SES was not related to delinquency. These researchers also argue that it does not make good logical sense to consider how SES may impact delinquenparent are attributed to SES. Although some theorists have pointed outcy or illegal drug usage without also examining how delinquency and illegal drug usage impacts SES. As a result, according to Friedman and Ali (1997), the influence of SES can be overestimated.

Other social scientists have asserted that the definition of SES is often too vague. Wieczorek and Hanson (1997) argue that SES factors are often confused with geographical factors. Warren, Sheridan, and Hauser (1998) point out that income levels in one geographic vicinity cannot be adequately compared with income levels in another. For example, $80,000 in one area of the country will be sufficient to buy a nice house and a new full-size car. In other areas of the country, $80,000 will only serve as a 25 percent down payment on the same quality house. Prandy (1998) argues that the whole classification system of income, education, and occupational status needs to be reexamined to more accurately reflect reality. A great deal of what is defined as SES is subjective in nature. For example, in terms of determining educational level, almost no attempt is made to differentiate between the quality of colleges and schools. A person with a master's degree in hotel management from a school in its first few years of existence is viewed as having a higher education level than an undergraduate in the top 5 percent of the class at Harvard. A person who has a high school diploma and graduated with straight As from one of America's best private schools is ranked no higher than an individual who barely graduated from an inner-city high school. The status of various occupations has changed considerably over time. For example, the emergence of the Internet has significantly raised the status of computer networking experts. The status of certain occupations not only varies with time, but with geographical location.

THE ISSUE OF CAUSALITY

Although social scientists have been reluctant to acknowledge that SES is at least as much a "catchall" variable, as it is a causal variable, researchers in other fields are beginning to recognize this. Researchers in the disciplines of health and medicine, in particular, have started to analyze the degree to which SES is as much an effect as it is a cause. Meddings and colleagues (1998) presented evidence indicating that medical conditions can influence SES and vice versa. In an article appearing in the *New England Journal of Medicine,* Jeffrey Sobal (1994) produced data that indicated that the stigma associated with obesity affects socioeconomic status. Sobal proposed that the direction of causality between obesity and socioeconomic status may actually change over time. Stunkard and Sorenson (1993) have found similar results to Sobal's. In another article, Sobal (1991) argued that a wide range of physical variables impact SES. Medical researchers have been quick to point out that models which assume that socioeconomic status is primarily a causal variable are too simplistic (Adler, 1995; Gortmaker et al., 1993; Heinstrom, 1999; Kaufman and Cooper, 1999; Sobal, 1991).

Medical researchers also point out that one should not overlook the causal factors that are at work from an early point in life, which are often difficult to obtain information on. For example, van de Mheen, Stronks, and Mackenbach (1998) argue that childhood factors such as health can ultimately impact the adult level of SES that a person experiences years later. Morag and colleagues (1998) claim that even this depiction of events simplifies a very complex situation, because the health and health care that a child receives can impact that person psychologically. The psychological well-being of a person can also impact the SES level. Research indicates that especially if certain health conditions are chronic, this can have a considerable impact on one's SES level (van de Mheen et al., 1999).

It should not surprise us that medical researchers are ahead of social scientists in addressing what SES truly measures as well as other issues regarding the direction of causality. Natural science research was in existence long before social science research emerged. Social scientists have long imitated some of the techniques used by natural scientists to more fully establish themselves as a true science. The true nature of SES is an area of endeavor in which social scientists can clearly learn from the techniques used by those in medical research.

In the social science fields, the one obviously most related to the medical profession is the field of psychology. Although most aspects of psychology are thought of as strictly a social science, there are certain facets of psychology, such as psychiatry, that clearly rest within the medical domain. This being the case, psychologists have been among the first social scientists to examine the issue of causality as it relates to SES and other issues. Huang (1999) found that psychological factors and issues regarding self-esteem and locus of control explain much of the differences that are found among people at different levels of SES. Marmot and colleagues (1998) obtained results similar to Huang's findings. In an article published in the *British Journal of Psychiatry,* Garralda and Bailey (1988) examined children who were referred to psychiatric centers. They sought to determine what were the real family causes behind the depressed levels of family SES. Even in the case of SES, one can argue that SES is as much a product of many social causes as it is a causal variable. They found that family support and psychosocial stress exerted a downward pressure on SES.

The Direction of Causality

Medical and psychological researchers have demonstrated more concern about the "direction of causality" issue than the rest of the social sciences. Medical researchers increasingly use the term "reciprocal causality" (Adelmann, Antonucci, Crohan, and Coleman, 1990). That is, two variables can have a reciprocal or circular relationship of cause and effect upon each other. For example, lower intelligence could, on average, lower a family's SES level. The lower SES level, in turn, could impact the average intelligence of the people living in that family by reducing their access to educational resources and so forth. Kaufman and Cooper (1999) assert that social and physical realities certainly interact. For example, Hyland (1990) has shown that mood swings may increase the risk of asthma; but asthma may also increase the likelihood of mood swings. Indeed, among those researchers who have examined this issue is a growing belief that SES is really not a causal variable at all, but a variable that is so vast that it might be called the ultimate variable engaged in "reciprocal causality" or even the ultimate dependent variable, because it results from so many interacting factors (Adler, 1995; Backman and Palme, 1998; Gortmaker et al., 1993; Heinstrom, 1999; Kaufman and Cooper, 1999; Meddings et al., 1998; Morag et al., 1998; Sobal, 1991; Sobel, 1998; van de Mheen et al., 1999).

In an article in the *European Journal of Social Psychology,* Guimond and Palmer's (1990) results indicate that the kind of academic training one receives can influence the causal attributions one makes regarding social problems. Therefore, it is possible that the kind of academic training that researchers receive can influence their thinking about the direction of causality. Guth and colleagues (1999) reinforce these results by indicating that the methodology one uses in research can often determine the type of conclusions a researcher comes to about causality. Robinson (1992) goes even further by asserting that attributing causality to SES can be "politically useful." That is, to the extent that certain individuals view government programs designed to increase income and educational attainment as the only solution to most of society's problems, focusing on the effects of SES might be helpful in this regard.

Schweder (1986) argued that the direction of causality is too difficult to determine. He believes that social scientists are too quick to assume that certain variables are causal variables, although it is possible in certain circumstances. Freedman (1989) asserted that a researcher's assumptions about the direction of causality and other aspects of statistical models can taint the findings reported in those studies. Ultimately, a danger accompanies the assumption that SES is solely a causal variable. The long-term effects of misinterpreting issues of causality cannot be underestimated. Poor assumptions about causality can affect the ways that research is undertaken and the direction of that research for many years to come.

Increasingly, researchers in the field of psychology are acknowledging that determining the direction of causality is generally difficult and that assumptions about the direction of causality can bias the results (Chambers, 1986; Flett et al., 1985; Heinstrom, 1999; Wu and Cheng, 1999). For example, McLaren (1985) asserted that stress is a factor that can easily be a result of particular stimuli, but can also clearly cause certain types of behavior. In terms of SES specifically, a growing number of studies indicate that the level of SES can be a result of various other factors, rather than a primary cause (Gortmaker et al., 1993; van de Mheen et al., 1999; Zakrisson and Ekehammer, 1998). Ceci and Williams (1997) found that the level of one's intelligence impacts his or her eventual level of income. The results of a study by Hofstetter, Sticht, and Hofstetter (1999) indicate that one's knowledge of culture and politics also influences his or her level of SES.

Crane (1996) found that the influence of SES, as a causal variable, can be overestimated if mediating family factors are not taken into account. Dornbusch and Wood (1989) found that in controlling for family processes, social processes had less of an impact on children. Although these findings may be true, one should acknowledge that in most cases it is difficult to control for. Nevertheless, researchers should at least acknowledge that some family factors cannot be controlled for, which affect children's academic outcomes. With this statement in mind, Cummings (1995) argued that researchers need to more frequently utilize the experimental method in the study of the family. However, there are problems with an experimental approach, including the degree to which a family will act naturally in such a setting and whether one can actually obtain meaningful information in the short duration that experiments generally require.

In studies using SES, many researchers make heedless assertions about causality, without even entertaining the possibility that the direction of causality might be in the reverse or that there might be a third or fourth factor affecting both variables under study. Butler (1986), for example, examined the effects of SES on sixth graders' causal attributions for success and failure, without even considering how parental causal attributions affected the SES level. Lowry and colleagues (1996) studied the effects of SES on "chronic disease risk behaviors" on adolescents, without seriously considering the effects that parental "chronic disease risk behaviors" had on SES. Other studies have suffered from similar weaknesses in that they have also assumed that SES is a causal variable without considering what parental variables may influence SES (Briller and Miller, 1984). The assumption by many researchers that SES is solely a causal variable is likely to face greater scrutiny in the coming decades.

The notion of "self-concept" as a causal variable has faced a large degree of scrutiny since the mid-1980s. For many years "self concept" was regarded primarily as a causal variable. If this were true, increasing academic outcomes could be accomplished simply by improving the self-concept of many students. However, it has become increasingly unclear just what the direction of causality is between variables related to self-concept and academic achievement (Gama and Pinheiro, 1991; Marsh and Yeung, 1998; Young and Shorr, 1986). Piciga (1989) expressed concern about relying too much on variables such as SES to explain causality. Researchers have also not examined enough imaginative and logical alternative means of controlling for SES, which would address these issues (Allison and Furstenberg, 1989; Jeynes, 1998c).

Factors That Can Affect SES

Over the years researchers have found that family SES is frequently correlated with high levels of academic achievement. In many educational circles, social scientists assume that SES is the key causal variable. Nevertheless, research indicates that parents with a strong work ethic usually produce children with a high work ethic (Alson, McCowan, and Turner, 1994; Padhi and Dash, 1994). The research also indicates that parents with a high level of education are more likely to emphasize and inculcate the importance of education to their children (Cassidy and Lynn, 1991; Giorgi and Marsh, 1990). Therefore, parents who have a strong work ethic and emphasize the importance of obtaining a high level of education are more likely to produce children who have the same priorities. Surely, there are contributions that SES makes which are truly causal. Nevertheless, given that a plethora of factors influence SES, it is presumptuous to treat SES as solely a causal factor. In fact, one can argue that SES is more a product of a copious amount of other factors than it is a causal agent. To the extent that other factors such as family structure, parental intelligence, and parental determination (along with a vast array of other variables that affect SES) are what produced the high level of SES to begin with, one could certainly argue that the actual causes of the academic achievement rest with those factors rather than with SES. It is this kind of reasoning that has caused Sobel (1998), Adler (1995), Huang (1999), and others to assert that SES is not a causal variable, but a "catchall" variable. For example, if two parents are intelligent, there are any number of reasons to expect that their children will be intelligent. It is quite likely that the high level of parental intelligence will lead to a high SES. But it certainly makes sense to assert that parents of high intelligence are likely to raise children of high intelligence. The causal link appears weaker if one asserts that parents of high intelligence are more likely to earn a high level of income, go to a good school, and have a respectable occupation, and these facts are what cause their children to be so intelligent. Surely, a high level of income and a good job for the parent can have a favorable impact on the intelligence of a child. Nevertheless, the genetic and nurturing factors involved in a family would likely have a greater impact on a child's intelligence. If one were to ask college students at Ivy League schools what influences enabled them to become strong students and attend such prestigious institutions, few students would argue that it was their level of SES. Rather, these students would be well aware of the parental attention they received, the emphasis on hard work in their home, and the inculcating of certain values that were important to their success. They would know the factors (which often contribute to a higher family SES level) that made it possible for them to succeed.

Having said all of this, the purpose here is not to invalidate the use of SES variables. Rather, the purpose is to draw attention to the fact that SES is a "catchall" variable, which has considerably more value if one understands that it is often not primarily a causal variable. In many cases, there are other causal variables that ultimately impact SES. Unfortunately, these primary causal variables are not easily measured and, in fact, may sometimes be virtually impossible to measure. Therefore, the research community should use SES variables cautiously. Otherwise, researchers may frequently find themselves giving simple answers to complex problems. Certainly, there is a great temptation to attribute a great deal of influence to SES. SES can often account for much of the variance that occurs among the observations in a study. Almost without exception, a statistical model that can account for a high percentage of the variation among the observations is considered superior to a model that can account for only a low percentage of the variance. Because SES reflects such a large degree of what a person does and who he or she is, it therefore can account for a large degree of the variance in a given study. But this should not be confused with explaining the causal forces at work. Komrey and Dickinson (1996) and Bakeman and McArthur (1999) observe that a tremendous incentive occurs for researchers to use statistical models which are powerful both in the degree of statistical significance and in the degree to which they can account for the variance present in the study's observations (Begg, 1994; Cook and Campbell, 1979).

The Use of Models

From a statistical perspective, the preference for powerful models of the type just discussed makes very good sense. However, Loftus (1997) asserts that this emphasis can potentially do a great deal of harm, if not utilized carefully. A model or a specific variable that can account for a large percentage of the variance may or may not be causal in nature. Cook and Campbell (1979) and Wu and Cheng (1999) aver that, at the present time in the research community, there is a great deal of incentive to use models which can explain a high degree of the variance, but have little utility in terms of explaining causality. Generally, the variables that are often the best in accounting for the variance among observations in a study are those that are *both* the causes and results. SES is undeniably such a variable, although it is far more likely a result of other variables than it is a direct cause of various phenomena.

Sobel (1998) and other researchers questioned why SES is essentially considered as the ideal variable to use in social science research, when its very composition makes the conclusions of studies suspect. A large part of the controversy stems from issues related to statistical and theoretical convenience. First, social scientists have long sought to establish their discipline as equal to the natural sciences in terms of producing results which have a high level of consistency and predictability (Stewart, 1950). The utilization of a model that can account for a large portion of the variance is essential to accomplish this task. Models used in the natural sciences are generally able to account for a much higher percentage of the variance than models used in the social sciences. In the case of certain large studies undertaken in the social sciences, it is not unusual to have models and/or individual regression coefficients that are statistically significant at the .0001 level of probability, but that account for only 3 to 5 percent of the variance in the observations. Numerous researchers refer to these kind of results as "significant, but not meaningful." In other words, when a statistical relationship has clearly been established, but the degree to which the model accounts for the variance is very low, it is questionable whether the results have that much use in terms of impacting the real world.

Social scientists generally find it much easier to produce a model that yields statistically significant results than a model that accounts for a large portion of the variance. A statistically convenient way of increasing the amount of variance accounted for by the model is to include SES variables. As a result of the challenges just mentioned, a social scientist has a considerable degree of incentive to include SES as an explanatory variable in his or her study. The problem is that more than any other variable that one can use, SES reflects literally hundreds of personality traits and other realities of life which determine one's level of education, income, and occupation. An individual's income, occupation, and education say a lot about that person. This information communicates so much about a person that when most people describe themselves, they usually start by stating their occupation. One's occupation, in itself, frequently reveals a lot about an individual's priorities, personality, the challenges that they face, and so forth. Whether a person went to college and the highest level of education he or she was able to obtain also says a lot about an individual. People also refer to their educational background when they describe themselves and their upbringing. Individuals are less likely to describe themselves in terms of their income level. This is because income is regarded as a highly personal matter. However, it is beyond dispute that one's income level can often reflect various personality traits and individual circumstances.

PREDISRUPTION VERSUS POSTDISRUPTION VARIABLES

The whole issue of controlling for SES has special relevance for examining the effects of parental divorce. The vast majority of the studies examining the influences of divorce on the academic achievement of children have used the custodial parent's present SES level as the study's control for SES. This means of controlling for SES may be flawed. The act of divorce itself causes the income component of a family's SES level to decline. Some researchers assert that the consequence of simplistic approaches for controlling for SES is that the effects of divorce on academic achievement are underestimated. In fact, in their 1989 study, Allison and Furstenberg did not include income as a control because, as the authors observed, ". . . this is likely to be a consequence of prior divorce rather than a cause" (p. 542). Therefore, some social scientists argue that when one uses the postdisruption level of a custodial family's SES as a control, a considerable portion of the effects of divorce are attributed to SES. Ann Milne (1989), for example, states: ". . . to control [for SES] in this situation would be to remove variance that is truly attributable to father absence but that is pathed through SES" (p. 45). If one therefore uses a postdisruption SES measure as a control, part of the effects for divorce will be lost in this measure, because the postdisruption SES measure is itself a result of the act of divorce. Some social scientists, therefore, argue that when one uses the postdisruption level of a custodial family's SES as a control, a considerable portion of the effects of absence of a parent are attributed to SES. Although some theorists have pointed out that nearly all studies on divorce "overcontrol" for SES in this manner, some debate occurs regarding the best way to control for SES (Heyman, 1992; McLanahan and Sandefur, 1994; Milne, 1989; Milne et al., 1986; Furstenberg, Morgan, and Allison, 1987).

As a result of these issues, there are an increasing number of researchers who are looking for alternative ways of controlling for SES. Cherlin, Kiernan, and Chase-Lansdale (1995) and Allison and Furstenberg (1989) are among the social scientists who have acknowledged the value of using predisruption SES variables in assessing the effects of parental divorce on academic achievement. According to this perspective, using predisruption SES measures is the next logical step in finding more accurate effects for divorce. In terms of addressing issues of causality, it does not appear to be logical to use measures of SES which have already been impacted by a change in parental family structure. Obtaining a predisruption measure for SES would seemingly produce effects for divorce that are closer to reality, as well as more accurate effects for SES. Although obtaining pre-disruption measures for SES is the ideal, one should note that they are often hard to obtain. Therefore, it is necessary to address the question of whether these measures are worth obtaining. If the effects for divorce are the same whether predisruption or postdisruption measures are used, it really does not make much sense to go to all the trouble of obtaining the predisruption measures. Therefore, several questions arise regarding the utility of using predisruption measures for SES. First, the most important question is whether using predisruption SES measures truly yield different regression coefficients for divorce. Second, are pre-divorce SES measures accessible enough to enable their widespread usage? The attractiveness of using predisruption SES measures is that they can reveal how much of the influence of divorce is due to the change in family structure and how much is due to SES. Therefore, ideally, one would want to know the custodial family's SES level both before and after the divorce. In that way one could distinguish the decrease in the SES level that apparently resulted from the divorce.

In reality, in most studies, we do not know what the predisruption SES level was for the families who experienced divorce. However, in recent years, an increase occurred in the number of nationwide longitudinal data sets available (Ganong and Coleman, 1994). In the case of these data sets, researchers often know what the predisruption SES level was of the families who experienced divorce during the period that the study took place. In Chapter 5, the National Educational Longitudinal Study (NELS) data set for the 1988-1992 period will be used to help determine what the predisruption level of SES is for those parents divorced during the course of the study. Using predisruption SES measures should give a better overall picture of the impact of parental divorce upon the academic achievement of the adolescents in the study. Instead of using the postdisruption level of SES to control for SES, when divorce is primarily what changed the SES level, the predisruption level of SES could be used, which is unaffected by the divorce. Because families of lower SES generally have a higher propensity to divorce (Becker, Landes and Michael, 1977; Svanum, Bringle, and McLaughlin, 1982), one would expect that the addition of predisruption SES variables would lower the effects for divorce somewhat. But one would certainly not expect the extent of the reduction that would take place using a custodial family's postdisruption level of SES versus when no control for SES is used.

As was stated earlier, the most important question is whether using predisruption SES measures truly yield different regression coefficients for divorce than using postdisruption measures for SES. If the answer to this question is affirmative, the results would support the argument propounded by Cherlin, Kiernan, and Chase-Lansdale (1995), Milne (1989), and others that because divorce impacts the income element of SES, one will get different effects for divorce if predisruption SES measures are used. These assertions raise the question of whether using a predisruption control for SES is preferable to using a postdisruption control. One would think that, because divorce does generally produce a drop in the income element of SES, using a predisruption control for SES is preferable. Using a postdisruption control for SES risks understating the effects for divorce. During the 1970s and 1980s, for example, a number of social scientists using postdisruption controls concluded that children of divorce did not face much of an academic disadvantage at all (Acock and Kiecolt, 1989; Bane and Jargowsky, 1988; Svanum, Bringle, and McLaughlin, 1982). Part of the reason for this conclusion may rest in the way these researchers controlled for SES. Some researchers have attempted to determine the proportion of the effects for divorce that are explained by a reduced SES (especially income level) level, using postdisruption SES measures. Although the vast majority of these researchers acknowledge the causal link between divorce and income, this method is not as direct as using a predisruption control for SES.

Although controlling for SES is a daunting task, there are problems in the way that SES is generally controlled for and how it is used. When social scientists view SES as almost solely a causal agent, the solutions they present to the problems of divorced families are overly simplified and many of these solutions are introduced at the macro or governmental level. One can certainly argue that social science researchers are a contributing force to the philosophy that most of the world's problems should be solved at the governmental level. Increased funding and educational access can be a viable means of solving some of society's problems. Nevertheless, the efficaciousness of these methods can be overestimated when researchers interpret the significance of SES in this simplistic fashion. Social scientists can learn from the research techniques and concerns raised by those in the medical and natural sciences to improve research techniques. Acknowledging some of the problems in the conceptualization of what postdisruption SES reflects might be a good starting point.

Chapter 5

Problems Involving Analysis of Socioeconomic Status

In Chapter 4 we focused on some of the problems in controlling for SES in studies examining family structure. Recently, some researchers have made at least some attempt to use predisruption SES measures in determining the effects for divorce (Allison and Furstenberg, 1989; Cherlin, Kiernan, and Chase-Lansdale, 1995). According to this perspective, using predisruption SES measures is the next logical step in finding more accurate effects for divorce. Nevertheless, several questions arise regarding the utility of using this method. First, the most important question is whether using predisruption SES measures truly yield different effects for divorce than postdisruption measures. Second, are predivorce SES measures accessible enough to enable their widespread usage? The primary purpose of this study will be to address the first question, but the second question will also be addressed in the discussion section.

PREDISRUPTION SES VARIABLES

To properly ascertain how much of the influence of divorce is due to the change in family structure and how much is due to SES, some researchers argue that ideally we would want to know the custodial family's SES level both before and after the divorce. In that way we could distinguish the decrease in the SES level that apparently resulted from the divorce.

Unfortunately, we do not know what the SES level was for the vast majority of families who experienced divorce who participated in the NELS 1988-1992 study. Fortunately we do know what the predisruption SES level was for the families who experienced divorce during the 1988-1992 period during which the NELS study took place. Therefore, using the children of these families as our sample of children of divorce, we can determine what some researchers consider to be the more pure effects for divorce. Instead of using the postdisruption level of SES to control for SES, when divorce is primarily what changed the divorce level, we can use the predisruption level of SES which is unaffected by the divorce.

Two sets of analyses were done in the study presented in this chapter. The first set involved determining the effects for divorce (and remarriage) for all the students for whom family structure variables could be obtained. The effects for divorce were obtained for the eighth grade (1988) and the twelfth grade (1992) data sets. For this set of analyses when a control for SES was used, a postdisruption measure for SES was used. The effects for divorce were then compared for a model that included the postdisruption SES variables, versus one that did not control for SES. These analyses did not include an examination of the tenth grade (1990) data set, because this data set included no SES measure.

The second set of analyses included a subset of the students participating in the NELS study (1,103). This subsample included all the students who participated in the 1992 follow-up study, whose parents divorced during the course of the 1988-1992 study. For this subset of students, a predisruption SES measure was available. For this set of analyses when a control for SES was used, this predisruption measure for SES was used.

Because families of lower SES generally have a higher propensity to divorce (Svanum, Bringle, and McLaughlin, 1982; Becker, Landes, and Michael, 1977), we would expect that the addition of the three predisruption SES variables would lower the effects for divorce somewhat. However, we would certainly not expect the extent of the reduction that would take place using a custodial family's postdisruption level of SES versus when no control for SES is used.

RESULTS USING THE POSTDISRUPTION SES MEASURES

Using the postdisruption measures of SES or no SES variables at all did have a large bearing on the regression coefficients obtained for divorce. The results obtained using the basic model both with and without the postdisruption SES variables added for the eighth grade (1988) data set is shown in table 5.1. Table 5.1 indicates that using the basic model without the SES variables produced results favoring children from intact families that were all statistically significant at the .0001 level of probability (children from intact families are the base of comparison in all the studies in this book, except where noted). Measured in standard deviation units, the effects for the grades and tests ranged from −.33 for GPA to −.15 for the reading test. When the postdisruption SES variables were added into the equation, however, the regression coefficients obtained were considerably different. Only the effects for GPA and being left back a grade remained statistically significant at the .0001 level of probability. All the other effects were no longer statistically significant. Therefore, whether one includes the postdisruption SES measures or not has a tremendous influence on the perceived effects of divorce on academic achievement.

TABLE 5.1. Effects for Divorce by Year and Subject Using the Basic Model for the Eighth Grade (1988, N = 18,013)

Academic measure	Regression coefficients without the postdisruption SES variables added	Regression coefficients with the postdisruption SES variables added
Standardized tests		
Math	−.18****	−.01
Reading	−.15****	.00
Science	−.17****	−.03
Social Studies	−.16****	−.02
Composite	−.17****	−.01
Other measures		
GPA	−.33****	−.22****
Left back[a]	.19****	.12****

Source: Jeynes (1998c) p. 11. Reprinted by permission of The Haworth Press, Inc.

*p < .05, **p < .01, ***p < .001, ****p < .0001

[a] Logistic regression analysis was used.

Table 5.2 shows the contrasting results that emerge using the same analyses, except using the full model (which includes variables for race and gender) both with and without the postdisruption SES variables. The results indicate that the general pattern that we saw using the basic model also holds when using the full model. When the full model without the postdisruption SES variables was used, all the regression coefficients favored children from intact families and were statistically significant at the .0001 level of probability. Measured in standard deviation units, the effects for the grades and tests ranged from −.31 for GPA to −.11 for the reading test. When the full model included these postdisruption SES variables, only the regression coefficients for GPA and being left back a grade remained statistically significant at the .0001 level of probability. The remainder of the regression coefficients were not statistically significant at all. Overall, using the full model yielded effects that were slightly lower in absolute value than those effects that emerged using the basic model. Nevertheless, the same general pattern holds.

TABLE 5.2. Effects for Divorce by Year and Subject Using the Full Model for the Eighth Grade (1998, N = 18,012)

Academic measure	Regression coefficients without the postdisruption SES variables added	Regression coefficients with the postdisruption SES variables added
Standardized tests		
Math	−.12****	.01
Reading	−.11****	.01
Science	−.13****	−.02
Social Studies	−.12****	.00
Composite	−.12****	.01
Other measures		
GPA	−.31****	−.21****
Left back[a]	.18****	.12****

Source: Jeynes (1998c) p. 12. Reprinted by permission of The Haworth Press, Inc.

*p < .05, **p < .01, ***p < .001, ****p < .0001
[a] Logistic regression analysis was used.

A similar pattern that was found in the eighth grade (1988) also held for the twelfth grade (1992) data set. Table 5.3 lists the results obtained using the basic model both with and without the postdisruption SES variables added for the twelfth grade (1992) data set. The NELS study did not differentiate between children whose parents were divorced and those who were separated for the twelfth grade students. However, the pattern remained the same. Table 5.3 indicates that when using the basic model without the SES variables effects emerged favoring children from intact families that were all statistically significant at the .0001 level of probability, with the exception of GPA. Measured in standard deviation units, the effects for the test scores ranged from −.29 for the math test to −.19 for the reading test. In all the analyses in this study the effects for the math test were larger in their negative value than the effects for the reading test. However, when the postdisruption SES variables were added into the equation,

TABLE 5.3. Effects for Divorce/Separation for the Basic Family Structures Using the Basic Model for Twelfth Graders (1992, N = 13,002)

Academic measure	Regression coefficients without the postdisruption SES variables added	Regression coefficients with the postdisruption SES variables added
Standardized tests		
Math	−.29****	−.10***
Reading	−.19****	−.03****
Science	−.26****	−.09***
Social Studies	−.24****	−.06*
Composite	−.25****	−.06*
Other measures		
GPA	−.07**	−.05
Left back[a]	.15****	.05*
Basic Core[a]	−.15****	−.07*
Drop out[a]	.24****	NA

Source: Jeynes (1998c) p. 13. Reprinted by permission of The Haworth Press, Inc.

*p < .05, **p < .01, ***p < .001, ****p < .0001
NA: not applicable.
[a] Logistic regression analysis was used.

the different regression coefficients were obtained. None of the regression coefficients were statistically significant at the .0001 level of probability. In addition, the regression coefficients for GPA and the reading test were no longer statistically significant. Most of the other regression coefficients were statistically significant at the .05 level of probability, although the math and science tests produce statistically significant coefficients at the .001 level of probability. Again it is apparent that whether one includes the postdisruption SES measures or not has a tremendous influence on the perceived effects of divorce on academic achievement.

Table 5.4 lists the regression coefficients for the twelfth grade (1992) data set using the full model with and without the postdisruption SES variables. The effects for divorce are once again reduced when the postdisruption SES variables are included in the

TABLE 5.4. Effects for Divorce/Separation for the Basic Family Structures Using the Full Model for Twelfth Graders (1992, N = 13,002)

Academic measure	Regression coefficients without the postdisruption SES variables added	Regression coefficients with the postdisruption SES variables added
Standardized tests		
Math	−.19****	−.07*
Reading	−.11****	−.01
Science	−.16****	−.05*
Social Studies	−.16****	−.05
Composite	−.16****	−.04
Other measures		
GPA	−.08*	−.07*
Left back[a]	.12****	.07**
Basic Core[a]	−.13****	−.08**
Drop out[a]	.17****	NA

Source: Jeynes (1998c) p. 14. Reprinted by permission of The Haworth Press, Inc.

*p < .05, **p < .01, ***p < .001, ****p < .0001
NA: not applicable.
[a] Logistic regression analysis was used.

model. However, the basic core, GPA, and drop out regression coefficients show a less dramatic decline than the other measures. This confirms an overall trend that emerged in this study, i.e., that standardized test measures were more influenced than the nonstandardized test measures by the inclusion of the postdisruption SES variables in the analysis. Measures such as GPA, being left back a grade, dropping out of school, and taking the basic core set of courses are less influenced by the introduction of the SES variables than the standardized test scores.

When the full model without the SES variables is included, all the regression coefficients, with the exception of the one for GPA, are statistically significant at the .0001 level of probability. However, once the SES variables are included in the analysis, none of the effects are statistically significant at the .0001 level of probability. One should note, in fact, the regression coefficients for the reading, social studies, and the composite standardized tests are no longer statistically significant at all. The regression coefficients for the basic core set of courses and being left back a grade are statistically significant at the .01 level of probability rather than the .05 level that was the case using the basic model with the SES variables included. Although the regression coefficients for the math and science tests were statistically significant at the .001 level, the absolute values of even these effects were cut by nearly two-thirds. Once again, the effects of divorce for the math test were more negative than for the reading test, whether or not the postdisruption SES variables were included in the analysis.

OBTAINING EFFECTS FOR DIVORCE USING A PREDISRUPTION CONTROL FOR SES

Table 5.5 lists the regression coefficients for the effects for divorce for the basic model without the SES variables added versus the effects for divorce with the basic model with the predisruption SES variables added. The comparison of the regression coefficients indicates that controlling for predisruption SES mildly reduces the effects for divorce, but not as much as was the case when the postdisruption SES variables were used.

The inclusion of the predisruption SES variables reduced the effects for divorce between .01 to .06 of a standard deviation. In the

TABLE 5.5. Effects for Divorce Using the Basic Model for Twelfth Grade Students Whose Parents Experienced a Divorce During the 1988-1992 period (1992, N = 16,310)

Academic measure	Regression coefficients with the predisruption SES variables added	Regression coefficients without the predisruption SES variables added
Standardized tests		
Math	−.19****	−.25****
Reading	−.13****	−.17****
Science	−.17****	−.22****
Social Studies	−.17****	−.22****
Composite	−.17****	−.22****
Other measures		
GPA	−.07	−.08*
Left back[a]	.04	.07*
Basic Core[a]	−.17****	−.19****
Drop out[a]	.23****	.25****

Source: Jeynes (1998c) p. 16. Reprinted by permission of The Haworth Press, Inc.

*p < .05, **p < .01, ***p < .001, ****p < .0001
NA: not applicable.
[a] Logistic regression analysis was used.

cases of GPA and being left back a grade, the addition of the predisruption SES variables reduces the effect for divorce from statistically significant at the .05 level to being statistically insignificant.

The weak effect for being left back a grade is not surprising, because the variable measures any differences in being left back a grade over the course of one's schooling. Seemingly, a recent divorce would impact only the most recent school years. The absolute values of the regression coefficients for the math test measure again exceed the absolute value of the regression coefficients for the reading test measure.

Table 5.6 compares the results using the full model both with and without the three predisruption variables added. The effects are once again reduced using the full model (which adds variables for race and sex) when the three predisruption SES variables are included versus when they are not. However, when the full model is used the effect of

TABLE 5.6. Effects for Divorce Using the Full Model for Twelfth Grade Students Whose Parents Experienced a Divorce During the 1988-1992 period (1992, N = 16,310)

Academic measure	Regression coefficients with the predisruption SES variables added	Regression coefficients without the predisruption SES variables added
Standardized tests		
Math	−.17****	−.21****
Reading	−.12***	−.15****
Science	−.15****	−.18****
Social Studies	−.15****	−.19****
Composite	−.16****	−.20****
Other measures		
GPA	−.07	−.09*
Left back[a]	.04	.07*
Basic Core[a]	−.16****	−.19****
Drop out[a]	.23****	.24****

Source: Jeynes (1998c) p. 17. Reprinted by permission of The Haworth Press, Inc.

*p < .05, **p < .01, ***p < .001, ****p < .0001
NA: not applicable.
[a] Logistic regression analysis was used.

the added SES variables is even less than when using the basic model. Even the largest reduction in the effect with the addition of the SES variables is only .04 of a standard deviation.

As in the case of the basic model, the addition of the predisruption SES variables does affect how many of the academic measures produce statistically significant results. Using the full model without the three SES variables produces statistically significant results for all the academic measures. However, when the three predisruption SES variables were added, the effects for GPA and being left back a grade were no longer statistically significant. Moreover, the addition of the predisruption SES variables reduced the *extent* to which the effect for the reading test was statistically significant. When the predisruption SES variables were not included, this measure produced statistically significant results at the .0001 level. When the predisruption SES variables were included, the measure produced statistically significant results at the .001 level of probability. This confirms the general trend found in this study that the effects of divorce were less for reading measures than they were for measures of mathematics. In this case, when the predisruption SES variables were added, the coefficient was –.17 for the math test. In contrast, the regression coefficient was .12 for the reading test measure. The difference between these two coefficients (.05) exceeded the standard error for the divorce variable for both the math test (.03) and the reading test (.03). The regression coefficients for the science and social studies tests were –.15 of a standard deviation, falling in between the regression coefficients for the math and reading tests.

DISCUSSION

These findings indicate that a different pattern of effects for divorce emerges depending on whether one uses a predisruption or postdisruption control for SES. The results showed large differences between the effects for divorce when the SES variables were included versus when they were not included for those analyses that used postdisruption SES measures. In contrast, when predisruption SES measures were used, the differences were negligible. In the case of the full model, the differences in the effects averaged only .03 standard deviation units. For the subset of children of divorce whose parents divorced during the 1988-1992 period the addition of the three predisruption SES variables only reduced the effects for divorce from .01 to .06 of a standard deviation using the basic model, and between .01 to .04 of a standard deviation using the full model. This indicates that how one controls for SES makes a difference on the estimated effect of divorce. These findings support the argument propounded by Cherlin, Kiernan, and Chase-Lansdale (1995), Milne (1989), and others that because divorce impacts the income element of SES, one will get different effects for divorce if predisruption SES measures are used.

Nevertheless, the question arises whether using a predisruption control is preferable to using a postdisruption control. Given that divorce does generally result in a drop in the income element of SES, one would think that using a predisruption control for SES is preferable. Using a postdisruption control for SES runs the risk of understating the effects for divorce. In fact, during the 1970s and 1980s a number of social scientists using postdisruption controls concluded that children of divorce did not face much of an academic disadvantage at all (Acock and Kiecolt, 1989; Bane and Jargowsky, 1988; Svanum, Bringle, and McLaughlin, 1982). Perhaps the way in which these researchers controlled for SES explains part of their conclusions. Some researchers have attempted to determine the proportion of the effects for divorce that are explained by a reduced SES (especially income level) level, using postdisruption SES measures. Although the vast majority of these researchers acknowledge the causal link between divorce and income, this method is not as direct as using a predisruption control for SES.

However, there are two disadvantages to using a predisruption control for SES. First, the predisruption income element of SES is usually not available. Only with the advent of nationwide longitudinal studies has the possibility of using these measures become much easier. Using predisruption income measures outside this context is time consuming and probably requires that the researcher undertake a longitudinal study. This requires a great deal of effort, patience, and financial support. Second, a predisruption control for SES is probably a better control for SES, but it is not perfect. For example, if a married couple separates prior to divorce it is possible that the income that a custodial parent receives may have already dropped. In this case, even the predisruption income element of SES may be deflated. This also could lead to a slight understatement in the effects of divorce. One could argue that a preseparation control for SES would yield even more accurate results than a predisruption control for SES. Nevertheless, preseparation income measures would be even more difficult to obtain than those existing prior to divorce.

Family research would benefit if more social scientists utilized a predisruption control for SES in conjunction with a postdisruption control. Using a predisruption control SES probably yields effects for divorce that more closely reflect reality than using postdisruption measures. It would seem that with the increase in the sophistication of the nationwide data sets that are available, researchers should avail themselves of this meaningful way to control for SES.

Chapter 6

Determining the Effects of Remarriage

Over the past twenty-five years, social scientists have repeatedly documented the negative influence that divorce has on academic achievement (Cherlin, 1992; Hetherington, 1992; Jeynes, 1996; McLanahan and Sandefur, 1994; Shinn, 1978; Wallerstein, Corbin, and Lewis, 1988). Research on stepfamilies has lagged considerably behind that of divorce and is still a young area of study (Booth and Dunn, 1994; Furstenberg, 1988; Ganong and Coleman, 1994; Heyman, 1992; Jeynes, 1997). The primary reason for this is that many researchers and Americans, as a whole, believe that parental remarriage generally benefits children. First, remarriage introduces an additional caregiver who can help raise children. The assumption is that this additional caregiver would especially benefit children of divorce, if the stepparent was the same gender as the child. Second, remarriage generally substantially raises the SES level of a family and this should benefit any children involved.

The assumption that remarriage benefits children of divorce was so strong that many studies determined the effects for divorce on academic achievement by comparing the academic achievement of children of divorce from single-parent families to that of children from both intact families and families that had been reconstituted. Unfortunately, because of the structure of their research design, these studies can give us no information about the effects of remarriage following divorce on academic achievement (Heyman, 1992; Milne, 1989). In addition, until about twelve years ago, most studies that did distinguish children of divorce from reconstituted families from other family structures did not use a random sample of a definable population. As mentioned in Chapter 2, Ganong and Coleman (1984) evaluated thirty-eight studies specifically dealing with the effects of remarriage on children. Of these thirty-eight studies, only six used a random sample of a definable population. In recent years, researchers have accumulated a fair degree of evidence suggesting that remarriage may have various kinds of negative effects on children.

Some researchers even suggest that it may be remarriage following divorce, more than divorce itself, that most negatively affects children (Amato and Ochiltree, 1987; Baydar, 1988). Other research, indicates that probably *both* divorce and remarriage following divorce have a negative impact on children (Hetherington, 1992; Hetherington and Jodl, 1994; Kurdek et al., 1994; Hetherington, Stanley-Hagan, and Anderson, 1989). Finally, some researchers insist that the effects of remarriage following divorce are fairly mild overall compared to those of divorce (McLanahan and Sandefur, 1994; Zill and Nord, 1994). Which of these three possibilities is correct? While it may take years for the social scientists to address this question in the broadest sense, this study will attempt to answer it as it pertains to the academic achievement of children of divorce from single-parent and reconstituted families.

One of the primary ways the previous studies differ from one another is the extent to which they present their results in a way that considers the effects of SES or whether a basic data summary is given. For example, in the Amato and Ochiltree (1987) study, the researchers control for SES, and present their results with that in mind. Zill and Nord (1994), on the other hand, focus on presenting basic data summaries. Although Zill and Nord do recognize the influence of SES, their conclusions are founded on the basic data that resulted from their research. With this in mind, it may be that the results of past research of the relative effects of divorce and remarriage may be more consistent than they appear. The different results that emerge may be a result of the extent to which the effects of SES are taken into consideration.

The following discussion tests the prediction that whether it appears that divorce or remarriage has the primary negative impact on academic achievement depends on whether one controls for SES.

RESULTS FOR STUDY NUMBER 1

Whether the control for SES was included in the analyses had a notable influence on the relative effects that emerged for divorce and remarriage. Table 6.1 shows the effects for divorce and remarriage using the basic model both with and without the SES variables included for the eighth grade (1988) data set. When SES is not controlled for, it appears that it is divorce, not remarriage, that is exerting the main downward pressure on academic achievement. For all the academic measures the regression coefficients for divorce indicated a negative relationship between divorce and academic achievement that was statistically significant at the .0001 level of probability. The absolute value of these regression coefficients ranged from .33 for GPA to .15 for the reading test. Although the direction of the regression coefficients for remarriage indicate some negative impact on academic attainment in all cases, except for GPA, only one of these regression coefficients is statistically significant. In the case of the math standardized test, remarriage following divorce produced a regression coefficient of $-.06$ standard deviation units. This result was statistically significant at the .05 level of probability.

When the basic model *with* the SES variables is added into the regression equation, the absolute value of effects for remarriage increase

TABLE 6.1. Effects for Divorce and Remarriage for the Basic Family Structures Using the Basic Model for Eighth Grade (1988, N = 18,176)

Academic measure	Effects for divorce and remarriage without SES variables		Effects for divorce and remarriage with SES variables	
	Divorce	Remarriage	Divorce	Remarriage
Standardized tests				
Math	$-.18$****	$-.06$*	$-.01$	$-.11$****
Reading	$-.15$****	$-.01$	.00	$-.05$*
Science	$-.17$****	$-.03$	$-.03$	$-.07$*
Social Studies	$-.16$****	$-.04$	$-.02$	$-.09$**
Composite	$-.17$****	$-.04$	$-.01$	$-.09$****
Other measures				
GPA	$-.33$****	.05	$-.22$****	.02
Left back[a]	.19****	.01	.12****	.04

Source: Jeynes (1998b) p. 90. Reprinted by permission of The Haworth Press, Inc.

*p < .05, **p < .01, ***p < .001, ****p < .0001
[a] Logistic regression analysis was used.

considerably for standardized test scores particularly. As a result, for five of the seven academic measures, it is remarriage, not divorce, that produces the statistically significant effects. The largest effect occurs for the math test, which is statistically significant at the .0001 level of probability. The effects for all the other standardized tests are statistically significant as well, ranging in statistical significance from the .001 to the .05 level of probability. For the other two academic measures, it is divorce, not remarriage, which produces the statistically significant results. For both GPA and being left back, the regression coefficients remain statistically significant at the .0001 level of probability. Nevertheless, the inclusion of the SES variables in the analysis reduces the absolute value of the regression coefficients in each case. Overall, whether one controls for SES has a large bearing on whether it is divorce or remarriage that exerts the greater downward pressure on academic achievement. However, when SES is controlled for, in most cases, it is remarriage that exerts the greater downward pressure.

When the full model is used, the influence of either including or excluding the SES variables becomes even more obvious. Table 6.2 shows the effects for divorce and remarriage using the full model

TABLE 6.2. Effects for Divorce and Remarriage for the Basic Family Structures Using the Standard Full Model for Eighth Grade (1988, N = 18,176)

Academic measure	Effects for divorce and remarriage without SES variables		Effects for divorce and remarriage with SES variables	
	Divorce	Remarriage	Divorce	Remarriage
Standardized tests				
Math	−.11****	−.09**	.02	−.13****
Reading	−.10****	−.04	.01	−.07*
Science	−.12****	−.06	−.01	−.09**
Social Studies	−.11****	−.07*	.00	−.10***
Composite	−.11****	−.07*	.02	−.11****
Other measures				
GPA	−.29****	.04	−.20****	.01
Left back[a]	.17****	.02	.12****	.04

Source: Jeynes (1998b) p. 92. Reprinted by permission of The Haworth Press, Inc.

*p < .05, **p < .01, ***p < .001, ****p < .0001
[a] Logistic regression analysis was used.

both with and without the SES variables included for the eighth grade (1988) data set. Using this larger model, which includes controlling for race (with the four race variables: Asian, black, Hispanic, and American Indian/Alaska Native) and gender yielded similar values as were found in Table 6.1. There was, however, one significant difference. Even before the SES variables were added into the equation, the addition of the race and gender variables strengthen the effect of remarriage, while weakening the effect for divorce.

In the case of the full model, as with the basic model, when SES is not controlled for, it appears that it is divorce, not remarriage, that is exerting the main downward pressure on academic achievement. For all the academic measures, the regression coefficients for divorce indicated a negative relationship between divorce and academic achievement that was statistically significant at the .0001 level of probability. The absolute value of these regression coefficients ranged from .29 for GPA to .10 for the reading test. As noted, these regression coefficients for divorce were of a lower absolute value than those that emerged using the basic model. When the full model without the SES variables is used we once again note that it is divorce, and not remarriage, that is exerting the primary downward pressure on academic achievement. Although the full model produced smaller effects for divorce than did the basic model, it yielded larger effects for remarriage. When the SES variables were not included, the basic model yielded only one statistically significant effect for remarriage (the math test). However, with the addition of the race and gender variables in the full model, the effects for the composite test and the social studies test also become statistically significant. In addition, the effect for the science test barely misses statistical significance with a p value of .0515. These results indicate that whether one controls for race and gender can have a measurable impact on the size of the regression coefficient for remarriage.

Controlling for race, it turns out, emerges as an important step in understanding the effect for remarriage. National studies indicate that whites have a much higher rate of remarriage after divorce than their black and Hispanic counterparts (Chadwick and Heaton, 1992; McLanahan and Sandefur, 1994). This would mean that whites tend to have a higher representation among remarrieds than one would otherwise expect. This fact should be considered when determining the effects of remarriage on academic achievement. Therefore, controlling for race is important.

Gender is also important to control for, because divorce usually involves the father being absent from the home. This fact leads one to hypothesize that divorce could have a different impact on boys versus girls.

In Table 6.2 when the full model *with* the SES variables is added into the regression equation, the absolute value of effects for remarriage again increase considerably, especially for the standardized test scores. Once again, the result is that for the majority of the academic variables it is remarriage, and not divorce, that is exerting the primary downward pressure on academic achievement. For the standardized test scores the effects range from −.13 for the math test, to −.07 for the reading test. Throughout this study divorce and remarriage appear to impact the results of the math test more negatively than the reading test. A possible reason for this is discussed in a later section. The effect for remarriage also reached the .0001 level of statistical significance for the composite test, .001 for the social studies test, and .01 for the science test. Although remarriage exerted the primary downward pressure on academic achievement for most of the measures, divorce remained the primary agent exerting downward pressure on GPA and being left back a grade. The effects of divorce in each of these cases was statistically significant at the .0001 level of probability.

These results confirm those found in the basic model. That is, whether or not one controls for SES has a large bearing on whether it appears that it is divorce or remarriage that is exerting the primary downward pressure on academic achievement.

Although 1990 SES variables were not available for the tenth grade (1990) data set, the effects for divorce and remarriage, when the SES variables were not included, were very close to those in the eighth grade (1988) data set. In most cases, the effects for divorce for a given measure were slightly stronger favoring children from intact families, with all of the effects statistically significant at the .0001 level of probability. This raises the possibility that the academic disadvantages associated with being a child of divorce may become larger over time. It should also be noted that although the effects of adding the SES variables could not be measured for the tenth grade (1990) data set, simply adding the race and gender variables increased the relative negativity of the remarriage regression coefficients.

The same general pattern found in the eighth grade (1988) and tenth grade (1990) data sets held for the twelfth grade (1992) data set as well. Table 6.3 indicates the results obtained using the full model both with and without the SES variables added for the twelfth grade (1992) data set. The NELS study did not differentiate between children whose parents were divorced and those who were separated for the twelfth grade students. Nevertheless, the pattern remained the same. When the SES variables are not included divorce/separation, not remarriage, emerges as the primary factor exerting a downward pressure on academic achievement. For all eight of the academic measures, the regression coefficients for divorce/separation were statistically significant. In fact, all but one of the academic measures yielded statistically significant results at the .0001 level of probability. The effect for math was the largest at −.19. The effects for remarriage, on the other hand, produced statistically significant results for four of the eight academic measures.

TABLE 6.3. Effects for Divorce/Separation and Remarriage for the Basic Family Structures Using the Full Model for Twelfth Grade (1992, N = 13,002)

Academic measure	Effects without the SES variables included		Effects with the SES variables included	
	Divorce/ Separation	Remarriage	Divorce/ Separation	Remarriage
Standardized tests				
Math	−.19****	−.10**	−.07**	−.14****
Reading	−.11****	−.07	−.01	−.11*
Science	−.16****	−.09*	−.05*	−.13****
Social Studies	−.16****	−.07	−.05	−.11**
Composite	−.16****	−.09*	−.04	−.13****
Other measures				
GPA	−.08*	.04	−.07*	−.04
Left back[a]	.12****	.08*	.07**	.11**
Basic Core[a]	−.13****	−.07	−.08**	−.08*

Source: Jeynes (1998b) p. 95. Reprinted by permission of The Haworth Press, Inc.
*p < .05, **p < .01, ***p < .001, ****p < .0001
[a] Logistic regression analysis was used.

When the SES variables are included the overall pattern of the regression coefficients changes considerably. Remarriage is the primary factor exerting downward pressure on academic achievement. All the regression coefficients for remarriage produce statistically significant results with the exception of GPA. The regression coefficients for the math, science and composite tests are all statistically significant at the .0001 level of probability. For divorce/separation five of the eight regression coefficients are statistically significant. The regression coefficients for GPA and being left back a grade remain statistically significant for the twelfth grade (1992) data set just as they were for the eighth grade (1992) data set. Hence, the overall picture regarding the effects of divorce and remarriage appears extremely consistent. In addition, the regression coefficient for the basic core courses is also statistically significant. This academic measure is unique to the twelfth grade (1992) data set.

The results for the eighth grade (1988), tenth grade (1990), and twelfth grade (1992) grade data sets show considerable consistency. While divorce appears to be the primary agent exerting a downward pressure on academic achievement when the SES variables are excluded from the analysis, remarriage appears to be the primary agent when the SES variables are included. Therefore, the hypothesis is supported i.e., whether or not one controls for SES has a major impact on whether it appears that divorce or remarriage has the primary negative impact on academic achievement.

DISCUSSION

These results clearly demonstrate that how one views the relative impact that divorce and remarriage following divorce each have on academic achievement depends largely on whether one controls for SES. The analyses using models that did not control for the SES level of the custodial parent(s) produced results that indicate that divorce has a greater negative impact on educational achievement than does remarriage. On the other hand, the analyses using models that did control for SES produced results that indicate that remarriage has a greater negative impact on educational achievement than does divorce. These results shed a great deal of light on why various researchers have arrived at different conclusions regarding the relative impact of divorce and remarriage. Indeed, if one chooses to examine the literature carefully one will find that those who emphasize the negative impact of remarriage following divorce almost always control for SES, while those who emphasize the negative impact of divorce may or may not control for SES. Therefore, the controversy that has arisen in recent years regarding the relative influence of divorce and remarriage may have a simple explanation. The disagreements among researchers probably have to do more with methodology than anything else.

The question that emerges then, is, which way of examining the effects of divorce and remarriage is most appropriate? Certainly, in most studies, controlling for SES has become almost a reflex action. Social scientists generally assume that studies which control for SES are superior to those that do not. If we assume that controlling for SES is most appropriate in this case, then one would conclude that remarriage following divorce, more than the divorce itself, negatively impacts the academic achievement of children. Indeed, what the data in these analyses indicate is that children of divorce from reconstituted families perform poorly academically, given their level of SES. Research indicates that remarriage following divorce raises the SES level of a family almost to the same point as that of an intact family (McLanahan and Sandefur, 1994). Therefore, some theorists would expect that this would produce a substantial increase in the academic achievement of those children whose parents have experienced divorce. However, this is not what happens at all. Instead, the academic achievement of children from reconstituted homes is actually roughly the same as, or slightly less than, that of children of divorce from single-parent homes. These results do not deny that, in general, an increase in parental socioeconomic status may produce some benefit for children. Rather, what these results indicate is that any positive impact that we would normally associate with a rise in the SES level is more than canceled out by the negative impacts of remarriage.

A question still exists as to whether controlling for SES produces the clearest picture of the relative effects of divorce and remarriage. Herzog and Sudia (1971) were the first to emphasize the importance of controlling for SES. They asserted that those studies that do not control for SES overstate the effects of divorce. Nevertheless, as was pointed out previously, a number of social scientists argue that controlling for SES understates the effects for divorce.

A case could be made for each of the three perspectives mentioned in the literature review as representing the best summation regarding the relative effects of divorce and remarriage on academic achievement. How one views the relative effects of divorce and remarriage may depend on whether one believes it is appropriate to control for SES and how it should be done. It is probably overly simplistic to assert that *only* divorce or *only* remarriage following divorce negatively impact the academic achievement of children. The results of this analysis indicate that it would be best to recognize the challenges faced by both children of divorce from single-parent families and children of divorce from reconstituted families. Each have some challenges in common and other challenges that are totally unique to their respective family structures.

RESULTS FOR STUDY NUMBER 2

A supplementary analysis was undertaken to further understand the effects of parental divorce and remarriage as they are manifested in students from different combinations of racial and socioeconomic backgrounds. This analysis involved creating twelve categories with students matched on the basis of three variables: (1) family structure (intact, divorced and remarried, and divorced single-parent); (2) race; and (3) SES (low SES/lower fifty percentile or high SES/higher fifty percentile). The twelve categories consist of each combination of these three variables. Children were divided into one of two categories, depending on their race. One category was for white and Asian students, and the other category was for black, Hispanic, and Native American students. These distinctions were made because social scientists are generally most concerned about the achievement gaps, especially between white and minority students, blacks, Hispanics, and Native Americans.

Tables 6.4, 6.5, 6.6, and 6.7 list the average score obtained by each of the twelve categories of children for the standardized tests for math, reading, social studies, and science. The results indicate that for the standardized test results, children of divorce from reconstituted families generally do more poorly on these tests than their counterparts from intact or single-parent families, when matched for SES and race. These differences are often, although not always, statistically significant. The overall effects for a child living in a divorced-reconstituted family versus living in an intact family were statistically significant for all four of the standardized test measures. The effect for the math test is −1.30 points (sd = 10.22), p < .0001. The effects for the science and social studies tests are −.90 (sd = 10.13), p < .01 and −1.02 (sd = 10.06), p < .001 respectively. The smallest effect is for the reading test, −.67 (sd = 10.08), p < .05.

For all of these analyses, the Waller test was performed to test differences in the mean scores. Of the sixteen matched comparisons, children of divorce from reconstituted families scored lower in fourteen comparisons than children of divorce from single-parent families. In fact, on fifteen (including one tie) of the sixteen matched comparisons, children from reconstituted families scored the lowest of the

TABLE 6.4. Average Math Standardized Test Scores for Eighth Grade (1988) Students Matched by Race, SES Level (Higher Two Quartiles versus Lower Two Quartiles), and Family Structure (N = 18,176)

Race	SES level	Intact family	Reconstituted family	Single-parent family
White/Asian	High	55.2 A	53.7 B	54.8 A
	Low	49.0 DE	48.6 E	49.2 DE
Black/Hispanic and Native American	High	50.5 CD	49.3 DE	50.0 CD
	Low	45.2 F	44.8 F	44.7 F

Note: Different numbers with the same letter following those numbers are not statistically significantly different from each other.

TABLE 6.5. Average Reading Standardized Test Scores for Eighth Grade (1988) Students Matched by Race, SES Level (Higher Two Quartiles versus Lower Two Quartiles), and Family Structure (N = 18,176)

Race	SES level	Intact family	Reconstituted family	Single-parent family
White/Asian	High	56.1 A	53.6 B	55.2 A
	Low	49.1 DE	44.3 F	49.3 CD
Black/Hispanic and Native American	High	50.2 CD	48.6 DE	48.6 DE
	Low	48.1 F	43.7 F	44.5 F

Note: Different numbers with the same letter following those numbers are not statistically significantly different from each other.

TABLE 6.6. Average Science Standardized Test Scores for Eighth Grade (1988) Students Matched by Race, SES Level (Higher Two Quartiles versus Lower Two Quartiles), and Family Structure (N = 18,176)

Race	SES level	Intact family	Reconstituted family	Single-parent family
White/Asian	High	55.3 A	53.1 B	54.4 A
	Low	49.4 C	44.6 CD	49.6 C
Black/Hispanic and Native American	High	49.6 C	48.6 CD	48.8 CD
	Low	44.6 E	44.4 E	47.8 D

Note: Different numbers with the same letter following those numbers are not statistically significantly different from each other.

TABLE 6.7. Average Social Studies Standardized Test Scores for Eighth Grade (1988) Students Matched by Race, SES Level (Higher Two Quartiles versus Lower Two Quartiles), and Family Structure (N = 18,176)

Race	SES level	Intact family	Reconstituted family	Single-parent family
White/Asian	High	55.3 A	53.1 C	54.2 B
	Low	49.0 EF	48.4 F	49.7 EF
Black/Hispanic and Native American	High	50.4 D	49.5 DE	50.1 D
	Low	45.1 G	43.9 H	44.8 GH

Note: Different numbers with the same letter following those numbers are not statistically significantly different from each other.

three groups of children. Standardized test scores for children from reconstituted families are generally .5 to 3.0 points lower than for children from intact families, matching for race and SES. This translates into roughly .05 to .30 of a standard deviation unit. Standardized test scores for children from reconstituted families averaged about 1 point or .10 of a standard deviation lower than children from divorced single-parent families. The absolute point differential is generally, although not always, greater for those students in the high SES (versus the low SES) category. The interaction between family structure and race was not statistically significant.

Of the four standardized tests examined, living in a divorced-reconstituted home impacts academic achievement roughly the same across academic subjects, although it tends to affect math and science achievement slightly more than reading achievement. These differences are not statistically significant. It should be noted that even before controlling for race and SES (and gender), children of divorce from reconstituted families scored somewhat lower than children of divorce from single-parent families on all the standardized tests in this data set.

DISCUSSION

The findings of this analysis indicate depressed levels of achievement for children from divorced-reconstituted families when compared to children living in intact families and children of divorce from single-parent families. These findings do not support the assumption held by many educators that children of divorce from reconstituted homes are better off academically than children of divorce from single-parent homes. Remarriage following divorce does not necessarily have a positive impact and may actually have a negative impact on academic achievement. The fact that remarriage has the greatest negative impact on math achievement may point to the cumulative nature of learning math. That is, if adverse circumstances, such as changes in parental family structure, cause one to fall behind in math class, it is more difficult to catch up than in other subjects. Nevertheless, the differences among subjects that emerged were not statistically significant. Therefore, we should presently conclude that these differences are either minor or nonexistent.

The findings of this study challenge the belief held by some regarding the presumed natural benefits of remarriage following divorce. To the extent that some Americans support the idea of remarriage because they believe it benefits children of divorce, this study encourages us to call into question the assumption that remarriage benefits children academically. One would expect that as a result of the increase in SES level that generally accompanies remarriage, the academic achievement of children of divorce in reconstituted families would be higher than their counterparts in single-parent families. The findings of this study indicate that this is not the case. Rather, children of divorce from reconstituted families perform no better, and perhaps somewhat worse, than their counterparts in single-parent families. There appear to be two possible explanations for these results. First, one might argue that the increase in SES that generally accompanies remarriage does not usually benefit children living in this family structure. Second, although an increase in SES generally benefits children of divorce from reconstituted families, there are other factors involved in parental remarriage that exert a downward pressure on the educational achievement of children. A direct consequence of this is that the effects of these other factors neutralize the otherwise positive effects of an increase in SES. Given that numerous studies have demonstrated a strong relationship between the SES of a child's family and the child's academic achievement, the second explanation appears more plausible (McLanahan and Sandefur, 1994). To the extent that the latter explanation is true, the findings of this study suggest that more research needs to done regarding the possible stresses that children experience as a result of the parental remarriage. More acknowledgment that remarriage can be stressful to children can lead to greater sensitivity to the challenges that they face. Moreover, as our understanding increases regarding the stresses that these children face, educators and others can develop more effective means of intervention. Finally, more research needs to be done to address the possibility that an increase in family SES may produce less benefit in the lives of the children involved than was previously believed.

Chapter 7

Remarriage and Mobility

Considerable debate exists about why remarriage following divorce impacts academic achievement. Although myriad researchers have suggested a number of reasons for this relationship, there is uncertainty about the relative importance of each. McLanahan and Sandefur's (1994) study contributed a great deal of knowledge about the relative effects of divorce and remarriage on educational attainment. To date, most of the research examining the effects on children of living in a stepfamily has focused on psychological rather than educational effects. Downey (1995, p. 875) notes research that has examined the effects of remarriage following divorce on children "has focused on the social-psychological consequences of life in a stephousehold . . . [therefore] less is known about the academic performance of children in stephouseholds." McLanahan and Sandefur (1994) conducted a study analyzing stepfamilies from the High School and Beyond, and the Panel Study of Income Dynamics data sets. They found that stepfamilies were much more likely to move than their counterparts in intact families and single-parent families.

McLanahan and Sandefur (1994) then found that much of the reason behind the academic disadvantage experienced by stepfamilies was due to the mobility of the custodial family. McLanahan and Sandefur discovered that "economic and parenting resources accounted for a good deal of the difference between children in single-parent families and two-parent families, but not much of the difference between children in stepfamilies and two-parent families" (p. 126). They then concluded that it is the mobility of the custodial parent that is the primary variable which helps explain the academic disadvantage incurred by children living in stepfamilies. McLanahan and Sandefur asserted, "We have now identified a potential mechanism for explaining some of the disadvantages associated with living in a stepfamily. Previously, researchers have only been able to account for differences between children in single-parent and two-parent families" (p. 132). McLanahan and Sandefur are correct in their claim. Researchers now know a great deal more about the dynamics behind why living in a single-parent home impacts academic achievement in a different way than living in a stepfamily. For this reason, it is especially important to assess McLanahan and Sandefur's mobility theory.

McLanahan and Sandefur's mobility theory is important for another reason as well. To the extent that their theory is correct, action can be taken by parents and others to reduce the degree of stepfamily mobility. McLanahan and Sandefur note,

> These results are important because residential mobility is something many parents have a good deal of control over. It is always nice to identify a mechanism that can be manipulated, as opposed to something like parents' race or age that cannot be changed. Since many parents are in a position to reduce the number of times they move, and since judges are often in a position to limit or minimize residential mobility, these findings may be especially useful to parents in improving the lives of children. (p. 132)

Some research has suggested that family mobility has a negative impact on the academic achievement and the psychological well-being of children (Ingersal, Scamman, and Eckerling, 1989; Jalongo, 1995; Miller and Cherry, 1991).

This discussion will test McLanahan and Sandefur's hypothesis as it relates to children in divorced-reconstituted homes especially, but also how it relates to all children living in reconstituted families.

HYPOTHESES AND ANALYSES UNDERTAKEN

In this study, hypotheses were formulated, based on McLanahan and Sandefur's theory that mobility is the primary factor exerting a downward pressure on the academic achievement of children from reconstituted families. It was therefore hypothesized that children whose custodial parent moved during the NELS 1988-1992 data set period would fare less well academically than those children whose custodial parent did not move during the same period. The hypothesis was used to test both: (1) the effect of custodial parent mobility on the academic achievement of children of divorce from reconstituted families; and (2) the effect of custodial parent mobility on the academic achievement of all children from reconstituted families (including children from both reconstituted widowed and reconstituted divorced families). McLanahan and Sandefur's actual analysis consisted of a group of children from both reconstituted widowed and reconstituted divorced families. Children from reconstituted divorced families are generally examined more than children from reconstituted widowed families. Therefore, for the purposes of this study, children of divorce from reconstituted families were also examined separately from widowed reconstituted families.

For this particular analysis, the number of subjects that were in each category was as follows: students whose custodial parent remained single after the divorce for the entire length of the study (N = 457); those students whose parents had remarried following a divorce during the course of the study (N = 155); students whose custodial parent had remained single either following widowhood or divorce (N = 520); and those students whose custodial parent had remarried either after widowhood or divorce (N = 181). The first set of analyses compared the academic achievement of the first two groups and the second set of analyses compared the academic achievement of the latter two groups.

RESULTS

Table 7.1 shows the results when the No-SES model is used to assess the effects of the mobility of the custodial parent on the academic achievement of children of divorce from reconstituted families. The results indicate that when the No-SES model is used the regression coefficients for mobility do not reach statistical significance. Nevertheless, one should note that the direction of the effects are still in the direction one would expect. The effects for the standardized tests held in a pretty tight range. The largest regression coefficient in absolute value for the standardized tests was −.16 for the test composite. The smallest regression coefficient in absolute value was −.13 for the social studies test. Among the nonstandardized measures, the effect

TABLE 7.1. Effects for the Variables Used in the No-SES Model for Children in the Reconstituted Divorced Family Structure for the Entire (1988-1992) Period of the NELS Study (N = 612)

Academic measure	Math	Reading	Science	Social studies	Test composite	GPA	Left back[a]	Basic core[a]
Intercept	5.24****	5.16****	5.42****	5.33****	5.21****	.41****	3.03****	.56****
Mobile	-.15	-.14	-.14	-.13	-.16	-.11	.06	-.22
Mobile missing	-.81****	-.52****	.68****	-.65****	-.71****	-.06	-.71****	-.55****
Asian	.44	.55	.52	.27	.53	-.24	-.21	.12
Hispanic	-.12	-.10	-.20	-.02	-.12	.26	-.04	-.07
Black	-.66****	-.50**	-.82****	-.44*	-.63***	.18	-.17	.14
Native American	-.60	-.45	-.61	-.64	-.56	-.29	.35	-.10
Gender	-.09	.11	-.34****	-.19*	.01	.00	-.14	.02

Source: Jeynes (1999d) p. 133. Reprinted by permission of The Haworth Press, Inc.
*p < .05, **p < .01, ***p < .001, ****p < .0001
[a]Logistic regression analysis was used.

for taking the basic core set of courses approached, but did not reach statistical significance. The effects for GPA and being left back a grade were not statistically significant. It should be noted that some of the effects for some of the race variables were not statistically significant, even though they were relatively large. This is probably due to the small number of students from certain racial groups, especially among Native Americans.

The inclusion of the three SES variables into the equation slightly increases the absolute values of the regression coefficients for mobility, as well as their corresponding F-values. Nevertheless, the effects are still not great enough to reach statistical significance (see Table 7.2). The effects for the standardized tests range from −.17 for the math test, and the test composite to −.15 for the reading, science, and social studies tests. These results indicate, once again, that the effects for parental mobility among divorced reconstituted families had a very consistent effect, although not statistically significant, on academic achievement across subjects.

The effects for the nonstandardized tests also fell short of statistical significance, but were all in the expected direction. The effect for taking the basic core set of courses neared, but did not reach statistical significance. The effects for GPA and being left back a grade were also not statistically significant.

Although the effects rose only slightly after the introduction of the SES variables this may indicate that children from families with a higher SES level have a slightly higher propensity to move than those with a lower SES level.

Table 7.3 shows the results when the No-SES model is used for all children coming from reconstituted families (including children who no longer lived with a natural parent either due to death or divorce). The absolute value of the effects increased slightly for a majority of the academic measures. None of the regression coefficients for mobility were statistically significant. The effects for the standardized tests were fairly tightly packed. The regression coefficients ranged from −.19 for the test composite, and the math test to −.14 for the science test. The regression coefficient for the basic core set of courses, which was the largest in absolute value for children of divorce from reconstituted families, was smaller (−.20 versus −.22) when this larger group of children was examined. Nevertheless, these two ef-

TABLE 7.2. Effects for the Variables Used in the SES Model for Children in the Reconstituted Divorced Family Structure for the Entire (1988-1992) Period of the NELS Study (N = 612)

Academic measure	Math	Reading	Science	Social studies	Test composite	GPA	Left back[a]	Basic core[a]
Intercept	4.79****	4.65****	4.89****	4.83****	4.70****	.40**	3.33****	.28****
Mobile	-.17	-.15	-.15	-.15	-.17	-.12	.07	-.14
Mobile missing	-.69****	-.39**	-.55****	-.53****	-.57****	-.07	.64****	.48****
SES Quartile 2	.31*	.32*	.45****	.43**	.34**	.06	-.31*	.18
SES Quartile 3	.45***	.47***	.51****	.46***	.49****	-.04	-.33**	.31*
SES Quartile 4	.80****	.95****	.81****	.86****	.94****	-.02	-.37**	.49***
Asian	.44	.54	.51	.26	.53	-.25	-.20	.12
Hispanic	-.12	-.10	-.20	-.02	-.11	.26	-.06	-.05
Black	-.59***	-.43**	-.80****	-.41*	-.55***	.13	-.20	.22
Native American	-.38	-.20	-.39	-.43	-.31	-.37	.26	.03
Gender	-.10	.12	-.34****	-.19*	.01	.00	-.14	.01

Source: Jeynes (1999d) p. 134. Reprinted by permission of The Haworth Press, Inc.
*p < .05, **p < .01, ***p < .001, ****p < .0001
[a]Logistic regression analysis was used.

TABLE 7.3. Effects for the Variables Used in the No-SES Model for Children in the Reconstituted Divorced Family Structure for the Entire (1988-1992) Period of the NELS Study (N = 701)

Academic measure	Math	Reading	Science	Social studies	Test composite	GPA	Left back[a]	Basic core[a]
Intercept	5.24****	5.14****	5.36****	5.30****	5.20****	.40****	3.00****	.57****
Mobile	-.19	-.16	-.14	-.15	-.19	-.09	.07	-.20
Mobile missing	-.85****	-.58****	-.65****	-.67****	-.77****	.01	.74****	-.54****
Asian	.28	.14	.32	.29	.23	-.10	.03	.00
Hispanic	-.15	-.12	-.20	-.05	-.15	.28	-.09	-.11
Black	-.56***	-.46****	-.67****	-.35*	-.55***	.08	-.02	.00
Native American	-.49	-.44	-.65	-.72	.49	-.27	.18	.34
Gender	-.06	.18*	-.29***	-.13	.06	-.01	-.12	.05

Source: Jeynes (1999d) p. 136. Reprinted by permission of The Haworth Press, Inc.
*p < .05, **p < .01, ***p < .001, ****p < .0001
[a]Logistic regression analysis was used.

fects were not statistically significantly different from each other. Neither effect for mobility was statistically significant. All the effects for the nonstandardized measures were also not statistically significant.

When the SES Model was used (see Table 7.4), the regression coefficients for mobility for the children in this group did not differ much from when the No-SES Model was used. The regression coefficients for the test composite (–.19), the math test (–.19), and the basic core set of courses (–.21) all registered probability values of less than .10, but none of these were statistically significant. The regression coefficients showed almost no change from the values that were found using the No-SES model and the f-values showed only small increases.

Overall, none of the analyses produced statistically significant results. Therefore, the hypotheses were not supported. However, it should be noted that the regression coefficients were all in the direction expected by McLanahan and Sandefur's theory.

DISCUSSION

The findings in this set of analyses leads to the conclusion that the effects of mobility on reconstituted families overall and reconstituted-divorced families, specifically, has little or no impact on the academic achievement of children, contrary to the results that McLanahan and Sandefur's theory would have predicted. The effects of family mobility did not produce even one statistically significant result in any of the analyses that were used. It should be noted, however, that: (1) in all cases the effects were in the expected direction, and (2) some of the results approached statistical significance. Considered together, these results may indicate that mobility among divorced-reconstituted families impacts the academic achievement of children very mildly rather than having no impact at all. From these findings, it would appear that researchers should either look at other possible variables that impact academic achievement or develop a more sophisticated model which could possibly include family mobility as one of many factors that together have a major impact on the educational accomplishments of children of divorce from reconstituted families.

A case could be made for not including the family mobility variable in a more complex model. First, the effects that emerged for fam-

TABLE 7.4. Effects for the Variables Used in the SES Model for Children in the Reconstituted Divorced Family Structures for the Entire (1988-1992) Period of the NELS Study (N = 701)

Academic measure	Math	Reading	Science	Social studies	Test composite	GPA	Left back[a]	Basic core[a]
Intercept	4.75****	4.62****	4.83****	4.79****	4.60****	.46***	3.32****	.27*
Mobile	-.19	-.16	-.15	-.16	-.19	-.09	.08	-.21
Mobile missing	-.71****	-.42****	-.51****	.53****	-.60****	-.02	.66****	-.46****
SES Quartile 2	.33**	.31**	.43***	.43***	.35**	-.03	-.31**	.25
SES Quartile 3	.47****	.47****	.49****	.44***	.50****	-.08	-.33**	.35**
SES Quartile 4	.87****	.95****	.91****	.89****	.99****	.08	-.43**	.46***
Asian	.32	.19	.35	.32	.28	-.11	.04	.00
Hispanic	-.15	-.12	-.21	-.05	-.15	.22	-.11	-.09
Black	-.49**	-.38*	-.62****	-.31*	-.46**	.06	-.07	.07
Native American	-.28	-.20	-.46	-.55	-.26	-.30	.09	.45
Gender	-.06	.18*	-.28***	-.13	.07	-.11	-.12	.04

Source: Jeynes (1999d) p. 137. Reprinted by permission of The Haworth Press, Inc.
*p < .05; **p < .01; ***p < .001; ****p < .0001
[a]Logistic regression analysis was used.

105

ily mobility were small and not statistically significant. Second, equally important is the real possibility that family mobility may be as much of an effect as it is a cause. That is, to whatever extent mobility has any influence at all on the academic achievement of these adolescents, it may be a result of other factors which make it more likely for certain divorced reconstituted families to move. For example, it seems likely that custodial families would be more likely to move in a situation in which the circumstances preceding and/or following the divorce were especially unpleasant. Research indicates that former spouses are more likely to move away from each other when a lot of friction is present in their relationship (Wallerstein and Kelly, 1980). In order to understand the effects of family mobility on the academic achievement of these children, this issue needs to be addressed.

Certainly, many other factors may make reconstituted families more mobile which are a consequence of other phenomena rather than purely a causal factor that can be easily changed. For example, Prilik (1998), and Wineberg (1990, 1992) note that childbearing during the second marriage often has a major impact upon the reconstituted family's living circumstances. When families already have children from a previous marriage living under the same roof, the addition of children resulting from a second or third marriage can many times force a family to move, even if they do not want to. The stepfamily is also a very complex structure that is influenced by stepchildren, the new alliances and roles that develop in the context of an intricate web of new relationships (Ambert, 1989; Bray, 1999; Deater-Deckhard and Dunn, 1999; Filinson, 1986; Roberts and Price, 1989; Vemer et al., 1989), and the unpredictable conflicts that can arise in any of these new relationships (Hobart, 1991; Visher and Visher, 1988).

One of the most essential of these issues involves the relationship that a child has with his or her custodial parent and the stepparent. Although the notion that the mobility of a reconstituted family does harm to a child is a reasonable one, family mobility may reflect problems in the relationship between the child and his or her caretakers which preceded the move. It is not unusual for a family to move in reaction to problems that have developed in the life of a child, especially when it affects others in the same household (Wallerstein and Kelly, 1980). Clearly, there are certain reasons behind why reconstituted families move as frequently as they do. These reasons may not only affect the mobility of a family, but other measurable attributes as well.

With these problems in mind, it seems that there may be greater value in investigating the reasons why remarried custodial families move, rather than examining whether they move. This distinction is especially important, because the issue of family mobility has definite public policy implications. To the extent that family mobility among divorced reconstituted families *causes* the academic achievement of children to fall, then counselors and legislators could take action to discourage reconstituted families from moving. However, if family mobility is primarily a result of family stress and other factors, then such an approach could have either little effect or even be deleterious. As a result, although family mobility is a pertinent variable to examine, it appears to suffer similar limitations in using SES variables to using socioeconomic status as a variable. SES, like family mobility, is a pertinent variable, but it is a "catchall" variable. Family mobility is also a "catchall" variable, reflecting such factors as interpersonal tensions, the desire to forget the past, etc. To the extent that McLanahan and Sandefur (1994) found effects for family mobility and this analysis found directional, albeit statistically insignificant, effects for family mobility, these results may be a product of the underlying reasons *why* families move rather than the move itself.

In summary, the results of this set of analyses indicate that family mobility among divorced-reconstituted families does not seem to have the effect on the academic achievement that McLanahan and Sandefur's theory would lead one to expect. However, the consistent directional effects found in this study indicate that there may be another underlying variable at work, which is partially reflected by the family mobility variable, that could help explain why children of divorce from reconstituted families perform at relatively poor levels academically. Further research would do well to examine: (1) the degree to which the custodial parents have difficulty putting the past behind them, as variables which affect the academic achievement of children more directly than the mobility of the custodial family, and (2) the levels of tension present in the relationships between both the spouses from the previous marriage(s) and the present marriage(s).

Chapter 8

The Effects of Living with Neither Parent on Academic Achievement

Virtually all studies examining the effects of divorce on academic achievement include only children of divorce from single-parent families. There are a number of reasons why it is important to also examine children of divorce living with neither parent. First, accurate estimates of the effects for divorce on children can only be obtained if *all* categories of children of divorce are included. Limiting studies to include children *only* from single-parent families excludes important data on children from other types of families including: (a) the population of children of divorce from neither-parent families, or (b) the population of children of divorce as a whole. Second, children of divorce living with neither parent make up an increasing percentage of the population under the age of eighteen. Third, past research, using a variety of academic and nonacademic measures, indicates that children of divorce are more likely to "fall through the cracks" of American society (McLanahan and Sandefur, 1994; Muransky and DeMarie-Dreblow, 1995; Wallerstein and Corbin, 1999). As a result, there is a consensus within the research community that coming from a divorced home places a child "at risk" in terms of eventually engaging in various undesirable behaviors. Children of divorce are more likely to have low grades, drop out of school, have premarital sex, seek psychological help, become drug addicts, get divorced later in life, end up in prison, commit murder, etc. (Hetherington, 1999; Moore, 1995; Popenoe, 1993; Uhlenberg and Eggebeen, 1986). However, beyond this we have very little evidence indicating the extent to which children from neither-parent families may be at an even greater risk, the same risk, or perhaps even at less risk than children of divorce from single-parent families. Parents, educators, social workers, and other caregivers need to know the extent to which children of divorce from neither-parent families do or do not face unique needs that either go beyond or are different from those found in children of divorce from single-parent families. Analyzing the effects of divorce on the academic achievement of children of divorce from neither-parent homes is a major step in giving this family structure the attention it deserves.

Social scientists have consistently documented the downward impact that divorce exerts on the academic achievement of children of divorce from single-parent families (Cherlin, 1992; Hetherington, 1999; Hetherington and Clingempeel, 1992; Jeynes, 1998b; McLanahan and Sandefur, 1994; Wallerstein, Corbin, and Lewis, 1988). The research done by psychologists, sociologists, family researchers, and educators has contributed a great deal to the storehouse of knowledge regarding the effects of divorce on academic achievement (Avenevoli, Sessa, and Steinberg, 1999; Cherlin et al., 1991; Forehand, Biggar, and Kotchick, 1998; Hanson, 1999; Zill and Nord, 1994). Research on children of divorce from neither-parent families, however, has been virtually nonexistent (Jeynes, 1997). Two of the primary reasons for this are that:

1. Because children of divorce from neither-parent families are less common, it is difficult to obtain a sufficient sample of these children on which analyses can be done.
2. Children of divorce from single-parent families are more common than their counterparts in neither-parent families and therefore have received the most publicity.

The effects of divorce on children of divorce, as a whole, cannot be taken into account unless the effects of divorce on children living with *neither* parent are also considered. Therefore this analysis, which specifically examines children of divorce living with neither parent, is the next natural step in coming to a more complete understanding of the effects of divorce on children.

This study tests the hypothesis that children of divorce from *neither-parent* families will perform worse academically than (1) children from intact families, and (2) children of divorce from *single-parent families* even after one controls for SES. The relevant terms were defined as follows:

Divorced, single-parent—Any child whose natural parents had been divorced, and the custodial parent had since remained single (1,902 students in the 1988 data set and 1,552 students in the NELS 1992 data set).

Neither parent—Any child whose natural parents had been divorced and the child was living with neither parent (394 students in the 1988 data set and 306 students in the 1992 data set).

RESULTS

Tables 8.1 and 8.2 show the effects for divorce for children of divorce from both single-parent families and from neither-parent families for each of the academic measures, using the basic model without the SES variables. Table 8.1 lists the regression coefficients for the eighth grade (1988) data set and Table 8.2 lists the regression coefficients for the twelfth grade (1992) data set. These tables not only indicate whether the effects are statistically significant overall, but whether the effects for divorce for children from neither-parent families are different at a statistically significant level from children of divorce from single-parent families (using the Scheffé test). The results indicate that children of divorce from neither-parent families achieve at academic levels that are considerably below both children from intact families and children of divorce from single-parent families. In the vast majority of cases, the academic gap between children of divorce from neither-parent homes and children of divorce from single-parent homes is actually greater than the gap between children of divorce from single-parent families and children from intact families. As a general trend, the differences in academic achievement between children of divorce from neither-parent families and children from intact families are greatest for mathematics achievement and being left back a grade.

In Table 8.1, the absolute values of the regression coefficients were relatively similar for both the standardized and nonstandardized measures. For the standardized test measures, the effects for living in a neither-parent home ranged from −.65 of a standard deviation for the math test, to .−41 for the social studies test. Among the nonstandardized measures, the betas ranged from −.70 of a standard deviation

TABLE 8.1. Effects for Divorce by Academic Measure for Eighth Grade (1988) Children from Single-Parent and Neither-Parent Families Using the Basic Model

Academic measure	Betas for children in single-parent families	F for children in single-parent families	Betas for children in neither-parent families	F for children in neither-parent families
Standardized tests				
Math	−.16****	43.56	−.65****b	29.95
Reading	−.13****	29.11	−.44***b	13.70
Science	−.16****	42.15	−.63****b	27.58
Social studies	−.15****	36.37	−.41***b	11.81
Composite	−.16****	41.55	−.59****b	25.35
Nonstandardized measures				
GPA	−.31****	166.91	−.70****b	35.96
Left back[a]	.19****	54.36	.63****b	24.00

Source: Jeynes (1999a) p. 111. Reprinted by permission of The Haworth Press, Inc.

Note: Total N = 24,599; Subsample N = 2,296.
*p < .05, **p < .01, ***p < .001, ****p < .0001
[a] Logistic regression analysis was used.
[b] Statistically significantly different from effect for children of divorce from single-parent families.

for GPA, to .63 for being left back a grade. All the regression coefficients obtained for children living in neither-parent families were statistically significantly lower than both children of divorce from single-parent families and children from intact families. The effects for children of divorce living in a single-parent family reached a high of −.31 of a standard deviation for GPA. For the standardized tests, the effects ranged from −.16 for the math test to −.13 for the reading test. Although the effects for a child living in a neither-parent home are considerably larger than for a child living in a single-parent home, not all the effects for a child of divorce living in a neither-parent family reach the .0001 level of statistical significance, which we find for children of divorce from single-parent homes. This is due largely to the relatively small number of children in this family structure, when compared to the number of children of divorce living with one parent.

The pattern of effects for the twelfth grade (1992) data set (Table 8.2) was similar to that found in the eighth grade (1988) data set. The only difference is that the effects for GPA are not statistically significant. This may be due to the fact that the 1992 figures for GPA, unlike the 1988 figures, are not standardized. It should also be noted that unlike the standardized test results, GPA is self-reported. The effects for a child of divorce living with neither parent were roughly of the same magnitude for the twelfth grade (1992) data set as for the eighth grade (1988) data set. For the standardized test measures, the effects ranged from −.43 for the science test to −.57 for the composite test. The largest beta was .61 for the left back variable. With the exception of the GPA measure, all the effects for a child of divorce living with neither parent were different from children of divorce from single-parent families at a statistically significant level.

TABLE 8.2. Effects for Divorce by Academic Measure for Twelfth Grade (1992) Children from Single-Parent and Neither-Parent Families Using the Basic Model

Academic measure	Betas for children in single-parent families	F for children in single-parent families	Betas for children in neither-parent families	F for children in neither-parent families
Standardized tests				
Math	−.29****	108.65	−.54****b	58.10
Reading	−.19****	44.71	−.49***b	45.82
Science	−.26****	87.72	−.43****b	36.07
Social studies	−.24****	72.97	−.52****b	52.31
Composite	−.25****	84.25	−.57****b	61.00
Nonstandardized measures				
GPA	−.07	6.17	−.15	3.16
Basic core[a]	−.15****	34.82	−.48****b	50.52
Left back[a]	.16****	42.42	.61****b	97.95

Source: Jeynes (1999a) p. 112. Reprinted by permission of The Haworth Press, Inc.
Note: Total N = 18,726; Subsample N = 1,888.
*p < .05, **p < .01, ***p < .001, ****p < .0001
[a] Logistic regression analysis was used.
[b] Statistically significantly different from effect for children of divorce from single-parent families.

It is interesting to note that for children of divorce from both neither-parent and single-parent families, the effects for the math test have the largest absolute value among the standardized test measures. While the sizes of the regression coefficients for the other measures were not too far behind, it is nevertheless an interesting result. It may point to the fact that performing well in math depends on a linked accumulation of knowledge more so than in the case of the other subjects tested. That is, doing well in math during the tenth week of instruction, for example, depends largely on understanding the mathematical formulas and principles presented during the first nine weeks of instruction. Certainly, this is not the only possible explanation for this trend, and the differences are small, but this is one possible explanation for these results.

Tables 8.3 and 8.4 show the effects for divorce for children of divorce from both single-parent families and children of divorce from neither-parent families for each of the academic measures, using the full model both with and without the addition of the SES variables. Table 8.3 lists the regression coefficients for the eighth grade (1988) data set, and Table 8.4 lists the regression coefficients for the twelfth grade (1992) data set. The addition of the variables for race and gender generally reduce the effects for a child of divorce living with neither parent, when compared with the results using the basic model.

For the eighth grade (1988) data set, when the full model without the SES variables was used, the effects for living in a neither-parent family ranged from −.62 for GPA to −.20 for the social studies test. The effect for the social studies test was the only academic variable that was not statistically significant. The absolute values of the betas for the two nonstandardized measures were considerably larger than for the standardized tests. Most of the effects were also different to a statistically significant degree from children from single-parent families.

Using the same model for the twelfth (1992) grade data set yielded betas that were generally larger than for the eighth grade data set. Among the standardized test measures, the effects for living in a neither-parent family without the SES variables ranged from −.52 for the composite test to −.37 for the science test. The largest effect emerged for the left back academic variable, which was −.60 of a standard deviation. The effect for GPA was not statistically significant. All these betas, with the exception of GPA, were also different at a statistically significant level from those of children from single-parent divorced families.

TABLE 8.3. Effects for Divorce by Academic Measure for Eighth Grade Children from Single-Parent and Neither-Parent Families Using the Full Model Both with and without the SES Variables Included

Academic measure	Using the SES Model Betas for children in single-parent families	Using the No-SES Model Betas for children in neither-parent families	Using the No-SES Model Betas for children in single-parent families	Using the No-SES Model Betas for children in neither-parent families
Standardized tests				
Math	−.10****	−.40***[b]	.03	−.23*[b]
Reading	−.09****	−.23*	.03	−.06
Science	−.10****	−.38***[b]	.00	−.23*[b]
Social Studies	−.10****	−.20	.01	−.04
Composite test	−.10****	−.35**[b]	.03	−.17[b]
Nonstandardized measures				
GPA	−.28****	−.62****[b]	−.19****	−.49****[b]
Left back[a]	.17****	.57****[b]	.11****	.47****[b]

Source: Jeynes (1999a) p. 114. Reprinted by permission of The Haworth Press, Inc.
Note: Total N = 24,599; Subsample N = 2,296.
*p < .05, **p < .01, ***p < .001, ****p < .0001
[a] Logistic regression analysis was used.
[b] Statistically significantly different from effect for children of divorce from single-parent families.

When the full model including the SES variables was used, the effects for a child of divorce living with neither parent decreased, especially using the eighth grade data set. The left back and the GPA measures were the least influenced by the addition of the SES variables. The regression coefficients for GPA and being left back a grade in the eighth grade were −.49 and .47 respectively. Each of these effects were also different at a statistically significant level from their counterparts in single-parent families. Among the standardized test measures, the effects for the reading and social studies tests were no longer statistically significant either in comparison to children from intact families or children of divorce from single-parent families. The regression co-

TABLE 8.4. Effects for Divorce by Academic Measure for Twelfth Grade Children from Single-Parent and Neither-Parent Families Using the Full Model Both with and without the SES Variables Included

Academic measure	Using the SES Model Betas for children in single-parent families	Using the No-SES Model Betas for children in neither-parent families	Using the SES Model Betas for children in single-parent families	Using the No-SES Model Betas for children in neither-parent families
Standardized tests				
Math	−.19****	−.50****b	−.03	−.38****b
Reading				
Science	−.16****	−.37****b	−.05*	−.26****b
Social studies	−.16****	−.47****b	−.05*	−.35****b
Composite test	−.16****	−.52****b	−.05	−.39****b
Nonstandardized measures				
GPA	−.08**	−.15	−.08*	−.14
Basic core[a]	−.13****	−.46****b	−.08**	
Left back[a]	.12****	.60****b	.08**	− 40****b

Source: Jeynes (1999a) p. 115. Reprinted by permission of The Haworth Press, Inc.
Note: Total N = 18,726; Subsample N = 1,888.
*p < .05, **p < .01, ***p < .001, ****p < .0001
[a] Logistic regression analysis was used.
[b] Statistically significantly different from effect for children of divorce from single-parent families.

efficients for each of these two tests using this model were mildly negative. The effects for the math and science tests for neither-parent families had the largest negative regression coefficients at −.23.

The absolute value of the regression coefficients for children in neither-parent families was less effected by the addition of the SES variables in the case of the twelfth grade data set. The effects for the standardized tests ranged from −.39 for the composite test to −.26 for the science test. The left back variable produced the largest effect of .40. The effect for taking the basic core set of courses was −.40. The effect for GPA was not statistically significant. All of the effects were also different at a statistically significant level from those of children from single-parent divorced families.

In summary, the effects for a child of divorce living with neither parent are greater than the effects for living with a single parent. The effects of a child of divorce living with neither parent are also greater for the students in the twelfth grade than they are for the students in the eighth grade. This is especially apparent when race, gender, and SES are controlled for. The addition of the SES variables does decrease the absolute value of the regression coefficients. However, the vast majority of the regression coefficients remain statistically significant even when the SES variables are added.

DISCUSSION

The results generally support the hypothesis that children of divorce from neither-parent families perform at academically lower levels than either children from intact families or children of divorce from single-parent families. Measured in absolute numbers, the difference between children of divorce from neither-parent families and children of divorce from single-parent families is actually greater than between children of divorce from single-parent families and children from intact families. Some of this difference is attributable to the lower SES level of these children. Nevertheless, it is clear especially from the twelfth grade (1992) data set, that there are other major factors at work as well. Even attributing a certain share of the causal effects to SES is untenable, because divorce almost always causes a drop in the income aspect of SES and often the other aspects of the SES level as well (Jeynes, 1998c; Milne, 1989). The loss of *one* custodial parent in divorce, on average, exerts a downward pressure on a custodial family's SES level. However, the loss of *both* custodial parents from divorce would truly have a greater impact.

Numerous family scientists and psychologists would argue that many of these factors are similar to those at work in the lives of children living with a divorced single parent. For example, the lack of access to parents, lack of parental support, and other psychological effects that a broken home might have on children from single-parent families might affect children of divorce from neither-parent families as well. However, one can also argue that children of divorce in neither-parent families may face certain challenges which are unique to their family structure. Children living with neither parent, for example, may be more likely to live with a guardian that is unpleasant, nonsupportive, or even abusive. The fact that a child even lives with neither parent to begin with may point to the fact that the child came from a family in which the effects of divorce were especially pernicious. For example, a physically and/or emotionally abusive custodial parent may have forced the child into a situation in which there was no other choice but to live with neither parent. It may also be the case that neither of the child's natural parents wanted the responsibility of caring for the child. Indeed, there are a good number of extreme scenarios resulting from divorce, which could result in a child living with neither parent. The effects of this family structure on the academic achievement of children may have as much or more to do with the circumstances surrounding the divorce itself rather than the circumstances inherent in the resulting family structure. Additional research in this area should help uncover whether it is the circumstances surrounding the divorce or the resulting family structure that exerts the greatest downward pressure on academic achievement.

The results of this analysis should encourage researchers to examine more seriously children of divorce living with neither parent. The vast majority of studies of divorce exclude this group from their investigation. To overlook these children in these studies is to disregard the group of children most impacted by divorce. Such exclusion will clearly result in an understatement of the effects of divorce on academic achievement.

Added research needs to be done regarding the reasons why children of divorce from neither-parent families achieve at a low level academically. Although part of the cause can be traced to the impact of divorce on a custodial family's SES level, beyond this it is not clear. The lower achievement levels can be traced to challenges distinct to living with neither parent or challenges that result from experiencing the severity of parental divorce which is, on average, greater than that experienced by children of divorce in single-parent families. As America experiences a continued increase in the diversity of its family structures, it befits society to understand the children who come from these family structures (McLanahan and Sandefur, 1994). Further research on children of divorce from neither-parent families would be a valuable step toward this end.

Chapter 9

The Effects of the Most Common Family Structures on Academic Achievement

Generally speaking, of all of the nonintact family structures researchers have examined over the past few decades, single-parent divorced families have received the greatest attention. Social scientists have consistently documented the downward impact that divorce exerts on academic achievement (Amato, 1993; Hetherington, 1999; Jeynes, 1998b; McLanahan and Sandefur, 1994; Wallerstein and Corbin, 1999). As the proportion of other family structures has grown, some social scientists have begun to study other less researched family structures as well. For example, as the population of never-married single mothers has grown, social scientists have examined the effects of this family structure on the well-being of children (Demo and Acock, 1996; Thomson, Hanson, and McLanahan, 1994). Zill and Rogers (1988) add, "the proportion of teen births outside of marriage almost doubled between 1970 and 1985, from 30 percent to 59 percent" (p. 81). These statistics actually do not totally address the problem of teenage sex, because pregnant teens today are much more likely to end their pregnancy by abortion than pregnant women of past generations (Zill and Rogers, 1988). Previously, many studies that examined the single unwed parent phenomenon often did not differentiate between this single-parent family structure and a divorced single-parent parent home when they did their analyses or stated their conclusions (Garfinkel and McLanahan, 1986; Rosenthal and Hansen, 1980). However, in most contemporary studies examining family structure, the vast majority of studies undertaken by social scientists have attempted to distinguish between different family structures as much as is reasonably possible (Hetherington 1999; Jeynes, 2000b; Ross, 1995).

Although researchers, overall, have devoted a larger percentage of their time examining the effects of children coming from never-married single-parent homes, there has been little attempt to examine the effects of cohabitation, remarriage, and parental separation on children. This is particularly true when it comes to investigating the effects of these parental family structures on the academic achievement of children. For example, social scientists have done a fair amount of research on cohabitation. However, most of the analyses have not focused on the effects of this family structure on the academic achievement of children (e.g., Loomis and Landale, 1994; Ross, 1995; Schoen and Weineck, 1993). In addition, although the number of American stepfamilies has increased considerably, there has not been as much research on stepfamilies as divorce. (Booth and Dunn, 1994; Furstenberg, 1988; Ganong and Coleman, 1994; Heyman, 1992; Jeynes, 1999b). Booth and Dunn (1994, p. ix) assert, "Compared to other family groups, the stepfamily has been neglected both with respect to research and policy." The number of studies on stepfamilies has increased since 1990. Nevertheless, the number of studies done on children from stepfamilies, especially as it relates to academic achievement, is relatively small (Ganong and Coleman, 1994; Heyman, 1992; Jeynes, 1999b). A primary reason for this is that many researchers and Americans believe that parental remarriage generally benefits children. First, remarriage introduces an additional caregiver and many social scientists simply assume that this would be especially beneficial if the stepparent was the same gender as the child. Second, remarriage generally substantially raises the SES level of a family and this too would be beneficial.

Compared to the number of studies done on divorce, the quantity of studies examining parental *separation* has been quite small. There are a number of studies on the effects of parental separation on the academic achievement of children (Jeynes, 2000; Maneker and Rankin, 1987; Morgan, 1988; Smith, 1990, 1992, 1995). These studies are valuable, but many of them do not fully differentiate between children from separated families and children of divorce (Smith, 1990, 1992). It is particularly important to distinguish between these family structures, because there are a large number of children whose parents separate, but never divorce. If one includes the couples who separate but never divorce, the marital dissolution rate is 60 percent rather than 50 percent (Hetherington and Jodl, 1994). Marital reconciliation is also far more common among couples who separate than couples who divorce. One can argue that for those children whose parents separate as the first step in the divorce process, the effects of separation on academic achievement would be particularly strong. Research indicates that the first stages of the divorce process are particularly difficult for children (Hetherington, 1999; Robinson, 1997).

The vast majority of studies that have been done on the effects of family structure on academic achievement or psychological adjustment have focused on two or three different family structures (e.g., Amato and Ochiltree, 1987; Hetherington and Clingempeel, 1992; Jeynes, 2000; Stevenson and Black, 1995; Simons et al., 1994). Although this is a profitable approach to examining the effects of family structure, the heightened diversity of family structures indicates that a broader approach is also appropriate. Little consensus exists among researchers regarding which family structures impact school achievement the most (Baydar, 1988; Hetherington and Clingempeel, 1992; Jeynes, 2000). It would be helpful to know the answer to this question for the following reasons: (1) it would be beneficial to know which children are likely to be the most at risk to most effectively help them perform well in schools; (2) knowing which family structures impact school achievement the most could give us insight into what kind of household adjustments are most difficult for children to make; and (3) a comparative study of this type may bring the research community a step closer to developing certain holistic models regarding the adjustments of children to changes in family structure, rather than merely relying on models which are specific only to a certain type of family structure.

THEORETICAL FRAMEWORK

There are three perspectives that have become the most prominent in explaining the effects of family structure on the academic achievement of children. The first perspective is the *absent parent* school of thought. This school of thought asserts that the absence of a natural parent has definitive and negative impacts on the psychological well-being of a child and one way these effects will manifest themselves is in academic achievement (Cherlin, 1997; Hetherington, 1989; Kelly,

1992). Those espousing this view assert that there are certain advantages that come with living with two natural parents which are very difficult, if not impossible, to duplicate if one of those parents is absent (Cherlin, 1992; Wallerstein, 1991; Wallerstein and Lewis, 1998; Zill and Nord, 1994). Relying on this perspective alone, one would expect that those family structures in which a child has the least access to an absent natural parent would have the largest impact on academic achievement. From this perspective, children coming from a widowed single-family structure, or children living with a never-married single or a divorced single parent would all suffer. Using this approach, one would anticipate that children living in a widowed single-family structure would suffer the most, because the child has no access at all to the natural parent. This school of thought would also predict that, generally speaking, children living with never-married single parents would be impacted more than children in divorced single households. This is because the former group of children usually have less access to their natural parents than children in the latter group. This school of thought would predict effects for the remarried and cohabitation family structures that are only somewhat greater than for their corresponding single-parent family structures. The larger effects would exist only to the extent that living in these family structures reduced the access children have to their natural parents to a greater extent than living in the corresponding single-parent family structure.

The second school of thought is the *socioeconomic* school of thought. Researchers from this school of thought emphasize that nonintact family structures, almost without exception, lower a family's socioeconomic status (Bane and Jargowsky, 1988; McLanahan and Sandefur, 1994; Neighbors, Forehand, and Armistead, 1992; Thomson, Hanson, and McLanahan, 1994). They argue that when a change in family structure takes place in which the income, employment, and educational resources are reduced, the negative effects that are normally associated with coming from a family of lower socioeconomic status are affected (Bane and Jargowsky, 1988; McLanahan and Sandefur, 1994). This school of thought would predict that family structures associated with the lowest socioeconomic status would be associated with the lowest levels of academic achievement. This perspective would predict that children living with a never-married single parent would especially be hard hit. Generally, never-married single families are often in dire straits financially. This perspective would also predict effects for living with a divorced or widowed single parent for similar reasons. Those holding to this socioeconomic perspective would predict that the act of remarriage or cohabiting would have an ameliorating impact on academic achievement and that the addition of another caregiver would generally increase socioeconomic status.

The third school of thought is the *nonparental adjustment* school of thought. Social scientists from this perspective assert that the presence of a caregiver who is not the child's natural parent is a source of stress for most children (Anderson and Rice, 1992; Hetherington and Clingempeel, 1992; Walsh, 1992; Zill and Nord, 1994). Many children demonstrate reluctance in accepting a new parental figure (Kelly, 1992; Visher and Visher, 1988). Children in blended families, specifically, often struggle with rivalries with their stepbrothers and stepsisters, as well as jealous feelings toward their the new stepparent (Anderson and Rice, 1992). Stepchildren often feel that the stepparent consumes a large portion of the time and energy of the natural parent (Amato, 1987; Kelly, 1992; Walsh, 1992). The presence of a stepparent often reduces the intimacy of the relationship that the children have with the biological parent (Hetherington, 1994; Walsh, 1992). Children also often suffer because remarriage often produces an increased tension between the biological parents (Walsh, 1992).

Researchers advocating this perspective focus their attention on the family structures that involve blended families or cohabitation. They would predict that even with the addition of an additional caregiver, the effects for these family structures will still be negative. They believe it is quite possible that the effects of children living in these family structures might even be larger than for children living in the corresponding single-parent family structures (i.e., the average child living in a divorced-remarried family structure might do worse academically than the average child living in a divorced single-family structure).

This chapter will present an exploratory analysis designed to contribute to a broader understanding of the effects of several of the most common family structures on the academic achievement of children. It is designed to not only answer some questions regarding the effects of family structure on the academic achievement of children, but to raise some interesting questions as well that will stimulate further research. It is also designed to explore the extent to which these three perspectives can or cannot explain the results of this analysis.

FAMILY STRUCTURE VARIABLES

Family structure variables were based on using the NELS 1988 and 1992 variables for marital status, family composition, and determining whether a parent was dead or alive.

In determining the family structure variables, any responses that were contradictory (e.g., responses that indicated the natural parents were married *and* that the natural father was dead) were deleted and included in a variable called "delete" to measure the effect for the observations that were deleted in various analyses. I will elaborate on this "delete" variable later in this section. Similarly, a variable called "missing" was designed to account for the effect of missing data for the family structure variable. The primary variables used in this analysis were:

- *Divorced single*—Any child whose natural parents had been divorced, and the custodial parent had since remained single.
- *Divorced remarried*—Any child whose natural parents had been divorced and whose custodial parent had remarried.
- *Widowed single*—Any child who had lost one of his natural parents due to death and whose custodial parent had remained single. It should be noted that it is possible that some children had a parent that was *both* divorced and dead. This group was coded as "yes" for the widowed variable, but not for the divorce variable.
- *Widowed remarried*—Any child who had lost one of his natural parents due to death and whose custodial parent had remarried.
- *Never-married single*—Applied to any mother-only or father-only family in which the parent had never married and was not cohabiting with another adult.
- *Cohabitation*—This variable applied to any living relationship in which the child resided in a household in which the couple

caring for the child was not legally married. Those custodial parents who were separated and cohabiting were coded as separated. This coding was based on the belief that in most cases separation from a parent would have a greater impact on the academic achievement of a child than the act of cohabiting.

- *Separation*—Any child who lived in a family in which the marital couple was separated, but not divorced, from each other.

The family structure variables were carefully designed so that a child would fit into one category alone. Therefore, for example, even though a never-married single parent may also be in a cohabitation relationship, for the purposes of this study such a family structure was defined as "cohabitation" and not "never-married single parent." The quantity of children in each family structure (in parentheses) included in this study are:

1. divorced single (1,902)
2. divorced remarried (2,395)
3. widowed single (339)
4. widowed remarried (47)
5. never-married single parent (394)
6. cohabitation (493)
7. separated (700)

A total of 13,986 students lived in intact families (U.S. Department of Education, 1992).

The family structure that the children were from generally had a marked impact on their academic achievement. Table 9.1 shows the regression coefficients using the basic model without the SES variables added. An examination of the regression coefficients of the seven family structure variables showed that coming from a home with a never-married single parent and coming from a home in which a widowed parent had remarried exerted the greatest downward pressure on the academic achievement of children. Among the achievement test measures, the effects for coming from a home with a never-married single parent ranged from $-.81$ for the composite test to $-.65$ for the social studies test. The effects for being left back a grade and GPA were smaller, $.37$ and $-.52$ respectively.

TABLE 9.1. Effects for Each of the Seven Main Family Structures for Each Academic Measure Using the Basic Model without the SES Variables for the Eighth Grade (1988) Data Set (N = 24,599)

Academic measure	GPA	Reading	Math	Science	Social studies	Composite test	Left back[a]
Intercept	4.00****	5.14****	5.70****	5.12****	5.15****	5.12****	3.01****
Divorced Single	–.31****	–.13****	–.16****	–.16****	–.15****	–.16****	.19****
Divorced Remarried	–.26****	–.14****	–.22****	–.19****	–.19****	–.20****	–.19****
Widowed Single	–.29****	–.21****	–.26****	–.24****	–.17**	–.26****	.31****
Widowed Remarried	–.37*	–.74****	–.69****	–.87****	–.82****	–.80****	.62****
Never-married Single	–.52****	–.71****	–.80****	–.79****	–.65****	–.81****	.37****
Cohabitation	–.49****	–.53****	–.58****	–.54****	–.54****	–.60****	.31****
Separated	–.40****	–.45****	–.57****	–.50*****	–.47****	–.52****	.31****
Deleted	–.33*****	–.40****	–.42****	–.44****	–.38****	–.44****	.24****
Missing	–.39*	–.29	–.22	–.34*	–.33*	–.29	.23

Source: Jeynes (2000b) p. 83. Reprinted by permission of The Haworth Press, Inc.
*p < .05, **p < .01, ***p < .001, ****p < .0001
[a]Logistic regression analysis was used.

The regression coefficients for the science (−.79) and math (−.80) tests were very close to each other. Generally, the betas for each family structure variable were quite close to one another across the academic achievement variables. All of these effects were statistically significant at the .0001 level of probability. For the achievement test scores, the effects for coming from a home in which a widowed parent had remarried ranged from −.87 for the science test to −.69 standard deviation units for the math test. It should be noted that in nearly every case, the effects for these family structures were also different at a statistically significant level, from the effects for all the remaining family structures.

The cohabitation family structure produced the third greatest impact on academic achievement. These families are those in which the parent(s) of the child was living together with another adult, but was not married. The regression coefficients for the standardized tests ranged from −.60 for the composite test to −.53 for the reading test. The effects for being left back a grade (.31) and GPA (−.49) were somewhat lower than those of the standardized tests, but were still statistically significant at the .0001 level of probability. Overall, the range of the regression coefficients were somewhat tighter for the cohabitation variable than was the case for the never-married single family structure variable. Nevertheless, for six of the seven academic measures, the absolute value of the regression coefficient for cohabitation was the third largest of the seven family structure variables examined. The only exception to this pattern was found for the left back regression coefficient. In this case, the effect for widowhood and the effect for separation (.31) were the same as for cohabitation.

Parental separation also had a strong negative impact on academic achievement. The effects for separation approached that of cohabitation. The impact of separation on the standardized test scores ranged from a high of −.57 for the math test to −.45 for the reading test. The regression coefficient for the composite test was −.52. The effects for being left back a grade and GPA were .31 and −.40, respectively.

One could be tempted to interpret these results as indicating that the period of the initial marital disruption is the most traumatic period (in terms of academic performance) for children who experience the marital dissolution of their parents. However, it should be noted that some separations last for a considerable length of time. Therefore, one cannot specifically make that argument from this data. The effects for separation far exceeded the effects for the death of a parent and rivaled the effects for children abiding in a cohabiting home.

The widowhood of a parent had a negative impact on the academic achievement of children as well. Among the standard test scores, the regression coefficients for the widowed single reached −.26 for both the math test and the composite test. The standardized test with the weakest effect was social studies with an effect of −.17. The effect of parental widowhood had a large relative impact on GPA and being left back. Most of the other family structures impacted standardized scores more than the nonstandardized measures. The regression coefficient for being left back was .31 and for GPA was −.29. In fact, the beta for being left back was the same as for the cohabitation and separated family structures.

In the divorce single variable, in contrast to most of the other family structure variables, GPA produced the largest effect. For the standardized test measures, the effects for divorce range from −.16 for both the math and science tests to −.13 for the reading test. As in the case for the widowed single variable, the effects for the nonstandardized test measures were larger than for the standardized test measures. The effects for GPA and being left back a grade were −.31 and .19 respectively.

With the exception of the GPA measurement, the effects for divorced remarried were at least as large as for the divorced single variable for each of the academic measurements. For the standardized tests, the effects for the divorced remarried variables were between .01 to .06 of a standard deviation larger than the effects for the divorced single variable.

For all the family structure variables, except the widowed remarried variable, the effects for the math test had a larger absolute value than the effects for the reading test. In addition, while the effects for the science test were generally close to that of the math test, the effects for the social studies test were generally close to that of the reading test.

The betas for students with "missing" family structure information tended to have negative regression coefficients well. This probably indicates that children from this category come from backgrounds that generally do not perform up to the norm academically. One possibility for this is that the sample of students in this category has a disproportionately large number of people coming from other than intact families. The various reasons for this could include the unwillingness of individuals to reveal that they live in a family structure that they do not particularly want to talk about. A disproportionate amount of children who come from other groups of people which tend to perform at below average levels academically could also be included in this group.

Recently, some researchers have asserted that children from less traditional family structures (e.g., children living with neither parent) need to be included in the analysis to get a more accurate account of the effects of divorce, separation, and other changes in family structure (Jeynes, 1999a). The recognition that children living with neither parent should be included in studying the impact of family structure is rather new. When children living with neither natural parent are added into the equation, only the coefficients for divorce and separation change discernibly. In fact, with the inclusion of children living with neither natural parent, the effects on standardized tests for separation are very close to the effects for cohabitation. Table 9.2 shows that with the inclusion of children living with neither parent, the regression coefficients for separation are very close to that for cohabitation. For the standardized test measures, the effects for cohabitation and separation are never more than .04 of a standard deviation apart. The absolute value of the regression coefficient is slightly larger for cohabitation on four of the five measures.

TABLE 9.2. Regression Coefficients with the Inclusion of Children Living with Neither Parent for the Cohabitation Family Structure Compared with the Separation Family Structure when All Children from These Family Structures Are Included for 1988 (N = 24,599)

Academic measure	Cohabitation	Parents separated
Reading	−.52****	−.48****
Math	−.58****	−.59****
Science	−.54****	−.52****
Social Studies	−.52****	−.50****
Composite test	−.60****	−.58****

Source: Jeynes (2000b) p. 86. Reprinted by permission of The Haworth Press, Inc.

*p < .05, **p < .01, ***p < .001, ****p < .0001
[a] Logistic regression analysis was used.

When the full model without the SES variables is used (Table 9.3), which includes variables for race and gender, both the relative and absolute sizes of the regression coefficients change. The three most prominent changes are: (1) the regression coefficients for the widowed remarried variable become the largest in absolute value of the seven family structures; (2) the regression coefficients for cohabitation now have higher absolute values than those of the never-married single variable; (3) the absolute values of the regression coefficients for the family structures declines.

Table 9.3 shows that the regression coefficients for most of the family structures remain rather large, even with the addition of the race and gender variables. The widowed remarried variable produced the largest effects. For the standardized tests, the effects ranged from −.73 for the science test to −.53 for the math test. The effects for being left back a grade and GPA were .53, respectively. Once again, these effects are different at a statistically significant level from the vast majority of the regression coefficients for the other family structure variables.

The betas for cohabitation emerge as the second largest regression coefficients for the standardized tests, in terms of absolute value, ranging from −.39 for the composite test to −.39 for the social studies and science tests. Although the effects for cohabitation were larger for the standardized tests than for the nonstandardized measures using the basic model without the SES variables, the same could not be said using the full model without the SES variables. The cohabitation family structure impacted GPA (−.42) more than it did any of the standardized test measures. The impact of cohabitation on being left back a grade was, however, still less in absolute value (.26) than for any of the standardized tests.

For the standardized test measures, the effects for the never-married single family structure ranged from −.33 for the composite and −.32 for science tests to −.26 for the social studies test. In the case of the cohabitation family structure variable, the betas for the standardized test measures were no longer larger than the effects for both of the nonstandardized measures. The never-married single family structure impacted GPA (−.36) more than it did any of the standardized test measures and the regression coefficient for being left back a grade was .23.

TABLE 9.3. Effects for Each of the Seven Main Family Structures for Each Academic Measure Using the Full Model without the SES Variables for the Eighth Grade (1988) Data Set (N = 24,599)

Academic measure	GPA	Reading	Math	Science	Social studies	Composite test	Left back[a]
Intercept	3.73****	4.96****	5.28****	5.42****	5.39****	5.12****	3.26****
Divorced Single	-.28****	-.09****	-.10****	-.11****	-.10****	-.10****	.16****
Divorced Remarried	-.25****	-.13****	-.19****	-.16****	-.17****	-.17***	-.29****
Widowed Single	-.25****	-.13*	-.16**	-.20****	-.09	-.15**	.28****
Widowed Remarried	-.30****	-.63****	-.53***	-.73****	-.69****	-.64****	.53****
Never-married Single	-.36****	-.30****	-.31****	-.32****	-.26****	-.33****	.23****
Cohabitation	-.42****	-.36****	-.35****	-.39****	-.39****	-.39****	.26****
Separated	-.31****	-.23****	-.29****	-.23*****	-.25****	-.28****	.24****
Deleted	-.27****	-.26****	-.27****	-.29****	-.24****	-.28****	.20****
Missing	-.34*	-.20	-.07	-.20	-.21	-.15	.20
Asian	.36****	-.03	.24****	.01	.06*	.11****	-.13****
Hispanic	-.26****	-.56****	-.60****	-.58****	-.56****	-.63****	.17****
Black	-.20****	-.62****	-.72****	-.71****	-.59****	-.72****	.21****
Native American	-.41****	-.68****	-.65****	-.74****	-.70****	-.72****	.26****
M......issing Race	-.27****	-.66****	-.71****	-.71****	-.70****	-.74****	.26****
Gender	.20**	.20****	-.04***	-.12****	-.09****	.08****	-.19****

Source: Jeynes (2000b) p. 88. Reprinted by permission of The Haworth Press, Inc.
*p < .05, **p < .01, ***p < .001, ****p < .0001
[a]Logistic regression analysis was used.

The effects for coming from a separated family also impacted academic achievement. For the standardized test measures, the betas ranged from −.29 for the math test to −.23 for the reading and science tests. The regression coefficients were .24 standard deviation units for being left back a grade and GPA, respectively.

The effects for the widowed single variable showed the same general pattern, as the effects for the other family structures, i.e., the effects were smaller using the full model without the SES variables than using the basic model without the SES variables. For the standardized test measures, the regression coefficients ranged from −.16 for the math test to −.09 for the social studies test. The betas for the nonstandardized tests were, in this case, both larger in absolute value: .28 and −.25 for being left back a grade and GPA, respectively.

The effects for divorced single and divorced remarried were smaller than for most of the other family structures. Once again, for all of the academic measures, except GPA, the effects for divorced remarried had a larger absolute value than for divorced single.

When the full model with the SES variables is used (Table 9.4), the regression betas decrease in their absolute value. This indicates that a considerable amount of the impact that living in these family structures has on the academic achievement of children is because nontraditional family structures tend to negatively impact the SES level of the families.

Using the full model with the SES variables (see Table 9.4), the widowed remarried and the cohabitation family structure once again impact the academic achievement of children to the greatest degree. For the widowed remarried family structure, even with the addition of the SES variables, the regression coefficients remained large in their absolute value. The regression coefficients ranged from −.58 for the science test to −.35 for the math test. Given the small sample size of this group, the level of statistical significance declined in nearly every case. Only the beta for the science test remained statistically significant at the .0001 level of probability. Among the nonstandardized measures, the effects were .48 for being left back a grade and −.16 for GPA. The effect for GPA was not statistically significant. Once again, the regression coefficients were different at a statistically significant level from most of the regression coefficients of the other family structure variables.

TABLE 9.4. Effects for Each of the Seven Main Family Structures for Each Academic Measure Using the Full Model with the SES Variables for the Eighth Grade (1988) Data Set (N = 24,599)

Academic measure	GPA	Reading	Math	Science	Social studies	Composite test	Left back[a]
Intercept	3.25****	4.36****	4.66****	4.88****	4.79****	4.46****	3.67****
Divorced	-.19****	.02	.02	.00	.01	.03	.11****
Divorced Remarried	-.19****	-.05*	-.10****	-.09****	-.09****	-.08****	.16****
Widowed Single	-.12*	.04	.02	-.01	.07	-.03	.19***
Widowed Remarried	-.16	-.46**	-.35*	-.58****	-.53****	-.44**	.48**
Never-married Single	-.17***	-.06	-.06	-.10*	-.01	-.06	.07
Cohabitation	-.26****	-.16****	-.13***	-.14***	-.13**	-.16****	.15****
Separated	-.18****	-.06	-.11**	-.07*	-.08*	-.10**	.15****
Deleted	-.20****	-.16****	-.17****	-.20****	-.15****	-.18****	.15****
Missing	.00	-.34	-.11	-.13	-.02	.05	.07

TABLE 9.4 (continued)

Academic measure	GPA	Reading	Math	Science	Social studies	Composite test	Left back[a]
SES Quartile 2	.23****	.29****	.27***	.25****	.30****	.30****	-.28****
SES Quartile 3	.42****	.52****	.50****	.46****	-.53****	.55****	-.42****
SES Quartile 4	.76****	.96****	-1.03****	.82****	.95****	1.07****	-.53****
Asian	.36****	-.03	.23****	.01	.05*	.11****	-.13****
Hispanic	-.05**	-.30****	-.34****	-.34****	-.31****	-.35****	.02
Black	-.05**	-.44****	-.52****	-.54****	-.41****	-.52****	.11****
Native American	-.27****	-.51****	-.46****	-.59****	-.53****	-.52****	.17**
Missing Race	-.13*	-.51****	-.55****	-.55****	-.52****	-.54****	.17**
Gender	.21****	.21****	-.02*	-.10****	-.07****	.10****	-.20****

Source: Jeynes (2000b) p. 88. Reprinted by permission of the Haworth Press, Inc.
*p < .05, **p < .01, ***p < .001, ****p < .0001
[a]Logistic regression analysis was used.

For the cohabitation family structure, some of the larger effects emerged for the nonstandardized measures. The effect for GPA was –.26 and for being left back a grade it was .15. The regression coefficients for the standardized test scores were generally somewhat smaller ranging from –.16 for both the composite test and the reading test to –.13 for the social studies and math tests.

The effects for separation generally impacted academic achievement to the third greatest degree. The effects for separation were larger for the nonstandardized test measures than they were for the standardized test measures. The effect for GPA was –.18 of a standard deviation and for being left back a grade it was .15. The regression coefficients for the standardized tests ranged from –.11 for the math test to –.06 for the reading test.

The betas for divorced remarried and widowed remarried were not as influenced by the introduction of the SES variables. Although divorce and the death of a parent cause the income aspect of SES to fall, the act of remarriage almost always increases the SES level of a family. Nevertheless, children of divorce from reconstituted families overall performed more poorly academically than their counterparts in divorced single-parent families. It is very intriguing to compare the overall patterns of effects for the two remarried variables (divorced remarried and widowed remarried). The regression coefficients for both of the remarried variables yield statistically significant effects for all the standardized test measures. In contrast, the regression coefficients for both divorced and widowed single yield statistically significant effects for all of the nonstandardized test measures, but none for the standardized test measures. Therefore, it is apparent that the act of remarriage, whether it is after divorce or widowhood, negatively impacts the achievement of these students on standardized tests. The regression coefficients for the two remarriage variables were also larger in absolute value for the left back measurement than for their single counterparts. In other words, a child coming from a widowed remarried family structure has a greater chance of being left behind a grade than a child coming from a widowed single family structure; and a child coming from a divorced remarried family structure had a greater chance of being left behind a grade than a child coming from a divorced single family structure.

These coefficients indicate that the addition of SES, race, and gender variables cause the following: (1) remarriage, more than divorce or widowhood, exerts a downward pressure on achievement on standardized tests; (2) divorce and widowhood, more than remarriage, exerts downward pressure on GPA and increases the likelihood of being left back a grade.

Adding the SES variables into the full model reduced the effects for a child living with a never-married single parent, particularly for the standardized test measures. The effects for one of the two non-standardized test measures remained statistically significant (GPA at −.17). The effects for being left back a grade were −.17. Most of the betas for the standardized test measures were not statistically significant.

DISCUSSION

When the full models were utilized (that is those including variables for race and gender or race, gender, and SES), the widowed remarried and cohabitation family structures generally had the largest negative impact on academic achievement. The results of this study indicate that while the death of a parent negatively impacts the academic achievement of children, the remarriage of the living parent worsens the child's academic achievement considerably. It is possible to conclude, based on the results of this study, that for a child whose parent has died, the addition of a nonbiological caregiver exerts more downward pressure on academic achievement than the death of the parent. The possible reasons for this will be discussed in a later section.

The results regarding the effects of the cohabitation family structure on the academic achievement of children are particularly interesting because family social scientists have probably examined the effects of this family structure the least of all. Cohabitation has certainly received much less attention than the never-married single parent family structure. The basic models showed that the effects for a child living with a never-married single parent are the largest. Indeed the effects are considerable, sometimes reaching .8 of a standard deviation. Including variables for race and gender produced results that indicate that cohabitation impacts the academic achievement of children even more than in a never-married single parent family structure. Although these results were rather unexpected, they may be consistent with recent research indicating that the addition of a nonbiological caregiver in a family may hurt the academic achievement of children (Jeynes, 1998b; McLanahan and Sandefur, 1994). This recent research has focused primarily on the act of remarriage, indicating that remarriage following divorce or widowhood may not have the positive effect on the academic achievement and psychological well-being of children that was once believed (Hetherington and Jodl, 1994; Jeynes, 1998b; Popenoe, 1994; Zill, 1994; Zill and Nord, 1994). Sometimes a cohabiting couple may, in fact, consist of a child's biological parents. However, to the extent that they usually do not, the presence of a nonbiological caregiver would help explain these results. Even if both parents are the biological parents, a child might question the parents' commitment to the present family unit, if the couple is not married.

The three theoretical perspectives presented earlier in the chapter, seem to contribute to helping to explain the results. The *absent parent* perspective helps explain why those children who have lost a natural parent by death, whether they live with a single parent or in a reconstituted home, perform poorly in academic achievement. One might argue that since a parent's death is almost always involuntary, their children could deal with this loss more easily than in the case of other family structures. However, the results do not support this notion, but are instead supportive of the absent parent perspective. Children in other family structures may have some degree of contact with the absent natural parent, the child living in a widowed family structure has none. The absent parent perspective also helps us understand why children living with never-married singles perform poorly academically. In the case of this family structure, one of the natural parents is often unavailable or available to the child only to a limited degree. A child's access to a natural parent is generally far less in this family structure than when a divorce has taken place.

It should be noted that the socioeconomic perspective was also helpful in interpreting these results. Once SES was controlled for, the effects for virtually every family structure were reduced considerably. The reduction in the effects for living with a never-married single are especially noteworthy in this regard. Without the addition of the SES variables, the effects for this family structure were among the largest of the family structures under consideration. However, with the introduction of the SES variables, the effects for the never-married single family structure are among the smallest of the family structure effects. The role of SES was also apparent in explaining a fairly large portion of the effects for living in a divorced single-parent family.

The *nonparental adjustment* perspective was an aid in understanding some of the results that the other two models could not. The socioeconomic and absent parent perspectives do not adequately explain why children in the reconstituted (divorced remarried and widowed remarried) and cohabitation family structures perform considerably worse than their counterparts in the corresponding single-parent family structures. The nonparental adjustment perspective asserts that the addition of a caregiver who is not a child's natural parent, necessitates adjustments that may have a negative impact on academic achievement. This perspective is especially helpful, given that once SES was controlled for, children from the widowed remarried and cohabitation family structures performed the worst academically among the family structures examined.

A general pattern in these results is that those family structures which include the presence of a nonbiological caregiver impact academic achievement more negatively than corresponding single-parent family structures that do not include a nonbiological caregiver. For example, children in reconstituted widowed families performed more poorly than children in widowed single-parent families; and children in reconstituted divorced families performed more poorly than children in single-parent divorced families. These results are consistent with recent research indicating the challenges that children face when adjusting to the presence of a nonbiological caregiver (Jeynes, 1998b; Kelly, 1992; Visher and Visher, 1988; Walsh, 1992).

Social scientists are increasingly recognizing just how many adjustments children must make to a new parental figure, the introduction of stepsisters and stepbrothers, and the decreased access the children may have to their natural parent (Amato, 1987; Anderson and Rice, 1992; Hetherington, 1994; Kelly, 1992; McLanahan and Sandefur, 1994; Visher and Visher, 1988; Walsh, 1992). In addition, remarriage often produces families that are more mobile and less stable than first-time marriages, which are also difficult realities for children to face (Booth and Edwards, 1992; McLanahan and Sandefur, 1994; Popenoe, 1994). As a result, many children from reconstituted homes become frustrated and show a greater tendency to be aggressive, anxious, and unhappy than children from intact families (Nunn, Parish, and Worthing, 1993; Wallerstein and Kelly, 1980).

It is possible that the negative impact the cohabitation family structure has on academic achievement is much the same as that of divorce followed by remarriage and widowhood followed by remarriage. First, in many cohabitation relationships only one of the adults is the child's biological parent. When this situation occurs, any children living in the household probably face many of the same disadvantages as in a household in which the child has only one biological parent. Even when both biological parents are present, cohabitation often involves a lower level of commitment by the adults to the continuation of family union and to any children that might abide in the household (Forste and Tanfer, 1996; Nock, 1995). Second, in those households in which one of the parents is not the natural parent, the same kind of friction and adjustments that often arise between stepparents and their stepchildren can develop between the child and the nonbiological parent.

Although the inclusion of the SES variables in the full model reduces the effects for most of the family structures, this fact may be somewhat misleading unless one considers that most of these family structures exert a downward pressure on SES. For example, the act of divorce almost by definition causes a reduction in a family's SES level. Therefore, controlling for SES probably understates the effects for each of these family structures. The fact that the inclusion of the SES variables reduces the effects for most of the family structures is at least in part due to the fact that the transition from one family structure to another often causes a drop in SES. It has often been argued, for example, that the increase in the number of children living in poverty since 1960 is largely a result of the considerable increase in single unwed parents and divorced parents (Uhlenberg and Eggebeen, 1986). To the extent that this is true, because these particular family structures cause a drop in SES, what appears to be largely a problem of SES in these families may have more to do with the family structures of these households than anything else. Acknowledging the socioeconomic limitations that children from these family structures face is essential to understanding their challenges.

When race and gender were controlled for, the effects for GPA tended to be larger than the effects for the standardized tests. To the extent that standardized tests are a more objective means of assessing academic achievement, one could argue that this indicates there is some degree of classroom bias directed against children from nontraditional family structures. Some social scientists have suggested that there exists a type of "Pygmalion effect" in the classrooms in which the expectations of the teachers manifest themselves in the academic output of the students (Rosenthal and Jacobson, 1968; Smith, 1995). An alternative explanation is that coming from nonintact families impacted the behavior of each child, as well as his or her academic abilities. If coming from a nonintact family increased the tendency for children to engage in disruptive behavior, this inclination would impact GPA more than standardized scores. However, as noted earlier, the effects for being left back a grade, the other nonstandardized test measure, were generally about the same or lower than the effects for the standardized tests. If the notion of classroom bias is correct, one would expect that the effects for the nonstandardized test measures would consistently exceed the effects for the standardized test measures. Given that this is not the case, it is unwise to conclude whether there is any evidence here suggesting the presence of classroom bias.

The findings from this study indicate that the family structure a child is from has a considerable impact on that child's academic achievement. While some of the effects are due to the impact that a given family structure has on SES, this study confirms the belief, held by most social scientists, that many other factors are at work as well. The fact that children from reconstituted and cohabitant families performed so poorly academically suggests that more research needs to be done on the impact of these family structures on the achievement and well-being of children.

Chapter 10

Longitudinal Analysis of the Effects of Remarriage Following Divorce on Academic Achievement

The number of studies on stepfamilies has increased since 1980. However, researchers generally agree that there remain two major deficiencies in these studies on the effects of remarriage following divorce on children. The first and foremost of these deficiencies is that there is a dearth of *longitudinal* studies on the effects of remarriage following divorce (Coleman and Ganong, 1990; Emery, 1988; Ganong and Coleman, 1994; Henry, 1996; Pasley and Ihinger-Tallman, 1987). Second is the low percentage of studies that have utilized a nationally representative random sample (Coleman and Ganong, 1990; Emery, 1988; Ganong and Coleman, 1994).

Very few studies exist that specifically examine the academic achievement of children of divorce from reconstituted families which also use a longitudinal design and a random sample. Given that this is the case, it is not surprising that a number of researchers are reluctant to accept the assertion that remarriage negatively impacts the academic achievement of children who have previously dwelled in a divorced one-parent home (Beer, 1992; Ferri, 1984; Ganong and Coleman, 1984).

Based on the National Education Longitudinal Study (NELS) 1988-1992 data set, this chapter presents a longitudinal design to assess the impact of remarriage following divorce on the academic achievement of children. It is very important for professionals in family sciences to know what effects remarriage following divorce generally have on the academic achievement of children from those families. The most effective forms of support, counseling, and intervention can take place only when those working with families have an understanding of these issues.

METHODS AND DATA SOURCES

Two sets of analyses were done in this study. The first set involved a subsample of 1,064 students who were analyzed using the General Linear Model (GLM) regression analysis. These students were children of divorce living in single-parent family structures in 1988 whose parents either remained in the divorced single-parent family structure from 1988 to 1992 (N = 606) or remarried during that same period (N = 458). Information on the family structure that children resided in was taken for all three (1988, 1990, and 1992) data sets. Students who had a parent die during this period were not included in the analysis. If these children had been included in the analysis, the effects obtained would have been biased, because it would not have been clear how much of the effects were due to the death of a parent and how much was due to the act of remarriage by the custodial parent.

A second set of analyses was performed to determine how children living with a parent who remarried following divorce during the 1988-1992 period performed academically compared with the remainder of those children of divorce who lived with a parent who remarried prior to 1988. This second set of analyses would give us greater insight into whether any effects for remarriage during the 1988-1992 period might to be due to the fact that the act of remarriage was a relatively recent event (less than four years).

MODELS

The models used in this analysis included two different combinations of the variables just listed. The No Previous Test Control Model included the variables for family structure, SES, race, gender, and missing data variables. The Previous Test Control Model included all these variables and also controlled for the test score each student obtained for the previous subject test taken in the eighth grade (1988). These variables were chosen for two reasons. First, each of these variables has been shown to have a considerable amount of influence on academic achievement and understanding the effects of family structure. For example, to the extent that there are any gender differences or differences in SES in the results of an academic measure, we want to make sure that the results are not due to a particular group (for example girls of high-SES students) being over- or underrepresented in a particular family structure. Second, the variables used in this model are those most commonly used by family researchers. This makes it easier for the results of this study to be understood in reference to the work that other researchers have done.

RESULTS

The findings of this study indicate that children of divorce whose custodial parent remarried during the course of the study fared somewhat worse academically than their counterparts remaining in divorced single-parent families. Table 10.1 indicates that in terms of average score, on all of the four standardized test measures, children of divorce whose custodial parent had remarried during the time of the study scored lower than children of divorce who remained with a single-parent the entire time. The largest difference between these scores was for the math test and the smallest difference was for the reading test.

Table 10.2 indicates that when SES, race, and gender were controlled for, all four of the differences listed in Table 10.1 were statistically significant. The betas for the math and science tests were the largest, among these effects, at −.11 and −.12 of a standard deviation, respectively. The regression coefficients for reading (−.10) and social studies (−.11) were smaller than for the math and science tests, but were still statistically significant. The family structure variables alone accounted for between 5 and 8 percent of the variance in the academic test scores.

TABLE 10.1. Mean Academic Measurements for the Twelfth Grade (1992) for Children from Reconstituted Families Whose Parents Remarried and Children Whose Custodial Parent Remained in a Single-Parent Divorced Home

Academic measure	Children entering reconstituted families in 1988-1992 (N = 458)	Children remaining in single-parent families 1988-1992 (N = 606)
Math	49.78 (9.32)	51.08 (9.57)
Reading	50.59 (9.52)	51.11 (9.56)
Science	49.99 (9.34)	50.80 (9.70)
Social Studies	50.47 (9.35)	51.11 (9.78)

Source: Jeynes (2000a) p. 139. Reprinted by permission of The Haworth Press, Inc.
Note: Standard deviations in parentheses.

TABLE 10.2. Effects for Each of the Family Structure Variables for Children in Divorced Single-Parent Families in 1988 Whose Parents Either Remained Single or Remarried During the 1988-1992 Period.

Academic measure	Effects for remarriage using the no previous test control model	Effects for remarriage using the previous test control model
Standardized tests		
Math	−.11****	−.09**
Reading	−.10****	−.04
Science	−.12****	−.06
Social Studies	−.11****	−.07*

Source: Jeynes (2000a) p.140. Reprinted by permission of The Haworth Press, Inc.
Note: *p < .05, **p < .01, ***p < .001, ****p < .0001

When the eighth grade (1988) corresponding subject test scores for each student was controlled for, the regression coefficients decreased in size. Table 10.2 shows that once the corresponding subject test scores were controlled for, only the effects for social studies and math remained statistically significant. The effects were −.07 and −.09 of a standard deviation, respectively. The effect for science (−.06) approached, but did not exceed statistical significance. The effect for reading (−.04) was also not statistically significant. Although SES level generally helped explain the changes in the test scores between 1988 and 1992, race usually did not. It should be noted that: (1) being black was associated with a statistically significant decline for two of the four standardized measures, and (2) the directional effects for each race, while usually not statistically significant, were almost always negative. One should also note that the effects for being Asian, while usually not statistically significant, were always negative. This may indicate that the tendency for Asian Americans to perform better academically than other races may decrease slightly between the eighth and twelfth grades.

The second set of analyses was undertaken to determine whether the effects for remarriage following divorce obtained in this study were a result of remarriage being a recent event. If that is the case, one would expect that children of divorce from recently blended families would perform more poorly than the remainder of the cohort of children of divorce from reconstituted homes. The results indicate that the children of divorce from recently reconstituted homes did not perform poorly academically when compared with the remainder of the children of divorce living in reconstituted homes. For the second set of analyses, Table 10.3 shows that on all of the four standardized test measures, children of divorce whose custodial parent had remarried during the time of the study obtained a higher mean score than the remainder of the cohort of children of divorce from reconstituted families. The largest difference between the two groups was for the reading test. The smallest difference between the two groups was for the math test. It should be noted, however, that when race, SES, and gender are controlled for, none of these differences in scores are statistically significant (see Table 10.4). The findings of this study support the notion that children from families with the recent marriage of a custodial parent do not perform more poorly than those who live with a parent who remarried earlier. It indicates that the results found in this sutdy were unlikely to be due to the recent occurrence of the parental remarriage.

DISCUSSION

The results of this study indicate that when race, SES, previous test score, and gender are controlled for, remarriage following divorce has somewhat of a negative impact on the academic achievement of

TABLE 10.3. Mean Academic Measurements for the Twelfth Grade (1992) for Children from Reconstituted Families Whose Parents Remarried During the Period of the Study (1988-1992) and the Remainder of the Children from Reconstituted Families Who Participated in the Study in 1992.

Academic measure	Children entering reconstituted families in 1988-1992 (N = 458)	Remainder of the cohort of children in reconstituted families (N = 1,094)
Math	49.78 (9.32)	49.54(9.85)
Reading	50.59 (9.52)	49.90 (9.67)
Science	49.99 (9.34)	49.720 (9.92)
Social Studies	50.47 (9.35)	49.85(9.79)

Source: Jeynes (2000a) p. 142. Reprinted by permission of The Haworth Press, Inc.

Note: Standard deviations in parentheses.

TABLE 10.4. Effects for Parental Remarriage Following Divorce, During the 1988-1992 Period, on the Academic Achievement of Children versus the Remainder of the Children from Reconstituted Families for the Twelfth Grade, Using the Previous Test Control Model (1992) (N = 1,562)

Academic measure	Betas for recent remarriage variable within model	F for family remarriage variable within model
Standardized measures		
Math	−.03	0.54
Reading	.02	0.15
Science	−.01	0.02
Social Studies	−.03	0.29

Source: Jeynes (in press). Reprinted by permission of The Haworth Press, Inc.

Note: *p < .05, **p < .01, ***p < .001, ****p < .0001

teenage children. The results of this study are particularly important, given that there are still large numbers of people in the general populace and some researchers who believe that remarriage following divorce benefits the academic achievement of children. The findings that emerge here clearly do not support this belief. When race, SES, gender, and previous test scores were controlled for, two of the four effects for academic achievement showed statistically significant effects in favor of children of divorce from families where the custodial parent had not remarried versus children of divorce whose custodial parent had remarried (see Table 10.2). Even those educational outcomes which did not yield statistically significant effects, usually resulted in effects that directionally favored children of divorce from single-parent families over children of divorce from reconstituted families.

One interesting finding is that remarriage had the greater negative impact on math achievement than it did on reading and science achievement. This may point to the cumulative nature of learning math. Hence, if certain circumstances (e.g., parental divorce or remarriage) cause one to fall behind in math class, it is more difficult to catch up than in other subjects. The finding that remarriage following divorce impacts math achievement more than reading achievement is consistent with other research (Kurdek and Sinclair, 1988). It is also possible that learning social studies may require more cumulative learning than reading and science, although this is less ostensible. Certainly, it is easier to learn European history if one also knows American and Asian history as well.

Some past studies have, in fact, indicated that while divorce negatively impacts certain measures of academic achievement, remarriage following divorce impacts others (Jeynes, 1998b; Smith, 1995). The Jeynes and Smith research indicates that divorce, more than remarriage following divorce, negatively impacts GPA and being left back a grade, while both remarriage and divorce negatively impact standardized test results and students' willingness to take basic core courses (Jeynes, 1998b). The findings of the Jeynes and Smith studies, in conjunction with other studies on the effects of parental remarriage (e.g., Baydar, 1988; McLanahan and Sandefur, 1994), would help explain why children of divorce from reconstituted families generally achieve at lower levels academically on virtually all measures than their counterparts in intact families. The analysis performed in this chapter focused on the effects of remarriage following divorce, rather than on the effects of divorce on academic achievement.

The primary limitation of the longitudinal aspect of this study is that it includes only those children whose custodial parent remarried during the course of the four years of the NELS 1988-1992 study. One might argue that the academic achievement of children whose custodial parent remarried during this relatively recent period of the children's lives would be depressed versus other children of divorce from reconstituted families who have lived in these families for a longer period of time. When the educational achievement of children of divorce who had *recently* entered reconstituted families is compared to children of divorce from blended families in the remainder of the sample, virtually no difference is found in achievement levels. The fact that no statistically significant differences emerged may indicate that the belief may be unfounded that the effects of remarriage on children decrease with time. It also appears to indicate that the results of this study are not due to the recent nature of the parental remarriage.

It should be noted that there are other possible explanations for this second set of results. One likely possibility is that the results may reflect an early occurrence of divorce among parents who remarried earlier. That is, it seems quite possible that the children of divorce who have lived in reconstituted families for longer periods of time experience parental marital dissolution at a younger age on average, than those children of divorce who recently entered reconstituted families. Past research by Hetherington and Clingempeel (1992) and others suggests that divorce has a more severe impact on children when it occurs earlier in a child's life (Cherlin, 1988). More longitudinal research needs to be done to obtain a greater understanding about whether the effects of remarriage on the academic achievement of children increase or decrease over time. Research suggests that the impact of family structure on academic achievement and psychological well-being of children over time may be much more complex and unpredictable than was once believed (Hetherington and Clingempeel, 1992; Hetherington, Stanley-Hagan, and Anderson, 1989; Love-Clark, 1984; Wallerstein and Blakeslee, 1989; Wallerstein, Corbin, and Lewis, 1988).

Although a longitudinal design, such as the one used in this analysis, is helpful, it probably understates the effects for remarriage. Those parents that remarry may be, on average, more fully recovered from their divorce and more psychologically stable than those who remain divorced. To the extent that this is true, the population of children of divorce in reconstituted families is probably not entirely comparable to children of divorce remaining in single-parent families. In addition, to the extent that children with educational and behavioral problems make the remarriage of a parent less likely, this also may contribute to the fact that the two groups of children are not entirely comparable.

For many centuries classical religious and philosophical writings have frequently declared that parental remarriage was an action to be avoided, often because of its painful impact upon children. Yet nationwide surveys such as the 1987 National Survey of Families and Households indicates that somehow our society has convinced itself otherwise (as cited in Chadwick and Heaton, 1992). Today, many Americans view remarriage as an action that is desirable if one is a single parent. Part of this mind-set rests in an honest desire to benefit any children of divorce. However, in most cases self-fulfillment is the primary reason why many people desire to remarry (Duberman, 1975; Messinger, 1984). Since 1980, various researchers have begun to question the notion that remarriage following divorce usually benefits children. Nevertheless, many of the studies undertaken during this period either did not used a longitudinal design or used a random sample to study the effects of remarriage.

The results of this study may even lead us to at least *question* whether remarriage benefits children in a more general sense. Grades and scores reflect much more than the intelligence of a child; they may reflect many other factors at work in a child's psychological well-being and happiness. Few would argue that the educational gap that exists between children from intact families and children from other family structures results primarily from a difference in intelligence. Rather, the gap reflects differences in levels of discipline, environmental stability, psychological well-being, and happiness. Schoolteachers know well, for example, that when a student's school achievement drops rather suddenly, a change in the child's emotional well-being and stability is often the cause.

One cannot conclude with certainty that this study indicates that remarriage adversely affects a child's psychological well-being and happiness. Nevertheless, the fact that many studies have found a high correlation between academic achievement and psychological well-being points to this possibility. Additional studies need to be done regarding the ways remarriage affects children psychologically, and the extent to which remarriage's impact on academic achievement reflects the altered psychological state of the child produced by remarriage.

Additional longitudinal research is needed to understand why the presence of an additional caregiver and the rise in family income that remarriage usually produces, does not have a generally beneficial impact on the academic achievement of children. Further research should also be done to examine the psychosociological aspects of remarriage which impact the academic achievement of children the most.

Chapter 11

Testing Other Important Hypotheses

This chapter includes the results of analyses, using the NELS 1988-1992 data set, which are based on some criticisms that various theorists have launched against previous studies performed on the effects of divorce and remarriage. A number of these criticisms are directed at certain assumptions that many researchers make before undertaking their analysis. Many of these assumptions are based on the belief that the effects of divorce and remarriage on children are almost purely a socioeconomic phenomenon. Many of these "socioeconomic theorists" believe that virtually all the effects of divorce can be explained by the fact that parental divorce is correlated with a low level of family socioeconomic status. Therefore, if one simply raises the socioeconomic status of a family of divorce, the effects of divorce on children will be nearly removed. In addition, these theorists aver that parental remarriage, which nearly always raises the income component (and perhaps other components) of socioeconomic status, will benefit children to that point that they will perform as well academically as children from intact families. We will examine three hypotheses that address these assumptions.

Over the years, many social scientists have included children from reconstituted families in the same category with children from intact families. The first hypothesis that we will investigate is the Proper Category Hypothesis.

THE PROPER CATEGORY HYPOTHESIS

Whether one includes reconstituted families in the same category as intact families or distinguishes these two family structures from each other, will affect the results obtained for the effect of family structure on academic achievement. Socioeconomic theory would as-

151

sert that these two groups of children do not need to be distinguished, because both kinds of families generally enjoy the benefits of two adults who can work. In addition, research has indicated that the SES levels of intact and reconstituted families are roughly the same (Chadwick and Heaton, 1992; McLanahan and Sandefur, 1994). Family structure theorists, on the other hand, assert that children from reconstituted families and intact families are in an entirely different family structure and should be differentiated accordingly. Children of divorce living in reconstituted families have experienced at least two disruptions in their family structure. Children from intact families have neither experienced the breakup of their family nor the introduction of a stepparent. Family structure theory would therefore predict that placing children from these two structural categories into the same group would produce smaller effects than if one distinguished these two family structures from each other. If this is true, this would indicate that studies that do not make such a distinction underestimate the effect of family structure on academic achievement.

Results of Proper Category Hypothesis Analysis

As predicted, how family structure is defined affects the kind of results obtained regarding the effects of divorce and remarriage. Researchers frequently make the mistake of grouping children of divorce from reconstituted families in the same category with children from intact families. If this definition of a divorced family is used, divorce has little or no impact on children.

When the basic model is used, a substantial difference emerges between the results found using the "insufficient family structure variable" and the divorce variable used in the analyses presented in this book. This is particularly important because most studies control for SES. All of the standardized test scores yielded statistically insignificant results when the SES variables were added. In fact, as Table 11.1 indicates, the regression coefficients for this "insufficient family structure variable" were sometimes not even negative. This is because children of divorce from reconstituted families, on average, scored the worst of all the three major family structures. This especially reduces the effect for family structure in this incomplete model because children from reconstituted families score especially low, given the socioeconomic level of the families that they come from.

TABLE 11.1. Effects for the Insufficient Family Structure Variable for the Basic Family Structures Using the Basic Model for Eighth Grade (1988) (N = 18,176)

Academic measure	Regression coefficient with SES variable added	Regression coefficient without SES variables added
GPA	−.19****	−.28****
Reading	.00	−.12****
Math	.01	−.14****
Science	−.02	−.14****
Social Studies	.00	−.13****
Composite	.01	−.14****
Left back[a]	.10****	.13****

*p < .05, **p < .01, ***p < .001, ****p < .0001
[a] Logistic regression analysis was used.

Regression coefficients were slightly positive for the math, reading, and social studies. In all cases, the regression coefficient was near zero. However, it should be noted that even using this insufficient model for family structure produces statistically significant effects for GPA and being left back a grade. The regression coefficients for these measures were −.19 and .10 standard deviation units, respectively. Each of these measures were statistically significant at the .0001 level.

The full model (see Table 11.2) which includes variables for race, gender, and SES yields similar results. With the exception of the effects for GPA and being left back a grade, the effects were not statistically significant. In fact, the regression coefficients for all the standardized tests, although statistically insignificant, are actually slightly positive. Once again, this trend emerges in part as a consequence of the fact that children of divorce from reconstituted families score especially low on standardized tests, given the high level of SES that the average reconstituted family enjoys. Analyses for the 1990 (tenth grade) data set were not performed, because no SES measures were taken for that year.

For the 1992 (twelfth grade) data set the same trend emerged as for the 1988 (eighth grade) data set. Table 11.3 compares the effects obtained for the "insufficient family variable" with and without the addition of the three SES variables. Once again, because the 1992

NELS questionnaire was structured differently than either the 1988 and 1990 questionnaires, the "insufficient family structure variable" includes children from single-parent structures which include both divorced and separated families. With this difference in mind, Table 11.3 shows that the results for the various academic measures are similar to those obtained using the 1988 data set.

TABLE 11.2. Effects for the Insufficient Family Structure Variable for the Basic Family Structures Using the Full Model for Eighth Grade (1988) (N = 18,176)

Academic measure	Regression coefficient for the full model with SES variables added
GPA	−.17****
Reading	.02
Math	.04
Science	.01
Social Studies	.02
Composite	.03
Left back[a]	.11***

*p < .05, **p < .01, ***p < .001, ****p < .0001
[a] Logistic regression analysis was used.

TABLE 11.3. Effects for the Insufficient Family Structure Variable (Including the Divorce/Separation Variation) Using the Basic Model for Twelfth Grade (1992) (N = 13,002)

Academic measure	Regression coefficient with SES variables added	Regression coefficient without SES variables added
GPA	−.04	−.05
Reading	−.04	−.19****
Math	−.10*	−.27****
Science	−.10*	−.26****
Social Studies	−.08*	−.23****
Composite test	−.08*	−.25****
Left back[a]	.07**	.14****
Basic Core[a]	−.06*	−.13****

*p < .05, **p < .01, ***p < .001, ****p < .0001
[a] Logistic regression analysis was used.

When the basic model is used without the SES variables added, all of the measures are statistically significant at the .0001 level of probability, except GPA. However, when the three SES variables are added, the effects are reduced substantially ranging from −.04 for GPA and the reading test to −.10 for the math and science tests.

When the full model is used with the three SES variables added, the different results produced by the "incomplete family structure variable" again become even more evident. Table 11.4 lists the regression coefficients using the full model with the SES variables. In the case of the full model, only two of the academic measures produced statistically significant results: being left back a grade and the basic core courses. The effects for these variables were .06, and −.06 respectively. Both of these measures were statistically significant at the .05 level of probability.

The twelfth grade (1992) data set overall had somewhat stronger effects than the eighth grade (1988) data set largely for two reasons: (1) The effects for the twelfth grade combined the effects for divorce and separation. As we will see in the second part of this section, the effects for separation are considerably larger than for divorce. Therefore, because the twelfth grade NELS questionnaire combined these

TABLE 11.4. Effects for the Insufficient Family Structure Variable (Including the Divorce/Separation Variation) Using the Full Model for Twelfth Grade (1992) (N = 13,002)

Academic measure	Regression coefficient with SES variables added
GPA	−.05
Reading	.00
Math	−.04
Science	−.03
Social Studies	−.03
Composite test	−.02
Left back[a]	.06*
Basic Core[a]	−.06*

*p < .05, **p < .01, ***p < .001, ****p < .0001
[a] Logistic regression analysis was used.

two family structures into one variable, the effects were larger than they would otherwise be if the variable included only the effects for divorce. (2) It is possible that the effects for divorce were larger for the twelfth graders (1992) than they were for the eighth graders (1988) four years earlier. Supporting this possibility is the fact that the effects for divorce are slightly higher for the tenth grade (1990) data set than the eighth grade (1988) data set.

Overall, if family structure is simply determined by whether a child lives in a two-parent or one-parent family, the effect of family structure is understated, especially when one controls for SES. The results indicate even more convincingly that the grouping of families simply on the basis of whether a child's parents are married does not sufficiently distinguish between family structures. This leads to different model coefficients than a model that distinguishes between distinct family structures. The insufficient family structure model also gives the false impression that divorce does not have as much of an effect as it actually does.

CUSTODIAL PARENT'S GENDER HYPOTHESIS

The custodial parent's gender hypothesis asserts that children from divorced father-only families will not achieve better academically than children in divorced mother-only families. Socioeconomic theory would predict that because father-only families generally have a higher SES level and income level, children of divorce from father-only families would perform better academically than children of divorce in mother-only families. Family structure theory, on the other hand, asserts that there is very little difference between the divorced mother-only and divorced father-only family structures. Therefore, the educational achievement of the children from each group should be about the same.

However, it should be noted that while the custodial parent's gender hypothesis is a null hypothesis, SES does impact academic achievement. Therefore, stating the hypothesis in this way understates the effect SES has. There may be some directional effects. Hence, while part of the effect of divorce exhibits itself through the SES variable, the influence of the SES variable is frequently overstated. The socioeconomic theory that predicts that children from divorced father-only families would perform better academically than children from mother-only families results from the fact that father-only families generally have a higher SES level than do mother-only families. The custodial parent's gender hypothesis predicts that there will be no statistically significant differences in the academic achievement of children from divorced mother-only families and divorced father-only families.

The Standard Basic Model for the 1988 Data Set

Table 11.5 shows the regression coefficients for living in a father-only family versus living in a mother-only family for children of divorce using the basic no-SES model. None of the regression coefficients for the 1988 (eighth grade) data set are statistically significant. The regression coefficients for GPA and being left back a grade show a statistically *in*significant negative effect for living in a father-only verses a mother-only arrangement. The regression coefficients for the standardized tests yield statistically insignificant positive effects.

TABLE 11.5. Effects for a Child Living in a Father-Only Family Rather Than a Mother-Only Family for All Three Data Sets Using the Basic Model Without SES Variables

Academic measure	1988 (8th grade) (N = 1,974)	1990 (10th grade) (N = 1,612)	1992 (12th grade) (N = 1,813)
GPA	−.05	NA	−.06
Reading	.04	−.17*	−.07
Math	.08	−.15*	.08
Science	.07	−.09	.10
Social Studies	.11	−.08	.00
Composite test	.06	−.17*	.00
Left back[a]	.12	.05	−.12
Basic Core[a]	NA	NA	−.10
Drop out[a]	NA	−.11	.09

*p < .05, **p < .01, ***p < .001, ****p < .0001
NA: not applicable.
[a] Logistic regression analysis was used.

The 1990 (tenth grade) data analysis (Table 11.5) also yields no evidence supporting the predictions of socioeconomic theory. In fact, three of the measures produced statistically significant results favoring children of divorce living in mother-only families. The measures for the standardized reading, math, and composite tests, all produced statistically significant results at the .05 level of probability. All the other measures of achievement with the exception of dropping out of school (1988-1990) produced negative effects as well, but they were not statistically significant. Overall, the effects for the standardized measures ranged from −.17 for the reading and composite tests to −.08 for the social studies test.

For both the 1988 and 1990 data sets the math and reading tests produced coefficients that least favored the father-only structure and most favored the mother-only structure. On the other hand, the social studies and science tests produced coefficients that least favored the mother-only structure and most favored the father-only structure.

The data analysis for the 1992 (twelfth grade) data set produced results roughly midway between the results found using the 1988 (eighth grade) and 1990 (tenth grade) data sets. However, none of the regression coefficients were statistically significant. Among the standardized measures, the science test produced the effect that most favored the father-only family structure. The value for dropping out of school produced the effect that most favored the divorced mother-only family structure.

It is clear from these analyses that children of divorce from father-only families do not enjoy an academic advantage over children of divorce from mother-only families. This result supports the custodial parent's gender hypothesis and is contrary to the results that socioeconomic theory would predict.

Table 11.6 shows the variables for the no-SES full model. The regression coefficients are much larger in favor of children in mother-only families versus father-only families (see Table 11.6). The addition of these variables into the regression equation makes it clear that even with the advantage of a higher average SES in a father-only family, there is no advantage for the child of divorce living in a father-only family as opposed to a child of divorce living in a mother-only family. In fact, nearly every regression coefficient goes in a direction favoring children from mother-only families rather than children from father-only families.

TABLE 11.6. Effects for a Child Living in a Father-Only Family Rather Than a Mother-Only Family for All Three Data Sets Using the Full Model Without SES Variables

Academic measure	1988 (8th grade) (N = 1,974)	1990 (10th grade) (N = 1,612)	1992 (12th grade) (N = 1,813)
GPA	−.07	NA	−.05
Reading	−.02	−.22**	−.15
Math	−.03	−.24***	−.03
Science	−.04	−.22***	−.04
Social Studies	.02	−.17*	−.09
Composite test	−.03	−.25***	−.10
Left back[a]	.12	.05	−.09
Basic Core[a]	NA	NA	−.11
Drop out[a]	NA	−.02	.12*

*p < .05, **p < .01, ***p < .001, ****p < .0001
NA: not applicable.
[a] Logistic regression analysis was used.

The regression coefficients for the tenth grade (1990) data set are particularly large in favor of children from mother-only families. Among the standardized test measures, the effects for the tenth grade data set varied from −.25 for the composite test to −.17 for the social studies test. The effects for the math, science, and the composite tests were statistically significant at the .001 level of probability. The reading test measure produced results that were statistically significant at the .01 level of probability and the social studies test produced statistically significant results at the .05 level of probability. Neither the eighth grade (1988) nor the twelfth grade (1992) data sets produced statistically significant results favoring the father-only family structure. In fact, although only one statistically significant result favoring mother-only families was produced for these two years (1988 and 1992), the regression coefficients almost always favored children from mother-only families. The most outstanding exception was the left back variable which yielded a −.09 regression coefficient for the twelfth grade. Although statistically insignificant, this variable points to the possibility that living in a father-only structure decreases the chance of a child being left back a grade. Nevertheless, a statistically significant result occurred for the twelfth grade (1992) data set. Living in a father-only (versus a mother-only) family increased the chances of dropping out of school.

Overall, the data seem to indicate that there is a small academic advantage to living in a mother-only rather than a father-only family structure. Given the results of the analyses using the basic and full models without the SES variables, the inclusion of the three SES variables should neutralize the effect of the measures that give children from father-only families an advantage and should increase the absolute value of the effects favoring children in the mother-only family structure. Table 11.7 lists the regression coefficients using the SES basic model.

Unfortunately, SES variables are not available for the 1990 data set which showed the strongest effects favoring mother-only families over father-only families. When the SES variables were added into the basic model equation (see Table 11.7), each of the regression coefficients made a definite move in the direction of favoring the mother-only family structure versus when the basic model was used without the SES variables included. The average movement for the eighth grade (1988) and twelfth grade (1992) data sets was about $-.07$ of a standard deviation. In fact, although most of the regression coef-

TABLE 11.7. Effects for a Child Living in a Father-Only Family Rather Than a Mother-Only Family for the Basic Model with SES Variables

Academic measure	1988 (8th grade) (N = 1,974)	1990 (10th grade) (N = 1,612)	1992 (12th grade) (N = 1,813)
GPA	−13*	NS	−.05
Reading	−.08	NS	−.11
Math	−.04	NS	.04
Science	−.04	NS	.06
Social Studies	.00	NS	−.04
Composite test	−.07	NS	−.04
Left back[a]	.18**	NS	−.09
Basic Core[a]	NA	NS	−.11
Drop out[a]	NA	−.01	NS

*p < .05, **p < .01, ***p < .001, ****p < .0001
NS: not available due to the absence of SES variables.
NA: not applicable.
[a] Logistic regression analysis was used.

ficients for the eighth grade basic model without the SES variables were positive (favoring children from father-only families), when the SES variables were included in the model almost all the coefficients were negative. With the three SES variables added, the effects for GPA and being left back a grade become statistically significant at the .05 and .01 level of significance, respectively.

The fact that the inclusion of the SES variables favors the mother-only family structure leads to the conclusion that, at the very least, the three academic measures which were statistically significant using the basic model without the SES variables for the tenth grade (1990) data set would be statistically significant with the inclusion of the three SES variables. In fact, given that the addition of the SES variables produced an average shift of −.07 in the regression coefficients for the 1988 and 1992 data sets, one could argue that virtually all of the academic measures for the 1990 data set would be statistically significant.

Table 11.8 lists the regression coefficients for the full model including the three SES variables. With the addition of the SES variables, the regression coefficients again make a general move in the direction of favoring the mother-only family structure. Although quite a few of the regression coefficients had an absolute value of at least .10, only two of the coefficients reached statistical significance. However, nearly all of these particular regression coefficients approach statistical significance. Once again, for the tenth grade (1990) data set, analyses including the SES variables could not be included because of the absence of SES data for this data set. Given that five academic measures were statistically significant using the full model *without* the SES variables, at least that many would almost certainly reach statistical significance with the inclusion of the SES variables.

THE DISTINCTION HYPOTHESIS

A considerable portion of the research addressing the influence of family structure on academic achievement fails to adequately differentiate between various kinds of single-parent family structures. Many of these studies simply divide families into three categories: (1) single-parent families; (2) intact families; and (3) reconstituted families. Moreover, a number of studies use the results of analyses

TABLE 11.8. Effects for a Child Living in a Father-Only Family Rather Than a Mother-Only Family for the Full Model with SES Variables

Academic measure	1988 (8th grade) (N = 1,974)	1990 (10th grade) (N = 1,612)	1992 (12th grade) (N = 1,813)
GPA	−.15	NS	−.06
Reading	−.09	NS	−.16*
Math	−.10	NS	−.03
Science	−.10	NS	−.04
Social Studies	−.05	NS	−.09
Composite test	−.10	NS	−.10
Left back[a]	.16**	NS	−.09
Basic Core[a]	NA	NS	−.10
Drop out[a]	NA	−.01	NS

*p < .05, **p < .01, ***p < .001, ****p < .0001
NS: not available due to the absence of SES variables.
NA: not applicable.
[a] Logistic regression analysis was used.

that use these structures to conclude that remarriage has a positive impact on academic achievement (and even more specifically, that remarriage following divorce has a positive impact on academic achievement).

Unfortunately, research that uses these broad structures and then makes these conclusions compares apples with oranges. Included in the single-parent family structure are all kinds of single-parent families including a large number of unwed single parents and other single-parent family structures. Family structure theory would predict that children living with an unwed parent would perform worse academically than children of divorce in single-parent families. To the extent that loss of parental presence reduces academic achievement, a parent who was never present to begin with would hurt academic achievement that much more.

To make any kind of conclusion regarding the effects of remarriage on academic achievement, one must compare the academic achievement of children of divorce from single-parent families with children of divorce in reconstituted families. Including children from other single-parent family structures in an equation that is designed to determine the effect of remarriage following marital dissolution generally, or divorce specifically, totally changes the results. The inclusion of children living with an unwed parent (and other single-parent family structures) would considerably reduce the average academic level achieved by children from the single-parent family structure. The inclusion of these children artificially inflates the effect for remarriage relative to the single-parent family structure it is being compared to.

The distinction hypothesis predicts that when children from all kinds of single-parent families are compared to children from all kinds of reconstituted families, the results will show that children from reconstituted families will score higher in academic measures than children from single-parent families. Through this result, it will be shown that when family structure is defined in this broad way, the results will give the false impression that remarriage has a beneficial impact on the academic achievement of children of divorce.

When examining the effect of divorce and remarriage in the context of single-parenthood and reconstituted families generally, the children under examination fall into one of five categories: (1) children from intact families; (2) children of divorce in single-parent families; (3) children in single-parent families for reasons other than divorce (most of the children in this group live with unwed mothers); (4) children of divorce in reconstituted families; and (5) children who live in reconstituted families whose parents are not divorced. Often, research studies examine the effect of single-parenthood by comparing the levels of academic achievement of children from group 1, with all children from single-parent families (groups 2 and 3), and all children from reconstituted families (groups 4 and 5). Family structure theory would assert that lumping groups 2 and 3 into one category and groups 4 and 5 into another category is inappropriate, because it does not properly distinguish between family structures. Family structure theory avers that one can only ascertain the effects of remarriage on children of divorce by *specifically examining children of divorce*. It would claim that combining children from nondivorced single-parent homes (most of which live with unwed mothers, i.e., group 3) in the same category with children of divorce from single-parent homes (i.e., group 2), will give the impression that remarriage has a positive effect on the academic achievement of children, because it will artificially depress the average achievement levels of the children that the children from reconstituted families are being compared to. Family structure theory would predict that children living with unwed mothers, for example, would fare considerably worse than children of divorce because most of them have scarcely had any access to the noncustodial parent.

Family structure theory therefore predicts that when all children in the categories of intact (group 1), single-parent (groups 2 and 3), and reconstituted families (groups 4 and 5) are examined, children from reconstituted families will perform better academically than children from single-parent homes. However, when only children of divorce are examined along with intact families, this advantage favoring children in reconstituted homes will disappear. This indicates that when socioeconomic theorists fail to differentiate between children of divorce and children of unwed mothers and other family structures, it can give the misleading impression that children of divorce from reconstituted families achieve at higher levels academically than children of divorce in single-parent families. This distinction is important, because this misleading result would seem to support the prediction of the socioeconomic school of thought. This school of thought would predict that children of divorce from reconstituted families would achieve at higher levels due to the higher SES levels that usually result from remarriage. When these family structures are properly differentiated, this is not the case. Socioeconomic theory alone cannot explain these results and the fact that additional factors related to family structure, are sometimes at work.

Using the no-SES basic model, Table 11.9 lists the regression coefficients for the single-parent and reconstituted family variables using this "overly broad" model. The regression coefficients for all the academic measures, except GPA, show tremendous consistency from year to year. The regression coefficients for the reading test, for example, vary only between .07 and .09 standard deviation units. The coefficients for the math test vary even less, from between .06 and .07 standard deviation units. The coefficients for the science test range from .08 to .10 standard deviation unit and the composite test measure ranges from .07 to .08 standard deviation units.

TABLE 11.9. Effects for the Reconstituted Family Variables for All Children Using the "Overly Broad" Basic Model Without the SES Variables for All Three Data Sets

Academic measure	1988 (8th grade) (N = 23,635)	1990 (10th grade) (N = 16,304)	1992 (12th grade) (N = 17,100)
GPA	.07*	NA	−.06
Reading	.09***	.07*	.08*
Math	.06**	.06*	.07*
Science	.08***	.10***	.09**
Social Studies	.04	.02	.09**
Composite test	.08***	.07*	.08**
Left back[a]	−.02	.00	−.01
Basic Core[a]	NA	NA	.00
Drop out[a]	NA	−.03	−.03

*p < .05, **p < .01, ***p < .001, ****p < .0001
NA: not applicable.
[a] Logistic regression analysis was used.

Nearly all the effects were in the positive direction, as predicted by the hypothesis. The vast majority of these positive effects were statistically significant. The probability levels for these effects ranged from .001 to .05. Of the academic measures that were taken in all three of the three data sets, only the effects for being left back a grade never reached statistical significance. These results stand in marked contrast to the results that examined only children of divorce in single-parent and reconstituted homes. These latter results show a neutral or somewhat negative effect for remarriage using the same basic model.

Tables 11.10, 11.11, and 11.12 compare the effects for remarriage using the inappropriate "overly broad" model versus the model used in this study that examines specifically children of divorce. Table 11.10 compares the effects for the eighth grade (1988), Table 11.11 compares the effects for the tenth grade (1990), and Table 11.12 compares the effects for the twelfth grade (1992) data sets.

Tables 11.10, 11.11, and 11.12 show a noticeable difference between the effects for remarriage using the "overly broad" no-SES basic model and the no-SES basic model used in this study. In the case of the "overly broad" model for the 1988 data set, the direction of the

TABLE 11.10. Comparison of the Effects for the Reconstituted Family Variables for the "Overly Broad" Basic Model versus This Study's Basic Model (Without the SES Variables) for the Eighth Grade (1988) (N = 23,635)

Academic measure	Effects for remarriage using the "overly broad" basic model	Effects for remarriage using this study's basic model
GPA	.07**	.05
Reading	.09***	.01
Math	.06**	−.06*
Science	.08***	−.03
Social Studies	.04	−.04
Composite test	.08***	−.04
Left back[a]	−.02	.01

*p < .05, **p < .01, ***p < .001, ****p < .0001
[a] Logistic regression analysis was used.

effects indicate that remarriage has a positive effect. Not all the regression coefficients are statistically significant. In contrast, the regression coefficients for the basic model used in this study, which examines children of divorce, indicate a neutral to slightly negative effect.

The regression coefficients for the tenth grade (1990) data show a very similar pattern (see Table 11.11). The regression coefficients for the overly broad approach, with the exception of the left back measure indicate a positive effect for remarriage, although not all the effects were statistically significant. The regression coefficients for the basic model for this study, on the other hand, tend to show a neutral effect for remarriage.

For the twelfth grade (1992) data set (Table 11.12) the regression coefficients for the "overly broad" basic model once again generally indicate that remarriage has a positive effect. All the standardized test measures produced statistically significant effects. In contrast, this study's basic model's regression coefficients (although only one is statistically significant), *directionally* point to remarriage having a negative effect.

These results indicate that an inaccurate impression about the effects of remarriage can result if a distinction is not made regarding children of divorce from other types of single-parent families. Over-

TABLE 11.11. Comparison of the Effects for the Reconstituted Family Variables for the "Overly Broad" Basic Model versus This Study's Basic Model (Without the SES Variables) for the Tenth Grade (1990) (N = 16,304)

Academic measure	Effects for remarriage using the "overly broad" basic model	Effects for remarriage using this study's basic model
Reading	.07*	−.01
Math	.06*	−.02
Science	.10***	.03
Social Studies	.02	−.01
Composite test	.07*	−.02
Left back[a]	.00	.03
Drop out[a]	−.03	−.01

*p < .05, **p < .01, ***p < .001, ****p < .0001
[a] Logistic regression analysis was used.

TABLE 11.12. Comparison of the Effects for the Reconstituted Family Variables for the "Overly Broad" Basic Model versus This Study's Basic Model (Without the SES Variables) for the Twelfth Grade (1992) (N = 21,116)

Academic measure	Effects for remarriage using the "overly broad" basic model	Effects for remarriage using this study's basic model
GPA	−.06	−.04
Reading	.08*	−.03
Math	.07*	−.05
Science	.09**	−.02
Social Studies	.09**	−.03
Composite test	.08**	−.04
Left back[a]	−.01	.07*
Basic Core[a]	.00	−.06
Drop out[a]	−.03	−.01

*p < .05, **p < .01, ***p < .001, ****p < .0001
[a] Logistic regression analysis was used.

all, these results support the hypothesis that: (1) the "overly broad" model will produce different results than a model which only includes children of divorce, and (2) the "overly broad" model will produce results that could lead some to inaccurately conclude that remarriage has a positive effect on the academic achievement of children.

The accuracy of the hypothesis is only partially substantiated when the "overly broad" full model excluding the SES variables is used. In this case: (1) the "overly broad" full model still produced different results from a full model which deals specifically with children of divorce, but, (2) the negative effect of remarriage was stronger than expected. Not only did the full model produce stronger effects for remarriage than was anticipated, but the negative effect of remarriage following divorce played a large role in the effects for living in a reconstituted family being at or near zero when using the "overly broad" model.

Tables 11.13, 11.14, and 11.15 compare the effects for remarriage using the "overly broad" no-SES full model versus the specific no-SES full model used in this study. Table 11.13 compares the effects for the eighth grade (1988) data set, Table 11.14 compares the effects for the tenth grade (1990) data set, and Table 11.15 compares the effects for the twelfth grade (1992) data set.

Tables 11.13, 11.14, and 11.15 show a noticeable difference between the trend in effects for remarriage using the "overly broad" full model and the full model used in this study. The full model adds the race and gender variables into the regression equation. With these variables added, the full model used in this study shows several statistically significant negative effects for remarriage and several other negative effects which barely miss a statistically significant level. In contrast, when the "overly broad" model is used, remarriage affects academic achievement in a negative way.

Table 11.13 shows statistically significant effects for this study's full model for the math, social studies, and composite tests. In addition, the −.06 effect for the science test just missed being statistically significant with a p-value of .0515.

The full model effects for the tenth graders (1990, see Table 11.14) were all in the expected direction, although the largest effect only approached statistical significance at p-levels of .06 to −.10.

TABLE 11.13. Comparison of the Effects for the Reconstituted Family Variables for the "Overly Broad" Full Model versus This Study's Full Model (Without the SES Variables) for the Eighth Grade (1988) (N = 23,635)

Academic measure	Effects for remarriage using the "overly broad" full model	Effects for remarriage using this study's full model
GPA	.04	.04
Reading	.00	−.04
Math	−.03	−.09**
Science	−.04	−.06
Social Studies	−.04	−.07*
Composite test	−.02	−.07*
Left back[a]	.00	.02

*p < .05, **p < .01, ***p < .001, ****p < .0001
[a] Logistic regression analysis was used.

TABLE 11.14. Comparison of the Effects for the Reconstituted Family Variables for the "Overly Broad" Full Model versus This Study's Full Model (Without the SES Variables) for the Tenth Grade (1990) (N = 16,304)

Academic measure	Effects for remarriage using the "overly broad" full model	Effects for remarriage using this study's full model
Reading	.00	−.04
Math	−.02	−.06
Science	.01	−.01
Social Studies	−.04	−.05
Composite test	−.01	−.05
Left back[a]	.02	.04
Drop out[a]	−.02	−.01

*p < .05, **p < .01, ***p < .001, ****p < .0001
[a] Logistic regression analysis was used.

The effects for the twelfth graders (1992) were the largest of all (see Table 11.15). Statistically significant effects emerged for the math, science, composite test, and being left back a grade. All the other measurements, with the exception of GPA, neared statistical significance with p-levels of about .10 down to .06.

TABLE 11.15. Comparison of the Effects for the Reconstituted Family Variables for the "Overly Broad" Full Model versus This Study's Full Model (Without the SES Variables) for the Twelfth Grade (1992) (N = 17,100)

Academic measure	Effects for remarriage using the "overly broad" full model	Effects for remarriage using this study's full model
GPA	−.06	−.04
Reading	.00	−.07
Math	−.02	−.10**
Science	−.03	−.09*
Social Studies	.01	−.07
Composite test	−.01	−.09*
Left back[a]	.01	.08*
Basic Core[a]	−.01	−.07
Drop out[a]	−.01	.00

*p < .05, **p < .01, ***p < .001, ****p < .0001
[a] Logistic regression analysis was used.

When using the "overly broad" full model none of the effects were statistically significant in either the positive or negative direction. Even with the inclusion of children from other single-parent family structures, the effect of remarriage is still not positive. In addition, the differences in the regression coefficients between the "overly broad" full model and this study's full model are less than when the regression coefficients are compared using the "overly broad" basic model versus this study's basic model.

Nevertheless, it is clear that when an "overly broad" model is used, especially one that does not control for race and gender, the negative effects for remarriage can be underestimated, overlooked, or even misinterpreted as being positive.

Chapter 12

What Does It All Mean?

CONSEQUENCES OF UNDERESTIMATING INFLUENCE OF FAMILY STRUCTURE

Some of the issues that have been raised in this work are as follows: (1) the importance of adequately controlling for SES; (2) overlooking children of divorce living with neither parent; (3) not frequently examining children from some of the least traditional family structures; and (4) the methodological problems presented in Chapter 11 ultimately lead to understating the effects of parental divorce on children. This is a serious problem, because it can produce a research community and a public that is less sensitive than it should be to the needs of children from less traditional family structures. Americans have long maintained a belief that every child should be educated and literate and society has become more effective in utilizing some useful techniques to accomplish that goal. Nevertheless, the goal of maximizing education outcomes can only be accomplished if society identifies the specific challenges that face children from particular backgrounds.

To heighten awareness of the specific challenges that children from less traditional family structures face, social scientists need to keep certain issues in mind when undertaking research in this field.

1. Family scientists and educators should carefully examine issues of causality.
2. The effects of children living in certain family structures often go beyond our usual paradigms.
3. Social scientists need to examine children from a wider array of family structures, which more fully reflect the diversity of family structures that we have today.

4. Researchers need to address problems in methodology that can produce inappropriate conclusions about a given statistical analysis.

The first issue is that family scientists and educators should carefully examine issues of causality. For many years, social scientists have regarded SES as virtually the ultimate causal variable. There has been very little acknowledgment that SES is a "catchall" variable and is often a product of literally thousands of causal agents more than it is a causal variable. The social sciences have greatly contributed to the advancement of civilization today. Nevertheless, the social sciences are still developing. Hundreds of years from now, today's social scientists will likely be called "pioneers" in the field, and certain aspects of research will be considered primitive, especially social scientists' simplistic treatment of SES variables.

The chief danger of viewing the effects of parental divorce as almost entirely a SES phenomenon is that children of divorce will be viewed as facing no real handicap beyond the fact that they come from homes of low socioeconomic status. In other words, there is a danger that social scientists will view the problems faced by children coming from divorced and other less traditional family structures as being no different than children living with an intact family from an equally poor home. In reality, on average, many differences exist between these two groups of children. These differences include parental access, a sense of personal security, harmony, and psychological stability. Directing government funds into less traditional families and enabling them to receive greater job training may help ease the pain to some degree. Nevertheless, a high level of pain is often felt by children who have lost a parent or who do not even know who their parent is. There needs to be a greater acknowledgment that simply attempting to raise the SES level of children from these families will do little to redress this pain.

A second concern is that the effects of children living in certain family structures often go beyond our usual paradigms. For example, nearly every study that has examined the effects of parental divorce on children has compared the effects of children of intact versus divorced single-parent families. Certainly, this comparison includes most of the kinds of children who have experienced parental divorce. However, research shows that a considerable number of children of divorce end up living with neither parent. There are cases in which children of divorce live with a grandparent, an aunt, an uncle, with a neighbor, or in a foster home. Although most Americans are well aware of such circumstances, the children living in these environments are almost never included in studies which examine the effects of parental divorce on children. However, it is clear that to obtain accurate estimates of the effects of divorce, children in these circumstances need to be included in research. The reality of the matter is that on many occasions a custodial parent may not be able to care for one or more of his or her children. In other cases, it happens that neither parent has any desire to care for a child or children. The presence of children can be a sore spot for divorced parents, because the presence of a child can be a vivid reminder of the existence of a former spouse. Often, such a reminder evokes memories that the custodial parent would like to forget. Whether a child living with neither parent is a voluntary or involuntary act on the part of the custodial parent, the presence of this family structure is a reality of life.

Nearly all research studies have tended to underestimate the effects of family structure. For example, if using only twelfth grade standardized test scores as a means of comparison, students who have dropped out of school will not be included. Research indicates that children from less traditional family structures are more likely to drop out of school (Jeynes, 1997).

Research also indicates that children from less traditional family structures are also more likely to be held back a grade (Jeynes, 1998b). Therefore, even if one compares the achievement test scores of children from various family structures, this too could be a somewhat unfair comparison. To the extent that children from less traditional family structures are more likely to be held back a grade, the average age of children from less traditional family structures is likely to be higher than the average age of children from intact families. This age difference may even be larger, to the extent that children from intact families are also more likely to skip a grade.

Finally, it is likely that the children who have been hardest hit by parental divorce may actually be unavailable to study for the researchers. The 1988-1992 NELS data set makes a genuine attempt to keep track of as many student dropouts as possible. Still, it remains impossible to incorporate these dropout students in assessing any differences in grades and standardized tests, simply because they had already dropped out of school.

A third concern is that social scientists need to examine children from a wider array of family structures that more fully reflect the diversity we have today. Given that several family structures, such as cohabitation, remarried-divorced, never married single-parent, and others are growing at rapid rates, the research community needs to redouble its efforts to examine the effects of children living in these families. Only a small number of studies have examined the effects of children living in these family structures on their academic achievement. Although a reasonable amount of research has assessed the effects on adults living in these relationships, very little is known about the effects on children. As a result, the research community has very little definitive data in these areas, based on empirical evidence. Unfortunately, social science researchers often examine a given phenomenon after it has been widespread for ten years. This often puts us "behind the times," in terms of giving individual advice and policy recommendations. In fact, some would argue that researchers often are not able to come to conclusions about potentially harmful matters until the damage has already been done. If social scientists are to maximize the beneficial impact that their work on family structure can have, they need to apply themselves more quickly and more fully to studying the effects of these family structures that have become more common in recent years.

A fourth concern is that researchers need to address problems in methodology that can produce inappropriate conclusions about a given statistical analysis. In the past, researchers have frequently lumped together groups of children in a particular study, which really do not belong together. The primary example of this was combining children from intact and remarried families in the same category, which diminished the effects of divorce. In assessing the effects of divorce on academic achievement, the NAEP used this technique. Many particular research configurations reflect the fact that many social scientists believe that the effects of parental family structure are purely a socioeconomic phenomenon. The research presented in this book indicated that the effects from parental family structure go far beyond its impact on socioeconomic status. There needs to be a sufficient degree of distinguishing among parental family structures.

SENSITIZING EDUCATORS
TO THE CHALLENGES OF CHILDREN
FROM NONTRADITIONAL FAMILIES

Social scientists know relatively little about the impact of cohabitation, a never married single-parent, and living with neither parent on a child's academic achievement. The same is true regarding understanding the impact of parental family structure on other facets of children's lives. Ultimately, what social scientists do or do not know about the impact of various family structures will affect what educators know. On a daily basis, parents rely on the knowledge of teachers and principals to maximize the amount of knowledge that children can obtain. Some criticism has been aimed at teachers for not sufficiently knowing the subjects they teach (Darling-Hammond, 1997; Hirsch, Koppich and Krapp, 1998). Effective teachers not only possess knowledge of a given subject, but know how best to work with individual students. To the degree that parental family structure impacts academic achievement, teachers need to be sensitive to the home situations of their students. One can certainly argue that children from less traditional family structures represent a true disadvantaged minority. The disadvantage may or may not be evident at the economic level. Rather, they may be disadvantaged in terms of the access they have to their parents, their knowledge of who is actually their parent, the presence of a relative "stranger" in the house, and in the degree to which there is peace and harmony in their family situation.

In America, educators have been trained to be sensitive to obvious issues of race, ethnicity, and socioeconomic status. The parental family structure, or even the precise everyday family situation that a child comes from may not be so readily discerned. Obtaining information about a child's family structure may involve getting to know the child or getting to know various people who are familiar with the child. Obtaining information about how the specific family situation affects a child's life may take some time. On this basis, one can argue that becoming an efficacious teacher will become complex. Merely mastering a subject and being able to communicate that mastery to students is not sufficient. An effective educator must invest his or her life in the lives of the students. This probably takes more time and a higher level of commitment than the mastery of the subjects that one is required to teach. In all likelihood, some educators will drop out when they conclude the level of commitment required to be an effective teacher is too high.

In a broader sense, we as a society need to determine the most sensitive way to respond to the increased diversity of family structures.

- Is this trend healthy?
- Does the diversity of family structures benefit the adults involved, even though it may harm the children?
- To what degree should the will of the parents override any concerns our society may have about the impact on the children?
- What is our best response to these changing demographic realities?
- Should we limit ourselves to helping only those children who have already been hurt by divorce, cohabitation, or marital unfaithfulness? Or should our nation do more to attempt to prevent the hurt to begin with? Two options include eliminating no-fault divorce, and encouraging a waiting period before filing for certain divorces. Both of these actions would slow down the divorce process in some instances, allowing couples more time to think about their actions and get marital counseling. Such policies will discourage couples from getting a divorce, who might later regret their actions.
- Should our society encourage marital counseling more than we presently do?
- Should we teach about marital fidelity and responsible motherhood and fatherhood in the schools?

Few would disagree with the notion that we need to become more sensitive to the effects of family structure and its transitions on the lives of children. At some point, our society probably needs to more fully address just how this sensitivity should be implemented.

ALTERNATIVE WAYS TO CONTROL FOR SES

Of all the findings reported in this work, probably the most salient is the dramatic role that SES plays in assessing the effects of family structure. Three of the most notable findings are that:

1. Predisruption measures of SES yield very different effects for divorce than when postdisruption measures of SES are used.
2. If no control for SES is used it appears that divorce more than remarriage exerts downward pressure on academic achievement, whereas when SES is controlled for it appears that remarriage more than divorce exerts downward pressure on academic achievement.
3. If SES is not controlled for it appears that living with a never-married single parent exerts the most downward pressure on academic achievement, whereas when SES is controlled for it appears that cohabitation exerts the most downward pressure on academic achievement.

A number of the results indicated considerably different effects for divorce, depending on whether predisruption or postdisruption variables were used. These findings point to the need to examine cautiously just how researchers control for SES in a given study. Medical researchers, in particular, are questioning various assumptions many researchers have made regarding controlling for SES. The issue of causality and the fact that SES appears to be a "catchall" variable head the list of concerns. Even the predisruption variable has some shortcomings. Frequently, it is *after* the point of initial separation that family structure impacts SES than at the actual time of the divorce. In addition, it can be argued that in some cases, the initial impact that family structure has on SES actually precedes any change in family structure. For example, if a spouse is engaged in an extramarital affair that he or she knows will ultimately lead to divorce, this affair may impact a family's disposable income in a number of ways. First, depending on its nature, an affair can either decrease or increase the number of hours the participants spend at work, potentially affecting their pay. Second, the individual that a spouse is having an affair with can either be a drain on disposable income or be a source of additional income. In addition, many times official marital separation is preceded by de facto marital separation. In these cases, the impact of marital separation on SES might again precede the actual agreement to separate.

In stating that researchers need to examine new ways to control for SES, the purpose is not to assert that a perfect way exists to control for SES. Rather, it should be recognized that most researchers currently control for SES simplistically, given the complex nature of this variable. SES must be recognized as a "catchall" variable and often indicates consequences rather than causality. Researchers need to be more cautious about making bold statements of relationship, based on statistically significant effects for socioeconomic status. They are likely to reach conclusions that are also overly simplistic, which are the greatest danger in attempting to understand the effects of parental family structure on the lives of children. Rather, simplistic policies emerge as a result of these conclusions.

SUMMARY

The research studies presented in this book have attempted to examine the effects of family structure on the academic achievement of children from a number of different perspectives. The development of the study of the effects of parental family structure have been traced from its incipiency and the major debates and controversies that surround this field of study have been examined. The effects of divorce and remarriage using a variety of approaches have been identified and other, less common, parental family structures and their impact on the academic outcomes of children have been investigated. It is hoped that this work will not only contribute to the body of research that has already been done in this field, but will help improve the quality of future research and improve life for many families in the United States and abroad.

References

Acock, A. C. and Kiecolt, J. (1989). Is it family structure or socioeconomic status? Family structure during adolescence and adult adjustment. *Social Forces, 68*(2), 553-571.

Adelmann, P. K., Antonucci, T. C., Crohan, S. E., and Coleman, L. M. (1990). A causal analysis of employment and health in midlife women. *Women and Health, 16*(10), 5-20.

Adler, N. E. (1995). Socioeconomic status and health: Do we know what explains the association? *Advances, 11*(3), 6-9.

Ahlburg, D. A. and DeVita, C.J. (1992). New realities of the American family. *Population Bulletin, 47*(2), 2-44.

Allen, H. L. and Tadlock, J. (1986). "Pupil achievement as related to social class, gender, and number of parents in the household." Paper presented at Mid-South Educational Research Association, Memphis, Tennessee, November.

Allison, P. D. and Furstenberg, F. F. (1989). How marital dissolution affects children: Variations by age and sex. *Developmental Psychology, 25* (July), 540-549.

Alson, R. J., McCowan, C. J., and Turner, W. L. (1994). Family functioning as a correlate of disability adjustment for African Americans. *Rehabilitation Counseling Bulletin, 37*(4), 277-289.

Amato, P. R. (1987) Family processes in one-parent, stepparent, and intact families: The child's point of view. *Journal of Marriage and the Family, 49*(2), 327-337.

Amato, P. (1993). Children's adjustment to divorce: Theories, hypotheses, and empirical support. *Journal of Marriage and the Family, 55*(1), 23-28.

Amato, P. (1999). Children of divorced parents as young adults. In E. M. Hetherington (Ed.), *Coping with divorce, single parenting, and remarriage: A risk and resiliency perspective* (pp. 147-163). Mahwah, NJ: Erlbaum.

Amato, P. R. and Keith, B. (1991). Parental divorce and adult well-being: A meta-analysis. *Journal of Marriage and the Family, 53*(1), 43-58.

Amato, P. R. and Ochiltree, G. (1987). Child and adolescent competence in intact, one-parent, and stepfamilies, an Australian study. *Journal of Divorce, 10*(3/4), 75-96.

Ambert, A. M. (1989). *Exspouses and new spouses: A study of relationships.* Greenwich, CT: JAI.

Anderson, E. R., Hetherington, E. M., and Clingempeel, W. G. (1999). The dynamics of parental remarriage. In E. M. Hetherington (Ed.), *Coping with divorce, single parenting, and remarriage: A risk and resiliency perspective* (pp. 295-319). Mahwah, NJ: Erlbaum.

179

Anderson, E. R., Lindner, M. S., and Bennion, L. D. (1992). The effect of family relationships on adolescent development during family reorganization. *Monographs of the Society for Research in Child Development, 57*(2), 149-177.

Anderson, E. R. and Rice, A. M. (1992). Sibling relationships during remarriage. *Monographs of the Society for Research in Child Development, 57*(2), 149-177.

Avenevoli, S., Sessa, F. M., and Steinberg, L. (1999). Family structure, parenting practices, and adolescent adjustment: An ecological examination. In E. M. Hetherington (Ed.), *Coping with divorce, single parenting, and remarriage: A risk and resiliency perspective* (pp. 65-90). Mahwah, NJ: Erlbaum.

Ayoub, C. C., Deutsch, R. M., and Maraganore, A. (1999). Emotional distress in children of high-conflict divorce: The impact of marital conflict and violence. *Family and Conciliation Courts Review, 37*(3), 297-314.

Backman, O. and Palme, J. (1998). Social background and sickness absence: A study of a Stockholm court. *Acta Sociologica, 41*(4), 349-362.

Bakeman, R. and McArthur, D. (1999). Determining the power of multiple regression analysis both with and without repeated measures. *Behavior Research Methods, Instruments, and Computers, 31*(1), 150-154.

Baltes, P. B., Featherman, D. L., and Lerner, R. M. (1990). The impact of divorce on life-span development: Short and long term effects. In P. B. Baltes, D. L. Featherman, and R. M. Lerner (Eds.), *Life-span development of behavior* (pp. 107-150). Hillsdale, NJ: Erlbaum.

Bane, M. J. and Jargowsky, P. (1988). The links between government policy and family structure: What matters and what doesn't. In A. J. Cherlin (Ed.), *The changing American family and public policy* (pp. 219-255). Washington, DC: Urban Institute Press.

Barton, D. (1994). *America: To pray or not to pray.* Aledo, TX: Wallbuilder Press.

Baydar, N. (1988). Effects of parental separation and reentry into union on the emotional well-being of children. *Journal of Marriage and the Family, 50*(4), 967-981.

Becker, G. S., Landes, E. M., and Michael, R. T. (1977). An economic analysis of marital instability. *Journal of Political Economy, 85*(6), 1141-1187.

Beer, J. (1989). Relationship of divorce to self-concept, self-esteem, and grade point average of fifth and sixth grade school children. *Psychological Reports, 65*(3), 1379-1383.

Beer, W. R. (1992). *American stepfamilies.* New Brunswick: Transaction Publishers.

Begg, C. B. (1994). Publication bias. In H. Cooper and L. V. Hedges (Eds.), *Handbook of research synthesis* (pp. 399-409). New York: Russell Sage Foundation.

Bernard, J. (1942). *American family behavior.* New York: Harper & Brothers.

Biggs, C. (1986). "A comparison of the school adjustment of single-parent students versus two-parent students in grade four in the Xenia school district." (Doctoral diss., Miami of Obio University).

Block, J. H., Block, J., and Gjerde, P. F. (1986). The personality of children prior to divorce: A prospective study. *Child Development, 57*(4), 827-840.

Boes, S. R. (1995). "The relationships among parental marital status, selected inter-personal variables, and the career development of a college population." Paper presented at the Georgia Educational Research Association, Atlanta, GA, November.

Booth, A. and Dunn, J. (1994). Preface. In A. Booth and J. Dunn (Eds.), *Step-families: Who benefits? Who does not?* (pp. ix-x). Hillsdale, NJ: Erlbaum.

Booth, A. and Edwards, J. N. (1992). Starting over: Why remarriages are more un-stable. *Journal of Family Issues, 13*(2), 179-194.

Brady, G. H. and Forehand, R. (1988). Multiple determinants of parenting: Re-search findings and implications for the divorce process. In E. M. Hetherington and J.D. Arasteh (Eds.), *Impact of divorce, singleparenting, and stepparenting on children. (pp. 117-133). Mahwah, NJ: Erlbaum Associates.*

Bray, J. H. (1999). From marriage to remarriage and beyond. In E. M. Hetherington (Ed.), *Coping with divorce, single parenting, and remarriage: A risk and resil-iency perspective* (pp. 253-271). Mahwah, NJ: Erlbaum.

Bray, J. H. and Berger, S. H. (1993). Developmental issues in step-families research project: Family relationships and parent-child interactions. *Journal of Family Psychology, 7*(1), 76-90.

Briller, B. and Miller, S. (1984). Assessing academic achievement. *Society, 21* (September/October), 6-9.

Bronfenbrenner, U. (1979). *The ecology of human development.* Cambridge, MA: Harvard University Press.

Bruce, M. L. (1998). Divorce and psychopathology. In B. P. Dohenwend (Ed.), *Ad-versity, stress, and psychopathology* (pp. 219-232). New York: Oxford Univer-sity Press.

Buchanan, C. M., Maccoby, E. E., and Dornbusch, S. (1991). Caught between par-ents: Adolescents' experience in divorced homes. *Child Development, 62*(5), 1008-1029.

Bumpass, L. (1984). Children and marital disruption: A replication and update. *De-mography, 21*(February), 71-82.

Bumpass, L., Sweet, J., and Martin, T. C. (1990). Changing patterns of remarriage. *Journal of Marriage and the Family, 52*(3), 747-756.

Butler, R. (1986). The role of generalized expectancies in determining causal attri-butions for success and failure in two social classes. *British Journal of Educa-tional Psychology, 56*(1), 51-63.

Camara, K. A. and Resnick, G. (1988). Interpersonal conflict and cooperation: Fac-tors moderating children's post-divorce adjustment. In. E. M. Hetherington and J. D. Arasteh (Eds.), *Impact of Divorce, Single Parenting, and Stepparenting on Children* (pp. 3-21). Hillsdale, NJ: Erlbaum Associates.

Canziani, F. (1996). Possible children's reactions to their parents' divorce. *Giornale di Neuropsichiatria dell' Eta Evolutive, 16*(4), 255-282.

Carlsmith, L. (1964). Effect of early father absence on scholastic aptitude. *Harvard Educational Review, 34*(1), 3-21.

Carlsmith, L. (1973). Some personality characteristics of boys separated from their fathers during World War II. *Ethos, 1*(4), 466-477.

Cassidy, T. and Lynn, R. (1991). Achievement motivation, educational attainment, cycles of disadvantage and social competence: Some longitudinal data. *British Journal of Educational Psychology, 61*(1), 1-12.

Ceci, S. J. and Williams, W. M. (1997). Schooling, intelligence, and income. *American Psychologist, 52*(10), 1051-1058.

Chadwick, B. A. and Heaton, T. B. (Eds.) (1992). *Statistical handbook of the American family*. Phoenix, AZ: Oryx Press.

Chambers, W. V. (1986). Inferring causality from corresponding variances. *Perceptual and Motor Skills, 63*(October), 475-478.

Cherlin, A. J. (1978). Remarriage as an incomplete institution. *American Journal of Sociology, 84*(3), 634-650.

Cherlin, A. J. (1988). The changing American family and public policy. In A. Cherlin (Ed.), *The Changing American Family and Public Policy* (pp. 1-29). Washington, DC: Urban Institute Press.

Cherlin, A. J. (1992). *Marriage, divorce, and remarriage*. Cambridge, MA: Harvard University Press.

Cherlin, A.J. (1997). Remarriage as an incomplete institution. In Hutter, M. (Ed), *The family experience: A reader in cultural diversity*. Boston: Allyn & Bacon.

Cherlin, A. J. and Furstenberg, F. F. (1994). Stepfamilies in the United States: A reconsideration. *Annual Review of Sociology, 20*, 359-381.

Cherlin, A. J., Furstenberg, F. F., Chase-Landsdale, P. L., Kiernan, K. E. (1991). Longitudinal studies of effects of divorce on children in Great Britain and the United States. *Science, 252*, 1386-1389.

Cherlin, A. J., Kiernan K. E., and Chase-Lansdale, P. L. (1995). Parental divorce in childhood and demographic outcomes in young adulthood. *Demography, 32* (August), 299-318.

Coleman, J. S. (1989). The family, the community, and the future of education. In W. J. Weston (Ed.), *Education and the American family: A research synthesis* (pp. 169-185). New York: New York University Press.

Coleman, M. and Ganong, L. (1990). Remarriage and stepfamily research in the 1980s: Increased interest in an old family form. *Journal of Marriage and the Family, 52*(4), 925-940.

Collier, J. L. (1991). *The rise of selfishness in America*. New York: Oxford University Press.

Collins, L. E. (1981). "A study of locus of control in of intact, single-parent, and re-constituted families." (doctoral diss.), Georgia State University.

Cook, T. D. and Campbell, D. T. (1979). *Quasi-experimentation: Design analysis issues for field settings*. Boston: Houghton Mifflin.

Cooper, H. and Hedges, L. V. (1994). Potential limitations of research synthesis. In H. Cooper and L. V. Hedges (Eds.), *Handbook of research synthesis* (pp. 521-529). New York: Russell Sage Foundation.

Corsica, J. S. Jr. (1980). "The relationship of changes in family structure to the academic performance and school behavior." (doctoral diss., SUNY at Buffalo).

Cortes, C. F. and Fleming, E. S. (1968). The effects of father absence on the adjustment of culturally disadvantaged boys. *Journal of Special Education,* (4), 413-428.

Couch, A. and Lillard, D. R. (1997). Divorce, educational attainment and the earnings mobility of sons. *Journal of Family and Economic Issues, 18*(3), 231-245.

Crane, J. (1996). Effects of home environment, SES, and maternal test scores on mathematics achievement. *Journal of Educational Research, 89*(5), 305-314.

Cummings, E. M. (1995). Usefulness of experiments for the study of the family. *Journal of Family Psychology, 9*(2), 175-185.

Darden, E. C. and Zimmerman, T. S. (1992). Blended families: A decade of review, 1979 to 1990. *Family Therapy, 19*(1), 25-31.

Darling-Hammond, L. (1997). The quality of teaching matters most. *Journal of Staff Development, 18*(1), 38-41.

Davis, G. and Murch, M. (1988). *Grounds for divorce.* Oxford, England: Clarendon Press.

Dawson, D. (1991). Family structure and children's health and well-being: Data from the 1988 National Health Interview Survey on Child Health. *Journal of Marriage and the Family, 53*(3), 573-584.

Deater-Deckhard, K. and Dunn, J. (1999). The multiple risks and adjustment in young children growing up in different family settings: A British community study of stepparent, single mother, and nondivorced families. In E. M. Hetherington (Ed.), *Coping with divorce, single parenting, and remarriage: A risk and resiliency perspective* (pp. 47-64). Mahwah, NJ: Erlbaum.

DeGarmo, D. S. and Forgatch, M. S. (1999). Contexts as predictors of changing maternal parenting practice in diverse family structures. In E. M. Hetherington (Ed.), *Coping with divorce, single parenting, and remarriage: A risk and resiliency perspective* (pp. 227-252). Mahwah, NJ: Erlbaum.

Demo, D. H. and Acock, A. C. (1996). Family structure, family process, and adolescent well-being. *Journal of Research on Adolescence, 6*(4), 457-488.

Dineen, P. (1990). *Adolescent suicide: Prevention, postvention, and crisis management.* Washington, DC: U.S. Department of Education.

Dornbusch, S. M., Carlsmith, J. M., Bushwell, S. J., Ritter, P. L., Leiderman, P. H., Hastorf, A. H., and Gross, R. T. (1985). Single parents, extended households, and control of adolescents. *Child Development, 56*(2), 326-341.

Dornbusch, S. M., Ritter, P. L., Leiderman, P. H., Roberts, D. F., and Fraleigh, M. J. (1987). Relation of parenting to adolescent school performance. *Child Development, 58*(5), 1244-1257.

Dornbusch, S. M. and Wood, K. D. (1989). Family processes and educational achievement. In W. J. Weston (Ed.), *Education in the American family: A research synthesis,* (pp. 66-95). New York: New York University Press.

Downey, D. B. (1995). Understanding academic achievement among children in stephouseholds: The role of parental resources, sex of stepparent, and sex of child. *Social Forces, 73*(3), 875-894.

Downey, D. B. and Powell, B. (1993). Do children in single-parent households fair better living with same-sex parents? *Journal of Marriage and the Family, 55*(1), 55-71.

Dreman, S., Spielberger, C., and Fried, R. (1999). The experience and expression of anger in divorced mothers. Effects of behavior problems in children. *Journal of Divorce and Remarriage, 30*(3/4), 25-44.

Duberman, L. (1975). *The reconstituted family: A study of remarried couples and their children.* Chicago: Nelson Hall Publishers.

Dunlop, R. and Burns, A. (1995). The sleeper effect—myth or reality? *Journal of Marriage and the Family, 57*(2), 375-386.

Elliot, B. J. and Richards, M. (1991). Children and divorce: Educational performance and behavior before and after parental separation. *International Journal of Law and the Family, 5*(3), 258-276.

Ellis, J. B. and Russell, C. D. (1992). Implications of divorce on reasons for living in older adolescents. *Journal of Divorce and Remarriage, 18*(3/4), 197-205.

Emery, R. E. (1988). *Marriage, divorce, and children's adjustment.* Newbury Park, CA: Sage Publications.

Emery, R. E., Kitzmann, K. M., and Waldron, M. (1999). Psychological interventions for separated and divorced families. In E. M. Hetherington (Ed.), *Coping with divorce, single parenting, and remarriage: A risk and resiliency perspective* (pp. 323-344). Mahwah, NJ: Erlbaum.

Emery, R. E., Waldron, M., Kitzmann, K. M., and Aaron, J. (1999). Delinquent behavior, future divorce or nonmarital childbearing, and externalizing behavior among offspring: A 14-year prospective study. *Journal of Family Psychology, 13*(4), 568-579.

Ferri, E. (1984). *Stepchildren: A national study.* Atlantic Highlands, NJ: Humanities.

Filinson, R. (1986). Relationships in stepfamilies: An examination of alliances. *Journal of Comparative Family Studies, 17*(1), 43-62.

Fine, M. A., Coleman, M., and Ganong, L. H. (1999). A social constructivist multimodel approach to understanding the stepparent role. In E. M. Hetherington (Ed.), *Coping with divorce, single parenting, and remarriage: A risk and resiliency perspective* (pp. 273-294). Mahwah, NJ: Erlbaum.

Fitzpatrick, P. L. (1993). "A comparison of student performance of adolescents from one-and two-parent families." (doctoral diss., Wayne State University).

Flett, G. L.,Vrendenburg, K., Pliner, P., and Krames, L. (1985). Sex roles and depression: A preliminary investigation of the direction of causality. *Journal of Research in Personality, 19*(4), 429-435.

Forehand, R., Biggar, H., and Kotchick, B. (1998). Cumulative risk across family stresses: Short-term and long-term effects for adolescents. *Journal of Abnormal Psychology, 26*(2), 119-128.

Forgatch, M. S., Patterson, G. R., and Ray, J. A. (1996). Divorce and boys' adjustment problems: Two paths with a single model. In E. M. Hetherington and E. A.

Blechman (Eds.), *Stress, coping, and resiliency in children and families* (pp. 67-105). Mahwah, NJ: Erlbaum.

Forste, R. and Tanfer, K. (1996). Sexual exclusivity among dating, cohabiting, and married women. *Journal of Marriage and the Family, 58*(1), 33-47.

Fortes, M. (1933). Stepparenthood and juvenile delinquency. *Sociological Review. 25,* 153-158.

Freedman, D. A. (1989). "Statistical models and shoe leather." Paper presented at the American Sociological Association, San Francisco, August.

Friedman, A. and Ali, A. (1997). The interaction of SES, race/ethnicity and family organization of adolescents, in relation to severity of use of drugs and alcohol. *Journal of Child and Adolescent Substance Abuse, 7*(2), 65-74.

Furstenberg, F. F. Jr. (1988). Good dads and bad dads: Two faces of fatherhood. In A. J. Cherlin (Ed.), *The changing American family and public policy* (pp. 193-218). Washington, DC: Urban Institute Press.

Furstenberg, F. F. Jr. and Cherlin, A. J. (1991). *Divided families: What happens to children when parents part.* Cambridge, MA: Harvard University Press.

Furstenberg, F. F., Morgan, S. P., and Allison, P. D. (1987). Paternal participation in children's well-being after marital disruption. *American Sociological Review, 52*(5), 695-701.

Gabardi, L. and Rosen, L. A. (1992). Intimate relationships: College students from divorced and intact families. *Journal of Divorce and Remarriage, 18*(3/4), 25-56.

Gama, E. and Pinheiro, M. (1991). "School achievement and causal attribution patterns among low income students." Paper presented at the Annual Convention of the American Psychological Association, San Francisco, August.

Ganong, L. H. and Coleman, M. (1984). The effect of remarriage on children: A review of the empirical literature. *Family Relations, 33*(2), 389-406.

Ganong, L. H. and Coleman, M. (1994). *Remarried family relationships.* Thousand Oaks, CA: Sage Publications.

Ganong, L. H. and Coleman, M. (1999). *Changing responsibilities family obligations following divorce and remarriage.* Mahwah, NJ: Erlbaum.

Ganong, L. H., Coleman, M., Fine, M. A., and Martin, P. (1999). The stepparents' affinity-seeking and affinity-maintaining strategies with stepchildren. *Journal of Family Issues, 20*(3), 229-327.

Garfinkel, I. and McLanahan S. (1986). *Single mothers and their children.* Washington, DC: Urban Institute Press.

Garmezy, N. and Rutter, M., (Eds.) (1983). *Stress, coping and development.* Baltimore: Johns Hopkins University Press.

Garralda, M. E. and Bailey, D. (1988). Child and family actors associated with referral to child psychiatrists. *British Journal of Psychiatry, 53*(July), 81-89.

Gilner, M. W. (1988) "Research on family structure and school performance: A meta-analysis." (doctoral diss., St. Louis University).

Giorgi, L. and Marsh, C. (1990). The Protestant work ethic as a cultural phenomenon. *European Journal of Social Psychology, 20*(6), 499-517.

Glick, P. C. (1980). Remarriage: Some recent changes and variations. *Journal of Family Issues, 1*(4), 455-478.

Goode, W. J. (1982). *The family.* Englewood Cliff, NJ: Prentice-Hall.

Goode, W. J. (1992). World changes in divorce patterns. In L. J. Weitzman and M. Maclean (Eds.), *Economic consequences of divorce* (pp. 11-49). Oxford, England: Clarendon Press.

Gortmaker, S. L., Must, A., Perrin, J. M., Sobol, A. M., and Dietz, W. H. (1993). Social and economic consequences of overweight in adolescence and young adulthood. *New England Journal of Medicine 329*(14), 1008-1012.

Gottfredson, D. C., McNeil, R. J., and Gottfredson, G. D. (1991). Social area influences on delinquency: A multilevel analysis. *Journal of Research in Crime and Delinquency, 28*(2), 197-226.

Gould, M. S., Shaffer, D., Fisher, P., and Garfinkel, R. (1998). Separation/divorce and child and adolescent completed suicide. *Journal of the American Academy of Child and Adolescent Psychiatry, 37*(2), 155-162.

Grant, L. S., Smith, T. A., Sinclair, J. J., and Salts, C. J. (1993). The impact of parental divorce on college adjustment. *Journal of Divorce and Remarriage, 19*(1/2), 183-193.

Gross, D. W. (1982). Improving the quality of family life. In J. D. Quisenberry (Ed.), *Changing family lifestyles* (pp. 50-54). Washington, DC: Association for Childhood Education International.

Guidubaldi, J. and Perry, J. D. (1984). Divorce, socioeconomic status, and children's cognitive-social competence at school entry. *American Journal of Orthopsychiatry, 54*(3), 459-468.

Guidubaldi, J., Perry, J. D., Cheminshaw, H. K., and McLoughlin, C. S. (1983). The impact of parental divorce on children: Report of the Nationwide NASP Study. *School Psychology Review, 12*(3), 300-323.

Guimond, S. and Palmer, D. L. (1990). Type of academic training and causal attributions for social problems. *European Journal of Social Psychology, 20*(1), 61-75.

Guth, S., Schrecker, C., Thomas, W. I., Znaniecki, F., and Durkheim, E. (1999). "Two different approaches of sociological methodology." Paper presented at the Annual Convention of the American Sociological Association, Chicago, August.

Hannan, M. T., Tuma, N. B., and Groeneveld, L. P. (1977). Income and marital events: Evidence from an income-maintenance experiment. *American Journal of Sociology 82*(6), 1186-1211.

Hanson, T. L. (1999). Does parental conflict explain why divorce is negatively associated with child welfare? *Social Forces, 77*(4), 1283-1316.

Haskey, J. (1984). Social class and socioeconomic differentials in divorce in England and Wales. *Population Studies, 38*(3), 419-438.

Haurin R. J. (1992). Patterns of childhood residence and the relationship to young adult outcomes. *Journal of Marriage and the Family, 54*(4), 846-860.

Heinstrom, O. (1999). Does the work environment contribute to excess male mortality? *Social Science and Medicine, 49*(7), 879-894.

Henry, C. S. (1996). Review of *Remarried Family Relationships. Journal of Marriage and the Family, 58*(1), 252-253.

Herzog, E. and Sudia, C. (1971). *Boys in fatherless families*. Washington, D C: U. S. Department of Health Education and Welfare.

Hetherington, E. M. (1972). Effects of father absence on personality development in adolescent daughters. *Developmental Psychology, 7*(3), 313-326.

Hetherington, E. M. (1973). Girls without fathers. *Psychology Today, 6*(9), 47-52.

Hetherington, E. M. (1989). Coping with family transitions: Winners, losers, and survivors. *Child Development, 60*(1), 1-14.

Hetherington, E. M. (1992). Coping with marital transitions: A family systems perspective. *Monographs of the Society for Research in Child Development, 57*(2/3), 1-14.

Hetherington, E. M. (1993). An overview of the Virginia Longitudinal Study of Divorce and Remarriage with a focus on early adolescence. *Journal of Family Psychology, 7*(1), 39-56.

Hetherington, E. M. (1994). Siblings, family relationships, and child development: Introduction. *Journal of Family Psychology, 8*(3), 251-253.

Hetherington, E. M. (1999). Should we stay together for the sake of the children? In E. M. Hetherington (Ed.), *Coping with divorce, single parenting, and remarriage: A risk and resiliency perspective* (pp. 93-116). Mahwah, NJ: Erlbaum.

Hetherington, E. M., Camara, K., and Featherman, D. L. (1981). "Cognitive performance, school behavior and achievement of children from one-parent households." Paper presented at the Annual Conference of the National Institute of Education, Washington, DC.

Hetherington, E. M. and Clingempeel, W. G. (Eds.) (1992). Coping with marital transitions: A family systems perspective. *Monographs of the Society for Research in Child Development, 57*(2/3), 1-242.

Hetherington, E. M., Cox, M., and Cox, R. (1985). Long-term effects of divorce and remarriage on the adjustment of children. *Journal of the American Academy of Child Psychiatry, 24*(5), 518-530.

Hetherington, E. M. and Jodl, K. M. (1994). Stepfamilies as settings for child development. In A. Booth and J. Dunn (Eds.), *Stepfamilies: Who benefits? Who does not?* (pp. 55-79). Hillsdale, NJ: Erlbaum Associates.

Hetherington, E. M., Stanley-Hagan, M., and Anderson, E. R. (1989). Marital transitions: A child's perspective. *American Psychologist, 44*(2), 303-312.

Hett, G. G. (1983). Canadian children from single-parent families: Are they an overlooked minority? Washington, DC: U.S. Department of Education.

Heyman, J. R. (1992). "The relationship between family structure as defined by parental marital status, family structure histories, gender, and various academic outcomes for seventh grade students in private schools." (Doctoral dissertation, University of San Francisco), abstract in *Dissertation Abstracts International,* AAG 9316055.

Hirsch, E., Koppich, J. E., and Knapp, M. S. (1998). *What are states doing to improve the quality of teaching? A brief review of current problems and trends*. Seattle: University of Washington.

Hobart, C. W. (1991). Conflict in remarriages, *Journal of Divorce and Remarriage, 15*(1), 69-86.

Hobbs, F. and Lippman, L. (Center for International Research) (1990). *Children's well-being: An international comparison.* Washington, DC: U.S. Department of Commerce.

Hoem, J. M. (1997). Educational gradients in divorce risks in Sweden in recent decades. *Population Studies, 51*(1), 19-27.

Hoffman, J. P. and Johnson, R. A. (1998). A natural portrait of family structure and adolescent drug use. *Journal of Marriage and the Family, 60*(3), 633-645.

Hoffman, R. and Zippco, D. (1986). Effects of divorce upon school self-esteem and achievement of 10-, 11-, and 12-year old children. *Perceptual and Motor Skills, 62*(2), 397-398.

Hofstetter, C. R., Sticht, T. G., and Hofstetter, C. H. (1999). Knowledge, literacy, and power. *Communication Research, 26*(1), 58-80.

Huang, C. J. (1999). "Does skin color really matter? Questions concerning African Americans' self-images, racial identities, and attitudes toward race relations." Paper presented at the Annual Conference of the American Psychological Association, Boston, MA, August.

Hyland, M. E. (1990). The mood peak flow relationship in adult asthmatics: A pilot study of individual differences and the direction of causality. *British Journal of Medical Psychology, 63*(4), 379-384.

Ingersal, G. M., Scamman, J. P., and Eckerling, W. D. (1989). Geographic mobility and student achievement in an urban setting. *Educational Evaluation and Policy Analysis, 11*(1), 143-149.

Jalongo, M. R. (1995). Helping children cope with relocation. *Childhood Education, 71*(2), 80-85.

Jenkins, J. E. and Guidubaldi, J. (1997). The nature-nurture controversy revisited. Divorce and gender as factors in children's racial group differences. *Child Study Journal, 27*(2), 145-160.

Jeynes, W. H. (1996). Subtleties of distributions. *Rasch Measurement, 10*(3), 515.

Jeynes, W. H. (1997). "Assessing socioeconomic theory's explanation for the effects of divorce and remarriage on academic achievement." Doctoral dissertation, University of Chicago.

Jeynes, W. H. (1998a). A historical overview of the research on the effects of remarriage following divorce on the academic achievement of children. *School Community Journal, 8*(1), 23-30.

Jeynes, W. H. (1998b). Does divorce or remarriage following divorce have the greater negative impact on the academic achievement of children? *Journal of Divorce and Remarriage, 29*(1/2), 79-101.

Jeynes, W. H. (1998c). Examining the effects of divorce on the academic achievement of children: How should we control for SES? *Journal of Divorce and Remarriage, 29*(3/4), 1-21.

Jeynes, W. H. (1999a). The effects of children of divorce living with neither parent on the academic achievement of those children. *Journal of Divorce and Remarriage, 30*(3/4), 103-120.

Jeynes, W. H. (1999b). The effects of remarriage following divorce on the academic achievement of children. *Journal of Youth and Adolescence, 28*(3), 385-393.

Jeynes, W. H. (1999c). "The effects of the religious commitment of adolescents on their consumption of alcohol." Paper presented at the Annual Convention of the National Council on Family Relations Conference, Irvine, California, November.

Jeynes, W. H. (1999d). The role of family residential mobility in explaining the lower academic achievement of high school children from reconstituted families. *Journal of Divorce and Remarriage, 32*(1/2), 123-143.

Jeynes, W. H. (2000a). A longitudinal analysis on the effects of remarriage following divorce on the academic achievement of children. *Journal of Divorce and Remarriage, 33*(1/2), 131-148.

Jeynes, W. H. (2000b). The effects of several of the most common family structures on the academic achievement of eighth graders. *Marriage and Family Review, 30*(1/2), 73-97.

Kalter, N. (1977). Children of divorce in an outpatient psychiatric population. *American Journal of Orthopsychiatry, 47*(1), 41-51.

Kalter, N. and Rembar, J. (1981). The significance of a child's age at the time of parental divorce. *American Journal of Orthopsychiatry, 51*(1), 85-100.

Karney, B. R. and Bradbury, T. N. (1995). The longitudinal course of marital quality and stability. A review of theory, method, and research. *Psychological Bulletin, 118*(1), 3-34.

Kaufman, J. S. and Cooper, R. S. (1999). Seeking causal explanations in social epidemiology. *American Journal of Epidemiology, 150*(2), 113-120.

Kaye, S. H. (1988/1989). The impact of divorce on children's academic performance. *Journal of Divorce, 12*(2/3), 283-298.

Kelly, J. (1992). "Conflict and children's post-divorce adjustment: A closer look." Paper presented at the National Council for Children's Rights, Arlington, Virginia, April.

Kiernan, K. E. and Hobcraft, J. (1997). Parental divorce during childhood: Age at first intercourse, partnership, and parenthood. *Population Studies, 51*(1), 41-55.

Kinard, E. M. and Reinherz, H. (1986). Effects of marital disruption on children's school aptitude and achievement. *Journal of Marriage and the Family, 48*(2), 285-293.

Kleist, D. M. (1999). Single-parent families: A difference that makes a difference? *Family Journal Counseling and Therapy For Couples and Families, 7*(4), 373-378.

Komrey, J. D. and Dickinson, W. B. (1996). Detecting unit of analysis problems in nested designs: Statistical power and type I error rates of the F test for groups-within treatment effects. *Educational and Psychological Measurement, 56*(2), 215-231.

Kowalski, G. S. and Stack, S. (1992). The effect of divorce on homicide. *Journal of Divorce and Remarriage, 18*(1/2), 215-218.

Kurdek, L. A., Fine, M. A., and Sinclair, R. J. (1994). The relation between parenting transitions and adjustment in young adolescents: A multisample investigation. *Journal of Early Adolescence, 14*(4), 412-431.

Kurdek, L. A. and Sinclair, R. J. (1988). Relation of eighth graders' family structure, gender, and family environment with academic performance and school behavior. *Journal of Educational Psychology, 80*(1), 90-94.

Laosa, L. M. (1988). Ethnicity and single parenting in the United States. In E. M. Hetherington and J. D. Arasteh (Eds.), *Impact of divorce, single parenting, and stepparenting on children* (pp. 23-49). Hillsdale, NJ: Erlbaum Associates.

Lasch, C. (1977). *Haven in a heartless world.* New York: Basic Books.

Lawson, A. (1988). *Adultery: An analysis of love and betrayal.* New York: Basic Books.

Lazear, E. T. and Michael, R. T. (1988). *Allocation of income within the household.* Chicago: University of Chicago.

Lester, D. (1986).The interaction of divorce, suicide, and homicide. *Journal of Divorce, 9*(3), 103-109.

Lichtenstein, I. (1990). "Joint custodians' relative involvement in child care and interparental hostility as correlates of child adjustment after divorce." (doctoral diss., University of Cincinnati).

Lichtenstein, P., Harris, J. R., Pederson, N. L., and McClearn, G. E. (1993). Socioeconomic status and physical health, how are they related? An empirical study based on twins reared apart and twins reared together. *Social Science and Medicine, 36*(4), 441-450.

Link, B. G., Lennon, M. C., and Dohrenwend, B. P. (1993). Socioeconomic status and depression: The role of occupations involving direction, control, and planning. *American Journal of Sociology, 98*(6), 1351-1387.

Linker, J. S., Stolberg, A. L., and Green, R. G. (1999). Family communication as a mediator of children to divorce. *Journal of Divorce and Remarriage, 30*(1/2), 83-97.

Loftus, G. (1997). Psychology will be a much better science when we change the way we analyze data. *Current Directions in Psychological Science, 6*(1), 22.

Loomis, L. S. and Landale, N. S. (1994). Nonmarital cohabitation and childbearing among black and white American women. *Journal of Marriage and the Family, 56*(4), 949-962.

Love-Clark, P. (1984). "A meta-analysis of the effects of divorce on children's adjustment." (Doctoral dissertation, Texas A&M University) abstract in *Dissertation Abstracts International,* 41-721-606.

Lowry, R., Kann, L., Collins, S. J., and Kolbe, L. J. (1996). The effect of SES on chronic disease risk behavior among adolescents. *Journal of the American Medical Association, 276*(10), 792-797.

Luepnitz, A. (1978). Children of divorce. *Law and Human Behavior, 2*(2), 167-179.

Maccoby, E. E. (1992). The role of parents in the socialization of children: An historical overview. *Developmental Psychology, 28*(6), 1006-1017.

Maccoby, E. E., Buchanon, C. M., Mnookin, R. H., and Dornbusch, S. M. (1993). Postdivorce roles of mothers and fathers in the lives of their children. *Journal of Family Psychology, 7*(1), 24-38.

MacDonald, W. and DeMaris, A. (1995). Remarriage, stepchildren, and marital conflict: Challenges to the incomplete institutionalization hypothesis. *Journal of Marriage and the Family, 57*(2), 387-398.

Maddox, B. (1975). *The half-parent.* New York: M. Evans & Co.

Maneker, J. S. and Rankin, R. P. (1987). Correlates of marital duration among those who file for divorce: Selected characteristics in California, 1966-1976. *Journal of Divorce and Remarriage, 10*(1), 97-107.

Marmot, M. G., Euhrer, R., Ettner, S. L., Marks, N. F., and Bumpass, L. L. (1998). Contribution of psychosocial factors to socioeconomic differences in health. *Milbank Quarterly, 76*(3), 403.

Marsh, H. W. and Yeung, A S. (1998). Top-down, bottom-up, and horizontal models: The direction of causality in multidimensional, hierarchical self-concept models. *Journal of Personality and Social Psychology, 75*(2), 509-527.

Massey, E. P. (1987). "A study of home background factors related to school achievement of fifth grade boys from single parent and two parent homes." (Doctoral dissertation, University of Houston), abstract in *Dissertation Abstracts International,* 41-725-891.

McCombs, A. and Forehand, R. (1989). Adolescent school performance following parental divorce: Are there family actors that can enhance success? *Adolescence, 24*(96), 871-880.

McKee, D. H. (1992). "The effects of parental divorce on children: Four meta-analyses." (doctoral diss., Arizona State University).

McLanahan, S. (1999). Father absence and the welfare of children. In E. M. Hetherington (Ed.), *Coping with divorce, single parenting, and remarriage: A risk and resiliency perspective* (pp. 117-145). Mahwah, NJ: Erlbaum.

McLanahan, S. and Sandefur, G. (1994). *Growing up with a single parent: What hurts, what helps.* Cambridge, MA: Harvard University Press.

McLaren, N. (1985). The concept of stress: Comment. *Australian and New Zealand Journal of Psychiatry, 19*(4), 445-447.

Mechanic, D. and Hansell, S. (1989). Divorce, family conflict, and adolescents' well-being. *Journal of Health and Social Behavior, 30*(1), 105-116.

Meddings, D. R., Hertzman, C., Barer, M. L., Evans, R. G., Kazanjian, A., McGrail, K., and Sheps, S. B. (1998). Socioeconomic status, mortality, and the development of cataracts at a young age. *Social Science and Medicine, 46*(11), 1451-1457.

Mednick, B. R., Baker, R. L., Reznick, C., and Hocevar, D. (1990). The long-term effects of divorce on adolescent academic achievement. *Journal of Divorce, 13*(4), 69-88.

Messinger, L. (1984). *Remarriage: A family affair.* New York: Plenum Press.

Metcalf, K. and Gaier, E. (1987). Patterns of middle-class parenting and adolescent underachievement. *Adolescence, 22*(88), 920-928.

Miller, Y. F. and Cherry, J. W. (1991). *Kids on the move.* Silver Spring, MD: National Association of School Psychologists.

Milne, A. M. (1989). Family structure and the achievement of children. In W. J. Weston (Ed.), *Education in the American family: A research synthesis* (pp. 32-65). New York: New York University Press.

Milne, A. M., Myers, D. E., Rosenthal, A. S., and Ginsburg, A. (1986). Single parents, working mothers, and the educational achievement of schoolchildren. *Sociology of Education, 59*(3), 125-39.

Moles, O. (1982). "Trends in divorce and effects on children." Paper presented at the American Academy for the Advancement of Science, Washington, DC, January.

Moore, K. (1988). *Adolescent fertility: Facts at a glance.* Washington, DC: Child Trends, Inc.

Moore, K. (1995). *Facts at a glance: Report on 1992 data on teen fertility in the United States.* Washington, DC: Child Trends, Inc.

Morag, M., Yirmiya, R., Lerer. B., and Morag, A. (1998). Influence of socioeconomic status on behavioral, emotional and cognitive effects of rubella vaccination: A prospective, double-blind study. *Psychoneuroendocrinology, 23*(4), 337-351.

Morgan, L. (1988). Outcomes of marital separation: A longitudinal test of predictors. *Journal of Marriage and the Family, 50*(2), 493-498.

Muransky, J. M. and DeMarie-Dreblow, D. (1995). Differences between high school students from intact and divorced families. *Journal of Divorce and Remarriage, 23*(3/4), 187-196.

National Association of Elementary School Principals staff. (1980). One-parent children and their children: The school's most significant minority. *Principal, 60*(1), 31-37.

Neighbors, B., Forehand, R., and Armistead, L. (1992). Is parental divorce a critical stressor for young adolescents? Grade point average as a case in point. *Adolescence, 27*(107), 639-646.

Nigel, B. (1998). Sex differences in disposition toward kin, security of adult attachment, and sociosexuality as a function of parental divorce. *Evolution and Human Behavior, 19*(2), 125-132.

Nock, S. L. (1995). A comparison of marriages and cohabiting relationships. *Journal of Family Issues, 16*(1), 53-76.

Norman, G. (1995). *Wreck of the Alamo.* Beverly Hills, CA: Gerald, Inc.

Nunn, G. D., Parish, T. S., and Worthing, R. (1993). Perceptions of personal and familial adjustment by children from intact, single-parent, and reconstituted families. *Psychology in the Schools, 20*(2), 166-174.

Nye, I. (1952). Adolescent-parent adjustment: Age, sex, sibling number, broken homes, and employed mothers as variables. *Marriage and Family Living, 14*(3), 327-332.

Padhi, J. and Dash, A. S. (1994). The relation of parental attitudes to adolescent competence. *Psycho-Lingua, 24,* 33-42.

Pagani, L., Tremblay, R. E., Vitaro, F., Kerr, M., and McDuff, P. (1998). The impact of family transition on the development of delinquency in adolescent boys: A 9-year longitudinal study. *Journal of Child Psychology and Psychiatry and Allied Disciplines, 39*(4), 489-499.

Pasley, K. and Ihinger-Tallman, M. (1987). The evolution of a field of investigation: Issues and concerns. In K. Pasley and M. Ihinger-Tallman (Eds.), *Remarriage and stepparenting: Current research and theory* (pp. 303-313). New York: Guilford.

Peckham, W. (1989). Family environment, family form, and high school academic achievement. (doctoral diss., Texas Woman's University).

Piciga, D. (1989). Relationships between the development of physical causality, social causality, and logico-mathematic operations of the subject. *Anthropos, 20*(5/6), 130-148.

Phillips, C. P. and Asbury, C. A. (1993). Parental divorce/separation and motivational characteristics and educational aspirations of African-American university students. *Journal of Negro Education, 62*(2), 204-210.

Popenoe, D. (1993). American family decline 1960-1990: A review and appraisal. *Journal of Marriage and the Family, 55*(3), 527-542.

Popenoe, D. (1994). The evolution of marriage and the problem of stepfamilies: A biosocial perspective. In A. Booth and J. Dunn (Eds.) *Stepfamilies: Who benefits? Who does not?* (pp. 55-79). Hillsdale, NJ: Erlbaum Associates.

Prandy, K. (1998). Deconstructing classes: Critical comments on the revised social stratification. *Work, Employment, and Society, 12*(4), 743-753.

Preston, S. (1984). Children and the elderly. Divorce paths for America's dependents. *Demography, 21*(4), 435-457.

Prilik, P. K. (1998). *Becoming an adult stepchild: Adjusting to a parent's new marriage.* Washington, DC: American Psychiatric Press.

Roberts, T. W. and Price, S. J. (1989). Adjustment in remarriage: Communication, cohesion, marital, and parental roles. *Journal of Divorce, 11*(1), 71-92.

Robinson, J. B. (1992). Of maps and territories: The use and abuse of socioeconomic modeling in support of decision making. *Technological Forecasting and Social Change, 42* (September), 147-164.

Robinson, M. (1997). *Divorce as a family transition: When private sorrow becomes a public matter.* London: Karnac Books.

Roizblatt, A., Rivera, S., and Fuchs, T. (1997). Children of divorce: Academic outcome. *Journal of Divorce and Remarriage, 26*(3/4), 51-56.

Rosenthal, D. and Hansen, J. (1980). Comparison of adolescents' perceptions and behaviors in single- and two-parent families. *Journal of Youth and Adolescence, 9*(5), 407-417.

Rosenthal, R. and Jacobson, L. (1968). *Pygmalion in the classroom.* New York: Holt, Rinehart, and Winston.

Ross, C. E. (1995). Reconceptualizing marriage status as a continuum of social status. *Journal of Marriage and the Family, 57*(1), 129-140.

Salzman, S. A. (1987). "Meta-analysis of studies investigating the effects of father absence on children's academic performance." Paper presented at the annual meeting of the American Educational Research Association, Washington, DC, April.

Santrock, J. W. (1972). Relation of type and onset of father absence to cognitive development. *Child Development, 43*(2), 455-469.

Schlesinger, B. (1975). The one parent family in perspective. In B. Schlesinger (Ed.), *The One-Parent Family* (pp. 3-12).Toronto: University of Toronto.

Schoen, R. and Weineck, R. (1993). Partner choice in marriages and cohabitations. *Journal of Marriage and the Family, 55*(2), 408-414.

Schweder, T. (1986). Is it possible for the social statistician to tell what is the cause and what is the effect? *Tidsskrift-for-Samfunnsforskning, 27*(4), 357-369.

Scott-Jones, D. and Clark, M. L. (1986). The school experiences of black girls: The interaction of gender, race, and socioeconomic status. *Phi Delta Kappan, 67*, 520-526.

Shiller, V. (1986). Loyalty conflicts and family relationships in latency age boys: A comparison of joint and maternal custody. *Journal of Divorce, 9*(4), 17-38.

Shinn, M. (1978). Father absence and children's cognitive development. *Psychological Bulletin, 85*(2), 295-324.

Shok, N. J. and Jurich, J. (1992). Correlates of self-esteem among college offspring from divorced families: A study of gender-based differences. *Journal of Divorce and Remarriage, 18*(3/4), 151-176.

Short, J. (1998). Predictors of substance use and mental health of children of divorce: A prospective analysis. *Journal of Divorce and Remarriage, 29*(1/2), 147-166.

Shreeve, W., Goetter, W., Bunn, A., Norby, J., Stueckle, A.F., Midgley, T. K., and deMichele, B. (1986). Single parents and student achievements: A national tragedy. *Early Child Development and Care, 23*(2/3), 175-184.

Simons, R. L., Whitbeck, L. B., Beamon, J., and Conger, R. D. (1994). The impact of mother's parenting involvement by nonresidential fathers, and parental conflict on the adjustment of adolescent children. *Journal of Marriage and the Family, 56*(2), 356-374.

Smith, T. E. (1990). Parental separation and the academic self-concepts of adolescents: An effort to solve the puzzle of separation effects. *Journal of Marriage and the Family, 52*(1), 107-118.

Smith, T. E. (1992). Gender differences in the scientific achievement of adolescents: Effects of age and parental separation. *Social Forces, 71*(2), 469-84.

Smith, T. E. (1995). What a difference a measure makes: Parental-separation effect on school grades, not academic achievement. *Journal of Divorce and Remarriage, 23*(3/4), 151-164.

Smith, W. (1945). The stepchild. *American Sociological Review, 10*(2), 237-242.

Sobal, J. (1991). Obesity and socioeconomic status: A framework for examining relationships between physical and social variables. *Medical Anthropology, 13*(3), 231-247.

Sobal. J. (1994). Social and economic consequences of overweight in adolescence: Comment. *New England Journal of Medicine, 330*(9), 647.

Sobel, M. E. (1998). Causal inference in statistical models of the process of socioeconomic achievement. *Sociological Methods and Research, 27*(2), 318-348.

Solomon, D., Hirsch, J. G., Scheinfield, D. R., and Jackson, J. C. (1972). Family characteristics and elementary school achievement in an urban ghetto. *Journal of Consulting and Clinical Psychology, 39*(3), 462-66.

Stack, S. (1980). The effects of marital dissolution on suicide. *Journal of Marriage and the Family, 42*(1), 83-92.

Stack, S. (1989). Impact of divorce on suicide in Norway, 1951-1980. *Journal of Marriage and the Family, 51*(1), 229-238.

Stevens, J. H. Jr. (1982). Support systems for black families. In J. D. Quisenberry (Ed.), *Changing Family Lifestyles,* pp. 14-16. Washington, DC: Association for Childhood Education International.

Stevenson, M. R. and Black, K. N. (1995). *How divorce affects offspring: A research approach.* Madison, WI: Brown and Brenchmark.

Stewart, J. Q. (1950). The natural sciences applied to social theory. *Science, 111,* 500.

Stinnett, N. and DeFrain, J. (1985). *Secrets of strong families.* Boston: Little, Brown, and Company.

Stunkard, A. J. and Sorenson, T. I. (1993). Obesity and SES: A complex relation. *New England Journal of Medicine, 329*(14), 1036-1037.

Sutherland, H. E. G. (1930). The relationship between I.Q. and size of family in the case of fatherless children. *Journal of Genetic Psychology, 38*(1-4), 161-170.

Sutton-Smith B., Rosenberg, B. G., and Landy, F. (1968). Father absence effects in families of different sibling compositions. *Child Development, 39*(4), 1213-1221.

Svanum, S., Bringle, R. G., and McLaughlin, J. E. (1982). Father absence and cognitive performance in a large sample of six- to eleven-year-old children. *Child Development, 53*(1), 136-143.

Swartzman-Schatman, B. and Schinke, S. P. (1993). The effect of mid-life divorce on late adolescent and young adult children. *Journal of Divorce and Remarriage, 19*(1/2), 209-218.

Tate, D. and Gibson, G. (1980). Socioeconomic status and black and white intelligence revisited. *Social Behavior and Personality, 8*(2), 233-237.

Thomas, A. M. and Forehand, R. (1993). The role of paternal variables in divorced and married families: Predictability and adolescent adjustment. *American Journal of Orthopsychiatry, 63*(1), 126-135.

Thomson, E., Hanson, T. L., and McLanahan, S.S. (1994). Family structure and child well-being: Economic resources vs. parental behaviors. *Social Forces, 73*(1), 221-242.

Thomson, E., McLanahan, S., and Curtin, R. B. (1992). Family structure, gender, and parental socialization. *Journal of Marriage and the Family, 54*(2), 368-378.

Tittle, C. R. and Meier, R. F. (1991). Specifying the SES/delinquency relationship by social characteristics of contexts. *Journal of Research in Crime and Delinquency, 28*(4), 430-455.

Trovato, F. (1986). The relationship between marital dissolution and suicide: The Canadian case. *Journal of Marriage and the Family, 48*(2), 341-348.

Trovato, F. (1987) A longitudinal analysis of divorce and suicide in Canada. *Journal of Marriage and the Family, 49*(1), 193-203.

Twaite, J. A., Silitsky, D., and Luchow, A. K. (1998). *Children of divorce: Adjustment, parental conflict, custody, remarriage, and recommendations for clinicians.* Norvale, NJ: Jason Aronson.

Uhlenberg, P. and Eggebeen, D. (1986). The declining well-being of American adolescents. *The Public Interest, 82*(Winter), 25-38.

Umberson, D. (1992). Relationships between adult children and their parents: Psychological consequences for both generations. *Journal of Marriage and the Family, 54*(3), 664-674.

United States Department of Education. (1992). *National education longitudinal study, 1988: First follow-up, 1990. Vol. 1: Student data.* Washington, DC: U.S. Department of Education.

United States Department of Education. (1994). *National education longitudinal study, 1988: First follow-up, 1992. Vol. 1: Student data.* Washington, DC: U.S. Department of Education.

United States Department of Health. (1998). *Divorced families, 1997.* Washington, DC: Author.

United States Department of Justice. (1993). *Age-Specific Arrest Rate and Race-Specific Arrest Rates for Selected Offenses, 1965-1992.* Washington, DC: Author.

United States Department of Labor. (1967). *The Negro Family.* Washington, DC: Author.

Valkonen, T. (1993). Problems in measurement and international comparisons of socioeconomic differences in mortality. *Social Science and Medicine, 36*(4), 409-418.

van de Mheen, H. D., Stronks, K., and Mackenbach, J. P. (1998). A lifecourse perspective on socioeconomic inequalities in health: The influence of childhood socioecos and selected processes. *Sociology of Health and Illness, 20*(5), 754-777.

van de Mheen, H. D., Stronks, K., Schrijvers, C. T., and Mackenbach, J. P. (1999). The influence of adult ill health on occupational class mobility out of and into employment in the Netherlands. *Social Science and Medicine, 49*(4), 509-518.

Vemer, E., Coleman, M., Ganong, L. and Cooper, H. (1989). Marital satisfaction in remarriage: A meta-analysis. *Journal of Marriage and the Family, 51*(August), 713-725.

Visher, E. B. and Visher, J.S. (1988). *Old loyalties, new ties: Therapeutic strategies with stepfamilies.* New York: Brunner/Mazel.

Wadsby, M. and Svedin, C. G. (1996). Academic achievement in children of divorce. *Journal of School Psychology, 34*(4), 325-336.

Wallerstein, J. S. (1984). Children of divorce: Preliminary report of a ten-year follow-up of young children. *American Journal of Orthopsychiatry, 54*(3), 444-458.

Wallerstein, J. S. (1987). Children of divorce: Report of a ten-year follow-up of early latency-age children. *American Journal of Orthopsychiatry, 57*(2), 199-211.

Wallerstein, J. S. (1991). The long-term effects of divorce on children: A review. *Journal of the American Academy of Child and Adolescent Psychiatry, 30*(3), 349-360.

Wallerstein, J. S. and Blakeslee, S. (1989). *Second chances: Men, women, and children a decade after divorce.* New York: Ticknor and Fields.

Wallerstein, J. S., Corbin, S. B., and Lewis, J. M. (1988). Children of divorce: A 10-year study. In E. M. Hetherington and J. D. Arasteh (Eds.), *Impact of divorce, single parenting, and step-parenting on children* (pp. 197-216). Hillsdale, NJ: Erlbaum Associates.

Wallerstein, J. S. and Corbin, S. B. (1990). The child and the vicissitudes of divorce. In Galatzer-Levy, R. M. and Kraus, L. (Eds.), *The scientific basis of child custody decisions* (pp. 73-95). John Wiley and Sons.

Wallerstein, J. S. and Kelly, J. B. (1980). *Surviving the breakup.* New York: Basic Books.

Wallerstein, J. S. and Lewis, J. (1998). The long-term impact of divorce on children: A first report from a 25-year study. *Family and Conciliation Courts Review, 36* (3), 368-383.

Walsh, W. M. (1992). Twenty major issues in remarriage families. *Journal of Counseling and Development, 70*(4), 709-715.

Warren, J. R. Sheridan, J. T., and Hauser, R. M. (1998). Choosing a measure of occupational standing: How useful are composite measures in analysis of gender inequality in occupational attainment? *Sociological Methods and Research, 27*(1), 3-76.

Wasserman, I. M. (1984). A longitudinal analysis of the relationship between suicide, unemployment, and marital dissolution. *Journal of Marriage and the Family, 46*(4), 99-140.

Werner, E. E. and Smith, R. S. (1992). *Overcoming the odds: High risk children from birth to adulthood.* Ithaca, NY: Cornell University Press.

Wertlieb, D. (1997). Children whose parents divorce: Life trajectories and turning points. In I. H. Gotlib and B. Wheaton (Eds.), *Stress and adversity over the life course* (pp. 179-196). New York: Cambridge University Press.

White, L. (1994). Stepfamilies over the life course: Social support. In A. Booth and J. Dunn (Eds.), *Stepfamilies: Who benefits? Who does not?* (pp. 109-137). Hillsdale, NJ: Erlbaum.

Wieczorek, W. F. and Hanson, C. E. (1997). New modeling methods: Geographic information systems and spatial analysis. *Alcohol Health and Research World, 21*(4), 331-339.

Williams, D. R., Takeuchi, D. T., and Adair, R. K. (1992). Socioeconomic status and psychiatric disorder among blacks and whites. *Social Forces, 71*(1), 179-194.

Wilson, K., Zurcher, L. A., McAdams, D. C., and Curtis, R. L. (1975). Stepfathers and stepchildren: An exploratory analysis from two national surveys. *Journal of Marriage and the Family, 37*(3), 526-36.

Wineberg, H. (1990). Childbearing after remarriage. *Journal of Marriage and the Family, 52*(1), 31-38.

Wineberg, H. (1992). Childbearing and dissolution of the second marriage. *Journal of Marriage and the Family, 54*(4), 879-887.

Wood, J., Chapin, K., and Hannah, M. E. (1988). Family environment and its relationship to underachievement. *Adolescence, 23*(90), 283-290.

Worthington, E. L., Jr. (1988). Decision making in adolescent pregnancy: A review of intrapersonal and interpersonal factors. In G. P. Regier (Ed.), *Values and public policy* (pp. 119-180). Washington, DC: Family Research Council of America.

Wright, B. R., Caspi, A., Moffitt, T., Miech, R. A., and Silva, P. A. (1999). Reconsidering the relationship between SES and delinquency: Causation but not correlation. *Criminology, 37*(1), 175-194.

Wu, M. and Cheng, P. W. (1999). Why causation need not follow from statistical association: Boundary conditions for the evaluation of generative and preventive causal powers. *Psychological Science, 10*(2), 92-97.

Ximenes, R. A. and Araujo, T. V. (1995). Internal validity in cross-sectional studies: Comments based on an investigation of the association between socioeconomic factors and schistosomiasis. *Cadernos de Saude Publica, 11*(1), 118-127.

Young, T. M. and Shorr, D. N. (1986). Factors affecting locus of control in schoolchildren. *Genetic, Social, and General Psychology Monographs, 112*(4), 405-417.

Zakariya, S. B. (1982). Another look at the children of divorce: Summary report of the study of school needs of one-parent. *Principal, 62*(1), 34-37.

Zakrisson, I. and Ekehammer, B. (1998). Social attitudes and education: Self-selection or socialization? *Scandanavian Journal of Psychology, 39*(2), 117-122.

Zaslow, M. J. (1988). Sex differences in children's response to parental divorce: Research methodology and postdivorce family forms. *American Journal of Orthopsychiatry, 58*(3), 355-378.

Zaslow, M. J. (1989). Sex differences in children's response to parental divorce: Samples, variables, and sources. *American Journal of Orthopsychiatry, 59*(1), 118-141.

Zill, N. (1994). Understanding why children in stepfamilies have more learning and behavior problems than children in nuclear families. In A. Booth and J. Dunn (Eds.), *Stepfamilies: Who benefits? Who does not?* (pp. 97-106). Hillsdale, NJ: Erlbaum Associates.

Zill, N., Morrison, D. R., and Coiro, M. J. (1993). Long-term effects of parental divorce on parent-child relationships, adjustment, and achievement in young adulthood. *Journal of Family Psychology, 7*(1), 91-103.

Zill, N. and Nord, C. W. (1994). *Running in place.* Washington, DC: Child Trends.

Zill, N. and Rogers, C. C. (1988). Recent trends in the well-being of children in the United States and implications for public policy. In A. J. Cherlin (Ed.), *The changing American family and public policy* (pp. 31-115). Washington, DC: Urban Institute Press.

Index

Page numbers followed by the letter "t" indicate tables.

Order a copy of this book with this form or online at:
http://www.haworthpressinc.com/store/product.asp?sku=4565

DIVORCE, FAMILY STRUCTURE, AND THE ACADEMIC SUCCESS OF CHILDREN

_____ in hardbound at $49.95 (ISBN: 0-7890-1486-6)

_____ in softbound at $24.95 (ISBN: 0-7890-1487-4)

COST OF BOOKS_____

OUTSIDE USA/CANADA/ MEXICO: ADD 20%____

POSTAGE & HANDLING_____
(US: $4.00 for first book & $1.50 for each additional book)
Outside US: $5.00 for first book & $2.00 for each additional book)

SUBTOTAL_____

in Canada: add 7% GST____

STATE TAX____
(NY, OH & MIN residents, please add appropriate local sales tax)

FINAL TOTAL____
(If paying in Canadian funds, convert using the current exchange rate, UNESCO coupons welcome.)

❏ **BILL ME LATER:** ($5 service charge will be added)
(Bill-me option is good on US/Canada/Mexico orders only; not good to jobbers, wholesalers, or subscription agencies.)

❏ Check here if billing address is different from shipping address and attach purchase order and billing address information.

Signature_____

❏ **PAYMENT ENCLOSED: $_____**

❏ **PLEASE CHARGE TO MY CREDIT CARD.**

❏ Visa ❏ MasterCard ❏ AmEx ❏ Discover
❏ Diner's Club ❏ Eurocard ❏ JCB

Account # _____

Exp. Date_____

Signature_____

Prices in US dollars and subject to change without notice.

NAME_____

INSTITUTION_____

ADDRESS_____

CITY_____

STATE/ZIP_____

COUNTRY_____ COUNTY (NY residents only)_____

TEL_____ FAX_____

E-MAIL_____

May we use your e-mail address for confirmations and other types of information? ❏ Yes ❏ No
We appreciate receiving your e-mail address and fax number. Haworth would like to e-mail or fax special discount offers to you, as a preferred customer. **We will never share, rent, or exchange your e-mail address or fax number.** We regard such actions as an invasion of your privacy.

Order From Your Local Bookstore or Directly From
The Haworth Press, Inc.
10 Alice Street, Binghamton, New York 13904-1580 • USA
TELEPHONE: 1-800-HAWORTH (1-800-429-6784) / Outside US/Canada: (607) 722-5857
FAX: 1-800-895-0582 / Outside US/Canada: (607) 722-6362
E-mail: getinfo@haworthpressinc.com
PLEASE PHOTOCOPY THIS FORM FOR YOUR PERSONAL USE.
www.HaworthPress.com

BOF02

FORTHCOMING, NEW AND RECENTLY PUBLISHED BOOKS FROM THE HAWORTH PRESS

THE THERAPIST'S NOTEBOOK FOR FAMILIES

Over 250 Pages!

Solution-Oriented Exercises for Working with Parents, Children, and Adolescents
Bob Bertolino, PhD, and Gary Schultheis, MA
This book empowers mental health professionals with clear, practical, easy-to-use therapeutic exercises for working with parents, adolescents, children, and families. These exercises will improve your effectiveness with clients, helping them to explore possibilities, manage setbacks, find solutions, and create change in spite of difficult problems.
$39.95 soft. ISBN: 0-7890-1244-8.
Available Fall 2002. Approx. 313 pp. with Index.

DIVORCE, ANNULMENTS, AND THE CATHOLIC CHURCH

Over 225 Pages!

Healing or Hurtful?
Richard J. Jenks, PhD
The first published study on annulments with wide-scale usage of questionnaires and interviews. In addition to delivering a quantitative analysis of the responses to various questions (religious, social, or psychological), it explains in lay terms what annulments are and what the acceptable grounds are for annulment and takes you step-by-step through the process of obtaining one.
$49.95 hard. ISBN: 0-7890-1563-3.
$24.95 soft. ISBN: 0-7890-1564-1.
Available Summer 2002. Approx. 258 pp. with Index.

WOMEN'S STORIES OF DIVORCE AT CHILDBIRTH

Over 225 Pages!

When the Baby Rocks the Cradle
Hilary Hoge, MD
This landmark book examines the causes and consequences of divorce occurring during pregnancy or within a year of childbirth. This book will be extraordinarily helpful to counselors and mental health professionals, couples having difficulty with the transition to parenthood, new parents who are considering divorce, and survivors of divorce at childbirth.
$49.95 hard. ISBN: 0-7890-1291-X.
$22.95 soft. ISBN: 0-7890-1292-8.
Available Spring 2002. Approx. 270 pp. with Index.

CLINICAL EPIPHANIES IN MARITAL AND FAMILY THERAPY

A Practitioner's Casebook of Therapeutic Insights, Perceptions, and Breakthroughs
Edited by David A. Baptiste, Jr., PhD
This fascinating collection shows how one therapist handled clients stuck in the therapeutic process. Each of these turning points is also discussed by two other therapists representing divergent points of view.
Over 400 Pages!
$69.95 hard. ISBN: 0-7890-0105-5.
$34.95 soft. ISBN: 0-7890-1565-X.
Available Spring 2002. Approx. 430 pp. with Index.

DIVORCE, FAMILY STRUCTURE, AND THE ACADEMIC SUCCESS OF CHILDREN

Over 250 Pages!

William Jeynes, PhD
This comprehensive volume investigates the effects of nontraditional family structures, race, socioeconomic status, and mobility on children's emotional and educational well-being. Educators, theorists, sociologists, and psychologists will find this volume an essential resource.
$49.95 hard. ISBN: 0-7890-1486-6.
$24.95 soft. ISBN: 0-7890-1487-4.
2002. Available now. 298 pp. with Index.

COUPLES THERAPY, SECOND EDITION

Linda Berg-Cross, PhD
This groundbreaking book proposes a new integrative approach to successful marriage based on four cornerstones: resiliency, social support, adaptability, and self-fulfillment. Through clinical vignettes and up-to-date research, it makes the common conflicts and developmental stages of marriage understandable.
To view an excerpt online, find this book in our QuickSearch catalog at: www.HaworthPress.com.
Over 400 Pages!
$89.95 hard. ISBN: 0-7890-1453-X.
$49.95 soft. ISBN: 0-7890-1454-8. 2001. 460 pp. with 2 Indexes.

DIVORCE AND THE NEXT GENERATION

Perspectives for Young Adults in the New Millennium
Edited by Craig A. Everett, PhD
Offers helpful tables and figures, thorough literature reviews, and meta analysis as well as original research. The studies analyze such diverse factors as gender, age at divorce, and level of conflict in the marriage. The results may surprise you.
(A monograph published simultaneously as the Journal of Divorce & Remarriage, Vol. 34, Nos. 3/4.)
$49.95 hard. ISBN: 0-7890-1411-4.
$24.95 soft. ISBN: 0-7890-1412-2. 2001. 197 pp. with Index.

CLINICAL PRACTICE WITH FAMILIES

Supporting Creativity and Competence
Michael Rothery, PhD, and George Enns, MSW
This comprehensive volume offers insight and ideas for practicing family therapists in such essential areas as boundaries, ecomaps, support, family traditions, and goalsetting.
Over 200 Pages!
To view an excerpt online, find the book in our QuickSearch catalog at www.HaworthPress.com.
$69.95 hard. ISBN: 0-7890-1084-4.
$29.95 soft. ISBN: 0-7890-1085-2. 2001. 254 pp. with Index.

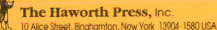
The Haworth Press, Inc.
10 Alice Street, Binghamton, New York 13904–1580 USA